Digital Photo Editing for Seniors

Addo Stuur

Digital Photo Editing
for Seniors

Learn how to edit your digital photos with ArcSoft PhotoStudio 5.5

www.visualsteps.com

This book has been written using the Visual Steps™ method.
Translated by Grayson Morris, Marleen Vermeij
Copyright 2005 by Visual Steps B.V.
Cover design by Studio Willemien Haagsma bNO

First printing: January 2005
ISBN 90 5905 064 9

Would you like more information?
www.visualsteps.com

Do you have questions or suggestions?
E-mail: info@visualsteps.com

Website for this book:
www.visualsteps.com/digital
Here you can register your book.

Register your book
We will keep you aware of any important changes that are necessary to you as a user of the book. You can also take advantage of our periodic newsletter informing you of our product releases, company news, tips & tricks, special offers, etc.
www.visualsteps.com/digital

Table of Contents

Foreword

Digital photography has soared in popularity in recent years. It appears as if the digital camera is supplanting the regular camera and its rolls of film. Increasingly, people are importing their regular snapshots into their computer. Now that you can have your photos put directly on a CD-ROM when you have your film roll developed there are even more reasons to get acquainted with a digital photo editing program.

Since the major advantage of digital snapshots is manipulation - the ability to crop, color-correct, remove red eye and otherwise fiddle with the image on a computer - it is no wonder that good photo editing software has become so important. The program *ArcSoft PhotoStudio* is really like an extensive photolab. It allows you to do things like retouch a photo or create a trick shot, things which used to be possible only for professional photographers.

In this book you'll receive detailed instructions on the program's basic techniques. Soon you too, can start working on your photos with skill and pleasure.

Last but not least, don't forget to visit the website for this book for current news and information: www.visualsteps.com/digital

I hope you enjoy the book!

Addo Stuur

P.S. Your comments and suggestions are most welcome. My e-mail address is: addo@visualsteps.com

Introduction to Visual Steps™

The Visual Steps™ manuals and handbooks offer the best instructions on the computer expressway. Nowhere else in the world will you find better support while getting to know the computer, the Internet, *Windows* and other computer programs.

Visual Steps™ manuals are special because of their:

- **Content**
  Your way of learning, your needs, your desires and your know-how and skills have been taken into account.
- **Structure**
  You can get straight to work. No lengthy explanations. What is more, the chapters are organized in such a way that you can skip a chapter or redo a chapter without worry. The small steps taken in Visual Steps also make it easy to follow the instructions.
- **Illustrations**
  There are many, many illustrations of computer screens. These will help you to find the right buttons or menus, and will quickly show you whether you are still on the right track.
- **Format**
  A sizable format and pleasantly large letters enhance readability.

In short, these are manuals that I believe will be excellent guides.

Dr. H. van der Meij

Faculty of Applied Education, Department of Instruction Technology, University of Twente, the Netherlands

What You'll Need

In order to work through this book, you'll need to have a few things on your computer.

The most important requirement for using this book is that your computer has the US version of **Windows XP**, **Me**, or **98**. You can check this yourself by turning on your computer and looking at the welcome screen.

You'll also need to have **ArcSoft PhotoStudio 5.5** on your computer. This program is included on the CD-ROM accompanying this book.

In Chapter 1, you'll read how to install this program and what the system requirements for running *ArcSoft PhotoStudio* are.

We recommend a printer. If you don't have a printer, you can just skip the printing tasks (Chapter 9).

You don't necessarily need additional devices such as a digital photo camera or a scanner.

In this book, you'll learn to use the program by working with several **practice photos** included on the CD-ROM accompanying this book.

ArcSoft PhotoStudio 5.5

Installing
Before you can get started with *ArcSoft PhotoStudio*, you'll need to install it on your computer. If you don't already have the program, you'll need to buy it. You'll read how to install the program in Chapter 1. Chapter 1 also tells you what the system requirements are for running *ArcSoft PhotoStudio* efficiently.

Registering
You can register your copy of the program online. You'll read more about this in Chapter 1.

Support
If you should encounter any problems with the program, you can contact the customer service department at *ArcSoft*:
www.arcsoft.com/en/support

More Information
You'll find current news, addresses for suppliers in the digital photo editing domain and more on the website for this book:
www.visualsteps.com/digital
Any errata for the book will also be listed on this website.

How to Use This Book

This book has been written using the Visual Steps™ method. It's important that you work through each chapter **step by step**. If you follow all the steps, you won't encounter any surprises. In this way, you'll quickly learn how to edit digital photos without any problems.

In this Visual Steps™ book, you'll see various icons. This is what they mean:

Techniques
These icons indicate which technique you should use:

☞	The mouse icon means you should do something with the mouse.
⌨	The keyboard icon means you should type something on the keyboard.
☞	The hand icon means you should do something else, for example turn on the computer.

Sometimes we give you a little extra help in order to work through the book successfully.

Help
You can get extra help from these icons:

⇨	The arrow icon warns you about something.
✖	The bandage icon can help you if something's gone wrong.
1	Did you forgot how to do something? The number next to the footsteps icon tells you where you can find it in the appendix *How Do I Do That Again?*

This book also contains a great deal of general information and tips about the computer and *ArcSoft PhotoStudio*. This information is in seperate boxes.

Extra Information
Information boxes are denoted by these icons:

📖	The book icon gives you extra background information that you can read at your convenience. This extra information is not necessary for working through the book.
💡	The light bulb icon indicates an extra tip for using *Windows* or *ArcSoft PhotoStudio*.

How This Book Is Organized

Chapter 1
This chapter explains how to install the program if you haven't already.
It also describes how to copy the practice files. You'll need these practice files to work through the rest of the chapters.

Chapters 2 through 6
These chapters cover all the important editing techniques. You aren't required to work through the chapters in this order, but we do recommend it.

Chapters 7, 8, and 9
You can work through these chapters on special effects, importing photos, and printing in your own order.

The Screen Shots

The screen shots in this book were made on a computer running *Windows XP* with *Service Pack 2*. If you have a different version of *Windows*, such as *Windows 98*, then from time to time the *Windows* screen shots may differ slightly from what you see on your screen. We will point out the places in the book where this could happen.

Test Your Knowledge

Have you finished reading this book? Test your knowledge then with the test *Digital Photo Editing*. Visit the website: **www.ccforseniors.com**

This multiple-choice test will show you how good your knowledge of digital photo editing is. If you pass the test, you'll receive your free computer certificate by e-mail.

Prior Computer Experience

This book assumes a minimum of prior computer experience. Nonetheless, there are a few basic techniques you should know in order to use this book:

- start up and shut down *Windows*
- click, double-click, right-click, and drag with the mouse
- start and stop programs
- type text

If you don't know how to do these things yet, you can read the book **Windows XP for Seniors** first.

US $ 19.95
Canada $ 26,95
ISBN 90 5905 044 4

Windows XP for Seniors has been specifically written for people who are taking their first computer steps at a later age. It's a real "how to" book. By working through it at your computer, you can learn all the information and techniques you need to enjoy working with your computer. The step-by-step method ensures that you're continually learning how to get the most out of your computer.

What You'll Learn
When you finish this book, you'll have the skills to:
- work independently with your computer
- write a letter using your computer
- create illustrations
- adjust your computer settings so you can work with it most comfortably

For more information, visit
www.visualsteps.com/winxp

For Teachers

This book is designed as a self-study guide. It is also well suited for use in a group or a classroom setting. For this purpose, we offer a free teacher's manual containing information about how to prepare for the course (including didactic teaching methods) and testing materials. You can download this teacher's manual (PDF file) from the website which accompanies this book: **www.visualsteps.com/digital**

1. Installing PhotoStudio

In this chapter, you'll learn:

- what *PhotoStudio 5.5* requires from your computer
- how to install the *PhotoStudio* program
- how to copy the folder containing practice files to your computer

⇒ **Please note:**

Is *ArcSoft PhotoStudio 5.5* already installed on your computer?
☞ **Then skip the section *Installing PhotoStudio***

System Requirements for PhotoStudio

It's fun to edit photos, but it does ask a lot from your computer—not only for the photos, which often take up quite a lot of space, but also for the photo editing programs themselves. It's no different for *PhotoStudio*.

The minimum system requirements in order to use *PhotoStudio 5.5* are:
- *Pentium* II or higher
- *Windows* 98SE/Me/2000/XP
- 64 MB RAM (128 MB recommended)
- 50 MB hard disk space for the standard installation
- a monitor set at resolution 800x600 or 1024x768 and "high color" or "true color"

The program won't operate very well if your computer just barely meets the minimum system requirements. Everything will go very slowly, and you'll also run a greater risk of the program "hanging" (no longer working) because there isn't enough available memory.

⇨ **Please note:**

Make sure you have at least 100 MB free space left on your hard disk after installing *PhotoStudio*. The program needs that much free space in order to work well.

Devices

You can load your photos directly into *PhotoStudio* from various sources such as a digital camera, a digital video camera, a webcam, or a scanner. The device must be *TWAIN* compatible. If it doesn't meet this standard, *PhotoStudio* won't automatically recognize it. Fortunately, most scanners do comply with the *TWAIN* standard. You can find out if your camera meets the standard in the manual you received with the camera. If it doesn't, you can always load your photos into *PhotoStudio* indirectly. First save the photos to your hard disk using your camera's software (consult the camera manual). Then you can open the photos in *PhotoStudio*.

Installing PhotoStudio

The program *ArcSoft PhotoStudio* is on the CD-ROM delivered with this book. Here's how you install the program:

☞ **Turn on your computer**

☞ **Insert the CD-ROM containing the program into your CD-ROM drive**

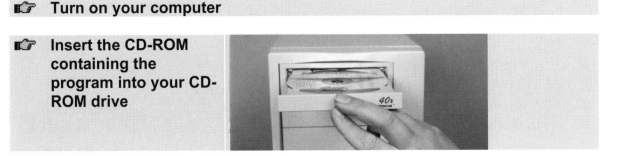

The following window will appear on most computers with *Windows XP*.

If you see this window:

☞ **Click on**

Open folder to view files using Windows Explorer

☞ **Click on** OK

Now you can continue on page 23.

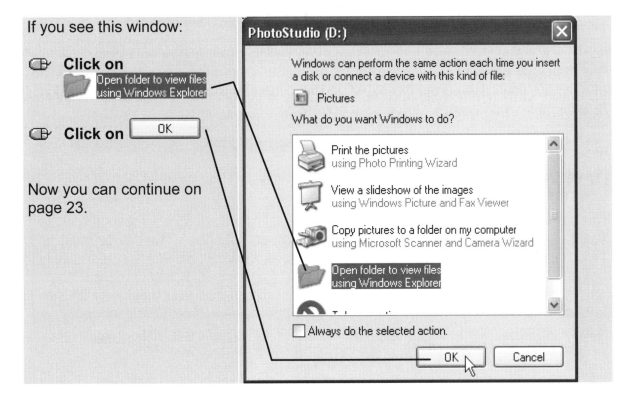

If you <u>don't</u> see the window, do the following:

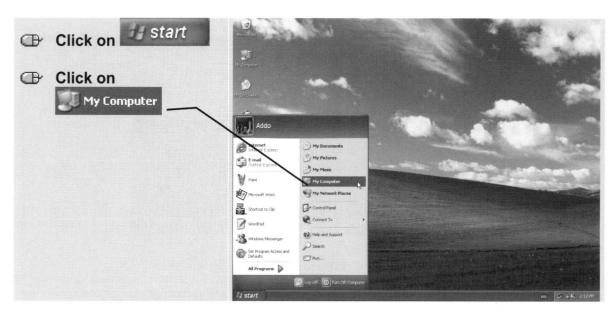

CB   **Click on** *start*

CB   **Click on**
        My Computer

Now the window *My Computer* opens and you see the contents of your computer. This may look different on your computer than in this example. Look for the CD-ROM drive where you inserted the CD-ROM. In this example, the CD-ROM is in drive D:. That might be a different letter on your computer.

CB   **Double-click on**
        PhotoStudio (D:)

HELP! What if I have Windows 98 / Me?

If you use *Windows 98* or *Windows Me*, the *My Computer* window looks a little different. The actions are the same, however.

You see the contents of the CD-ROM. This CD-ROM contains two folders: *My PhotoStudio Practice Files* and *PhotoStudio 5.5.*

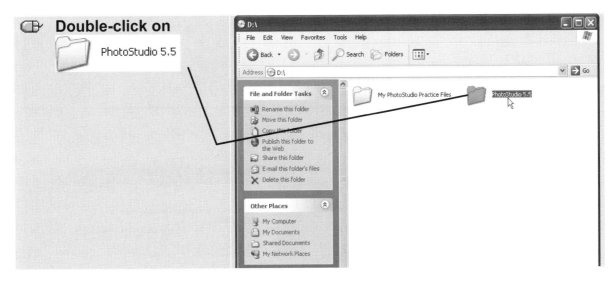

You see the contents of the folder *PhotoStudio 5.5.*

You see a window in which you can choose the desired language.

The installation is being prepared. You can see that in this window:

Now you see the window for the InstallShield Wizard.

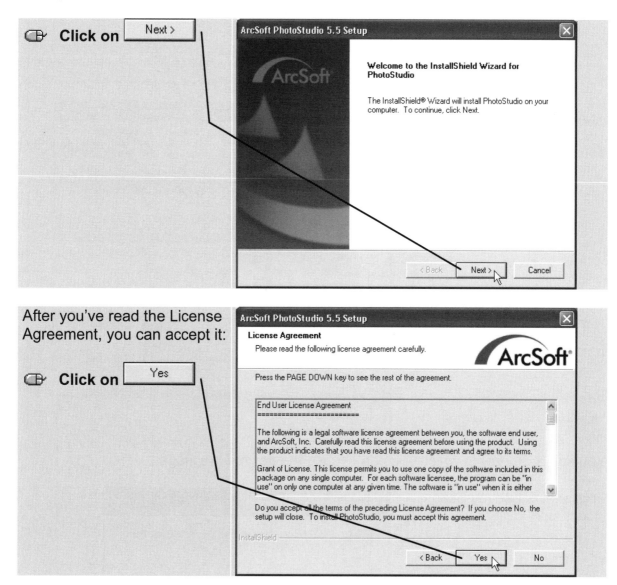

The program is installed on the hard disk drive C:. You can choose a different location in this window, but that isn't necessary.

Click on Next >

> **ArcSoft PhotoStudio 5.5 Setup**
>
> **Choose Destination Location**
> Select folder where Setup will install files.
>
> *ArcSoft*
>
> Setup will install PhotoStudio in the following folder.
>
> To install to this folder, click Next. To install to a different folder, click Browse and select another folder.
>
> Destination Folder
> C:\Program Files\ArcSoft\PhotoStudio 5.5   Browse...
>
> < Back   Next >   Cancel

Click on Next >

> **ArcSoft PhotoStudio 5.5 Setup**
>
> **Select Program Folder**
> Please select a program folder.
>
> *ArcSoft*
>
> Setup will add program icons to the Program Folder listed below. You may type a new folder name, or select one from the existing folders list. Click Next to continue.
>
> Program Folders:
> ArcSoft PhotoStudio 5.5
>
> Existing Folders:
> Accessories
> Administrative Tools
> Adobe
> Alarmclock
> Games
> PrintMe Internet Printing
> Real
> Startup
>
> < Back   Next >   Cancel

ArcSoft PhotoStudio is now copied to your hard disk and installed:

> **ArcSoft PhotoStudio 5.5 Setup**
>
> **Setup Status**
>
> *ArcSoft*
>
> PhotoStudio Setup is performing the requested operations.
>
> Installing:
> C:\...\{9DCCCCD2-F531-41D1-BF2F-B577FBD9694C}\data1.cab
>
> 2%
>
> Cancel

You see this window when the installation is finished:

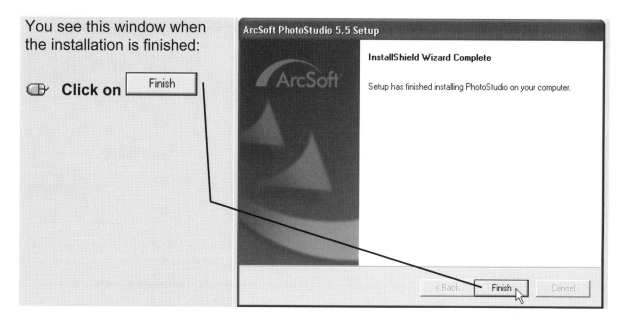

The installation is complete. Now you can copy the practice files for this book from the CD-ROM onto your hard disk.

Copying the Practice Files to the Hard Disk

Now you're going to copy the practice files. On your screen, you see a window showing the contents of the *PhotoStudio 5.5* folder on the CD-ROM. You want the folder containing the practice files.

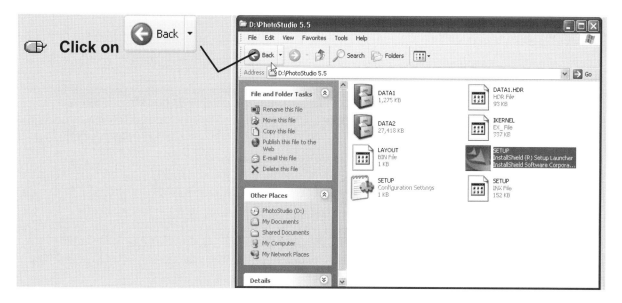

You see the two folders on the CD-ROM:

☞ **Right**-click on

My PhotoStudio Practice Files

Now a menu appears:

☞ **Click on** Send To

☞ **Click on** My Documents

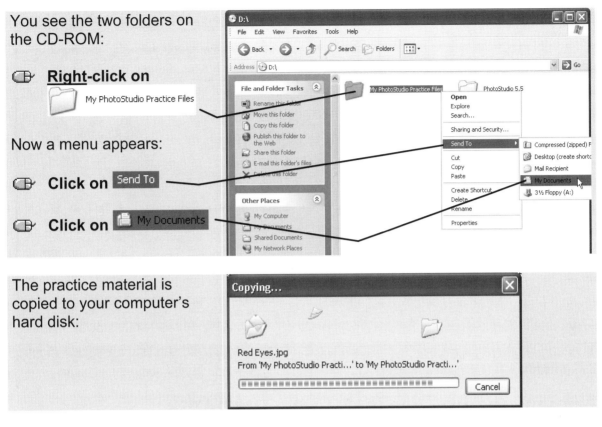

The practice material is copied to your computer's hard disk:

Have you finished copying?

☞ **Close the *My Computer* window** $\ell\ell$23

HELP! What if I have Windows 98 / Me?

If you use *Windows 98* or *Windows Me*, the *My Computer* window looks a little different. The actions are the same, however.

All the practice files have now been copied to the folder *My Documents*. Now you can start with Chapter 2.

The Website for This Book

On the website for this book, you'll find current news about the program and the book. It's a good idea to visit this website regularly so that you're always up to date on the latest state of affairs. Let's take a look at the website now.

☞ **Start *Internet Explorer***

☞ **Go to the web address** www.visualsteps.com/digital

You see the website for this book.

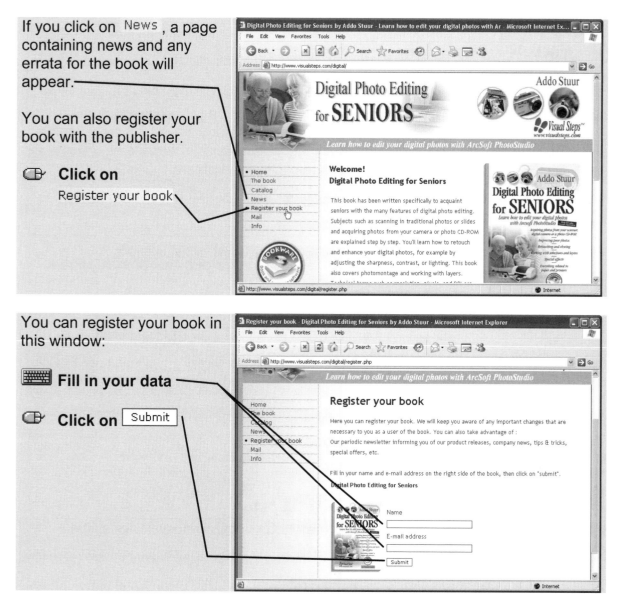

If you click on News , a page containing news and any errata for the book will appear.

You can also register your book with the publisher.

☞ **Click on**

    Register your book

You can register your book in this window:

⌨ **Fill in your data**

☞ **Click on** Submit

You'll receive an e-mail from the Visual Steps publishing house at the e-mail address you provided. This e-mail will tell you how to confirm your registration.
After registering, you'll receive the free Visual Steps Newsletter, a series of Tips & Tricks, and information about new publications and special offers, all via e-mail.

☞ **Close** *Internet Explorer*

Tips

💡 Tip

The Program Doesn't Work
The most common solution to problems with a program that doesn't work well is to remove the program from your hard drive (see the next page) and install it again. After this "fresh" installation, the problems are often already solved. If you still have problems with the program, you can check the manufacturer's website at **www.arcsoft.com** to see if they list a solution for your problem.

💡 Tip

Registering *ArcSoft PhotoStudio*
You can register the program *ArcSoft PhotoStudio* online or by fax or mail. Here's how you do it:

👉 **Click on** Internet

👉 **Click on**
Online Product Registration

Internet Explorer opens automatically:

👉 **Connect to the Internet**

👉 **Fill in your data**

Then you can choose whether you prefer to register online or print out a registration form and send it by fax or by mail:

👉 **Click on** Register online
or Register by fax/mail

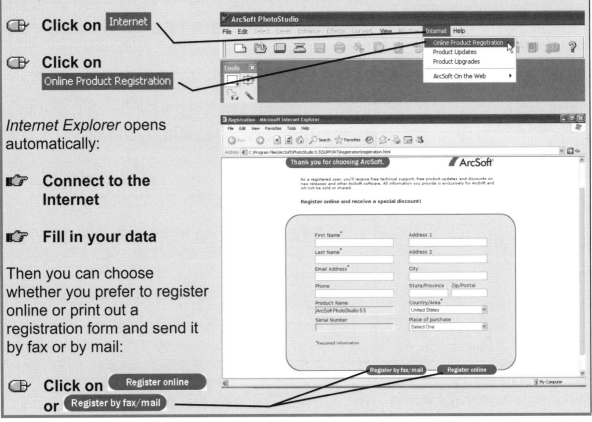

💡 Tip

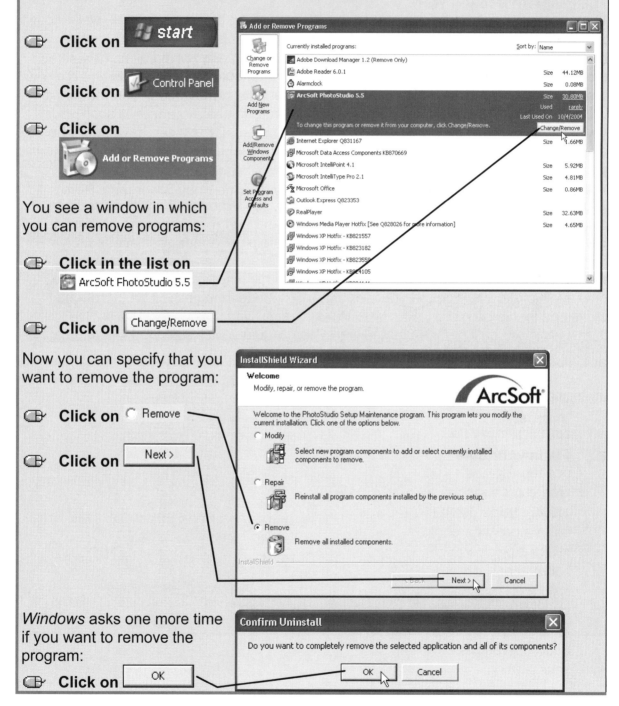

Uninstalling *ArcSoft PhotoStudio*

If for some reason you no longer use *ArcSoft PhotoStudio*, you can uninstall the program (remove it from your hard drive) as follows:

👆 **Click on** 🏁 *start*

👆 **Click on** Control Panel

👆 **Click on**
Add or Remove Programs

You see a window in which you can remove programs:

👆 **Click in the list on**
ArcSoft PhotoStudio 5.5

👆 **Click on** Change/Remove

Now you can specify that you want to remove the program:

👆 **Click on** ○ Remove

👆 **Click on** Next >

Windows asks one more time if you want to remove the program:

👆 **Click on** OK

2. Getting Started with PhotoStudio

Digital photography has soared in popularity. While the price of digital cameras has dropped, the image quality is steadily improving. In addtion there are more and more programs with which to edit your photos at home. You can even edit your photos if you don't have a digital camera. For instance, you can use a scanner to scan your vacation photos, thereby making digital copies of them. Or you can have your photos put on a CD when you have your film roll developed, which is another good way to get digital photos that you can edit with a photo editing program.

The program *ArcSoft PhotoStudio* features many tools for working with your digital photos. You can adjust the color balance in a photo and even eliminate parts of a photo that you don't want to be visible. With the help of various special effects, you can turn an otherwise simple photo into a masterpiece. With this program, many of the tools that a professional photographer has at his disposal in the darkroom are now available to you right on your computer. These techniques will be thoroughly explained in this book.
In this chapter you'll get acquainted with *PhotoStudio*. You'll start working with digital photos and learn just what a digital photo is made of.

In this chapter, you'll learn how to:

- start *PhotoStudio*
- use the palettes
- use the *Browser*
- create a new folder in the *Browser*
- move photos using the *Browser*
- open a practice photo
- rotate a photo
- zoom in and out
- crop a photo
- view a photo's dimensions
- enlarge and shrink a photo
- undo operations
- save a photo

Starting PhotoStudio 5.5

You start the program *PhotoStudio* as follows:

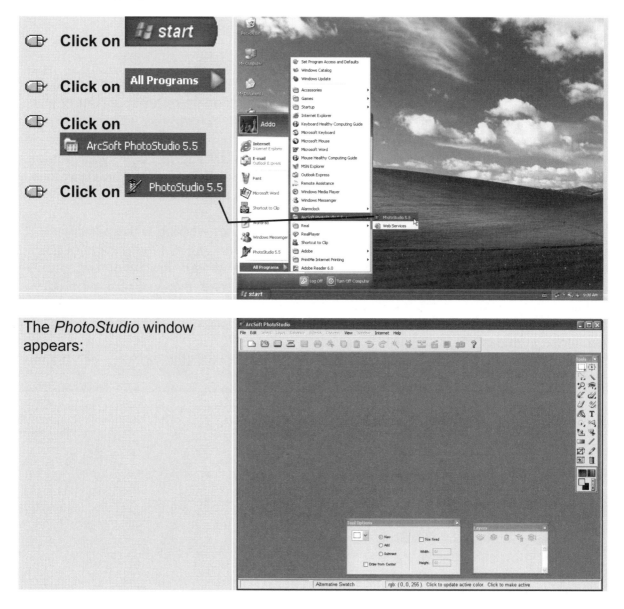

Now you're ready to work with *PhotoStudio*. In the following section, you'll become acquainted with three important palettes.

The Palettes

PhotoStudio is an extensive program with a great many features for editing photos. For many operations, you'll need the *PhotoStudio* palettes. In the *Tools Palette*, for example, you can select the tool you want to use for editing a photo.

You see the *Tools Palette* on the right-hand side of the window:

The tool *Rectangle Select* is automatically selected:

The *Options Palette* goes with the *Tools Palette:*

This palette displays additional options for using a particular tool.

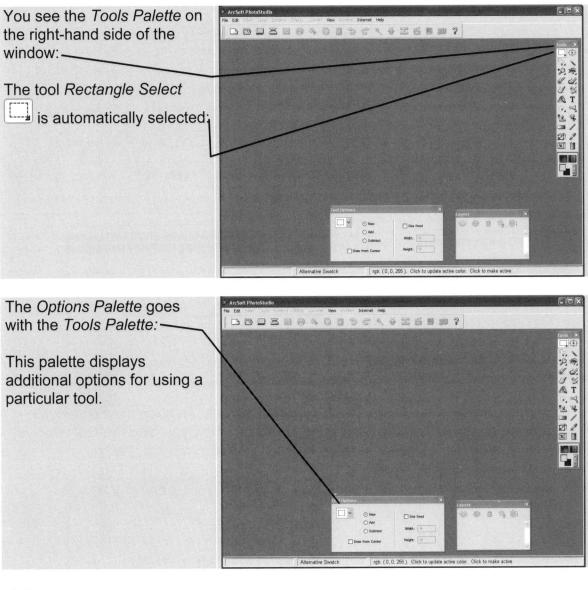

HELP! I don't have an *Options Palette*.

If you don't see the *Options Palette*, you can make it visible like this:

☞ **Click on** View **,** Show Options Palette

Every time you select a new tool, the content of the *Options Palette* is updated. You can give it a try for the *Zoom* tool.

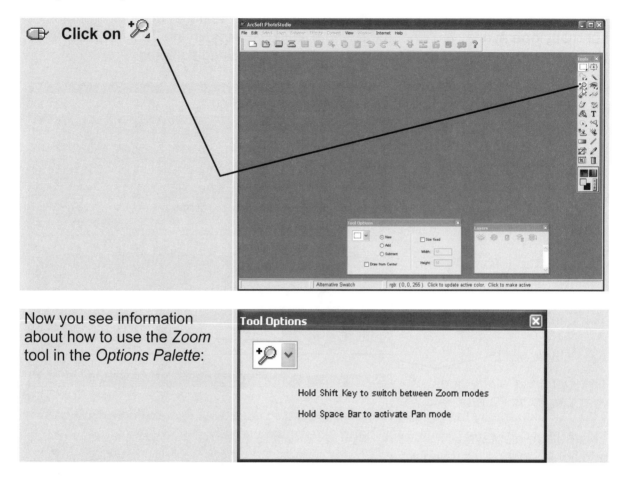

Now you see information about how to use the *Zoom* tool in the *Options Palette*:

You can hide the *Options Palette* when you don't need it. As soon as you select a new tool, the palette will automatically reopen. Here's how you hide the *Options Palette*:

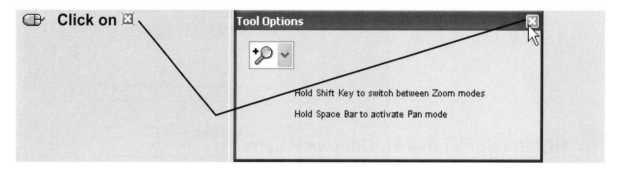

You see that the *Options Palette* is no longer visible:

☞ **Click on**

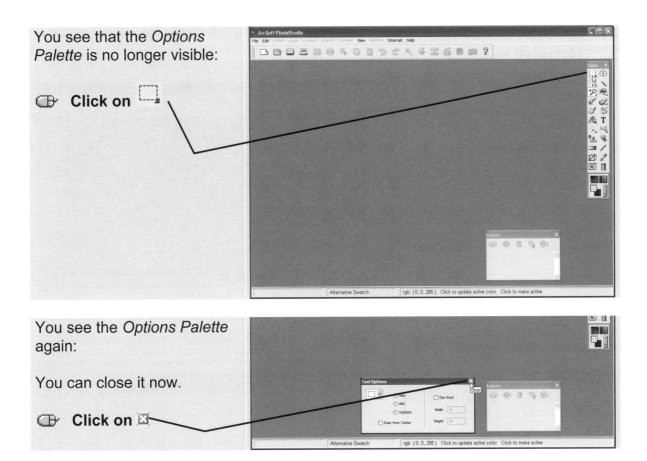

You see the *Options Palette* again:

You can close it now.

☞ **Click on** ⊠

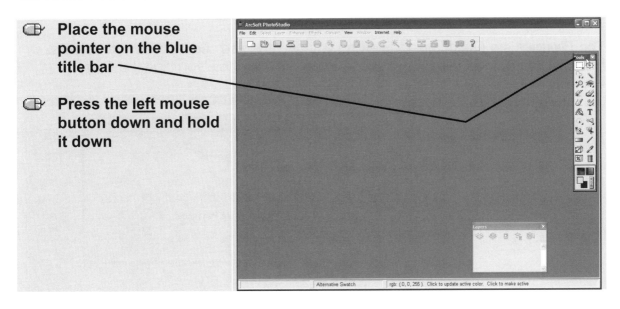

You can also easily move the palettes if they're in your way. For example, you can move the *Tools Palette* to the left-hand side of the window.

☞ **Place the mouse pointer on the blue title bar**

☞ **Press the left mouse button down and hold it down**

Drag the *Tools Palette* to the left side of the window

Release the mouse button

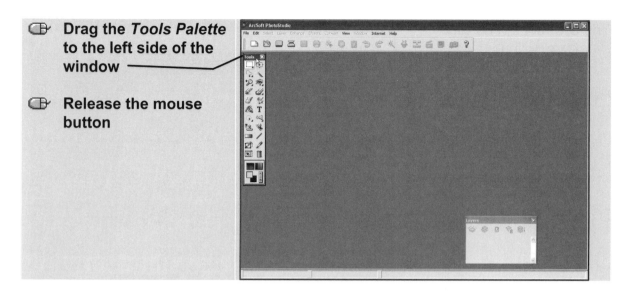

The third palette you see in the *PhotoStudio* window is the *Layers Palette*. You don't need this palette for the time being, so you can close it.

Click on ⊠

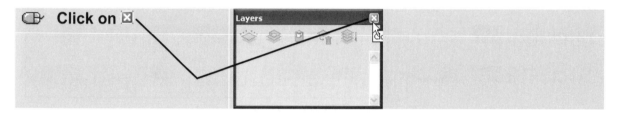

The Browser

The *Browser* is a useful tool for viewing your photos and sorting them into folders. Here's how you start the *Browser*:

Click on File

Click on Open Browser

The *Browser* opens:

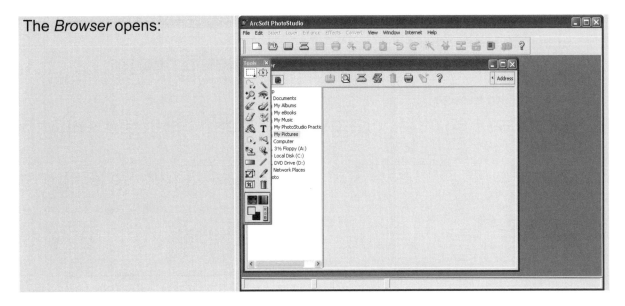

The *Tools Palette* is now on top of the *Browser* window. You can temporarily hide this palette.

☞ **Click on** View

☞ **Click on** Hide Tools Palette

The *Tools Palette* disappears.

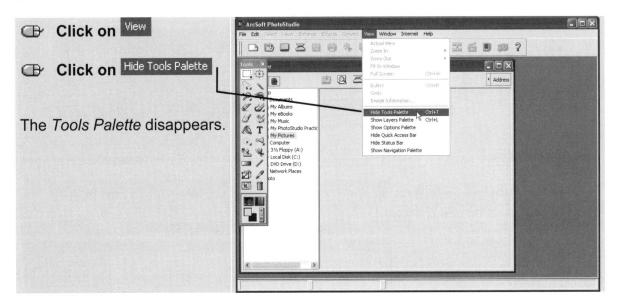

Now you see that the folder *My Pictures* is already open:

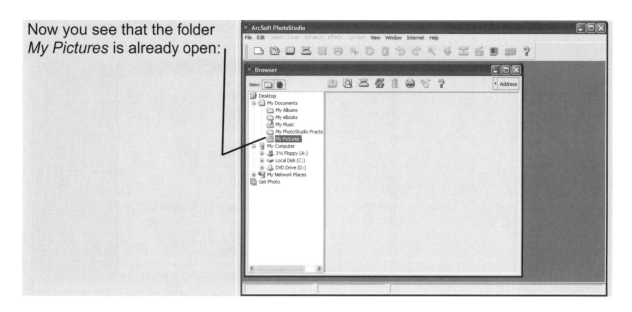

HELP! I don't see the *My Pictures* folder.

If you don't see the *My Pictures* folder in the *Browser*:

☞ **Click on** 🗀

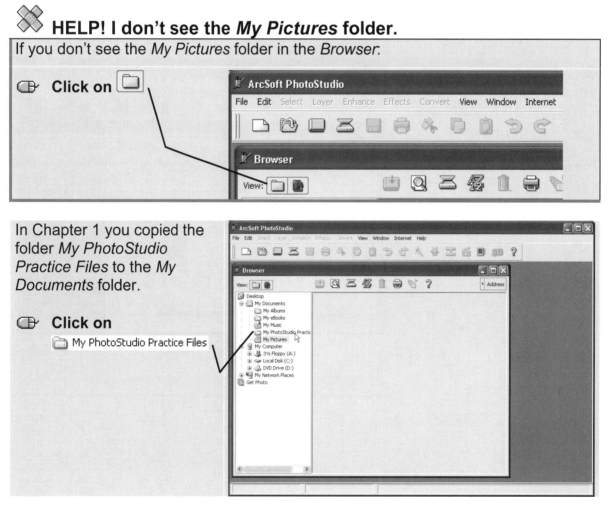

In Chapter 1 you copied the folder *My PhotoStudio Practice Files* to the *My Documents* folder.

☞ **Click on**

🗀 My PhotoStudio Practice Files

Now you see *thumbnails* (miniatures) of the practice photos for this book:

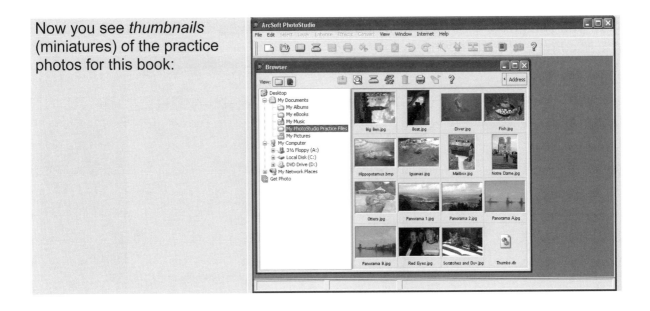

Creating Folders in the Browser

If you have a large collection of photo files, you can organize it by dividing it into different folders. Here's how you create a new folder in the *Browser*:

Right-click on
🗀 My PhotoStudio Practice Files

Click on New

The new folder is created.

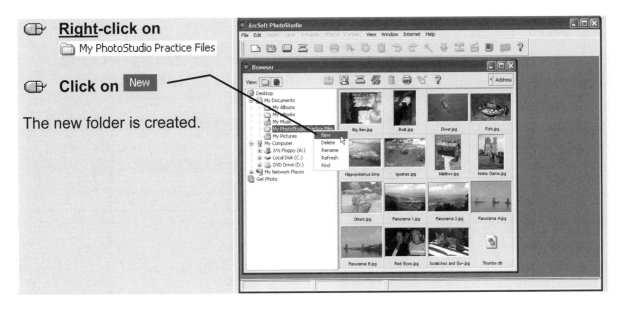

Now you can give the new folder a name.

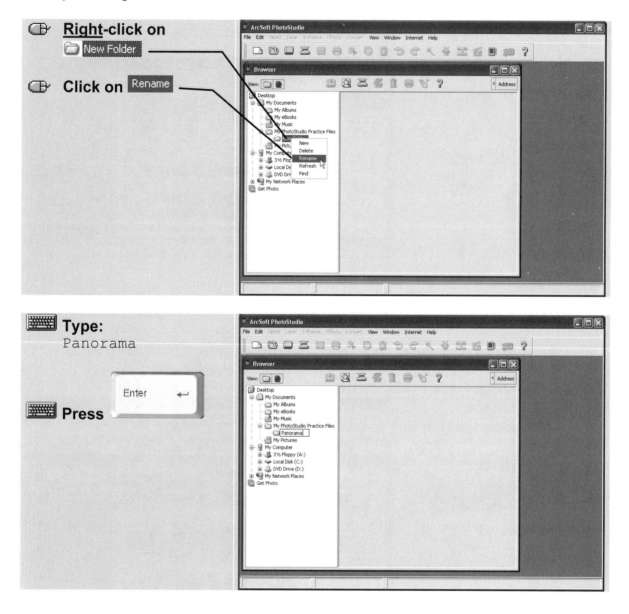

You'll use this folder shortly to store the four photo files *Panorama 1.jpg*, *Panorama 2.jpg*, *Panorama A.jpg* and *Panorama B.jpg*. But first, you're going to go back to the folder containing the practice files.

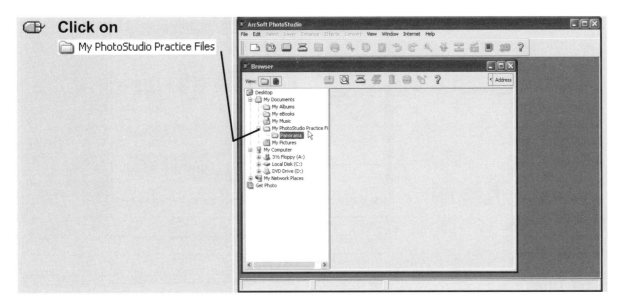

Moving Files to a New Folder

You first have to select the files you want to move to a new folder.

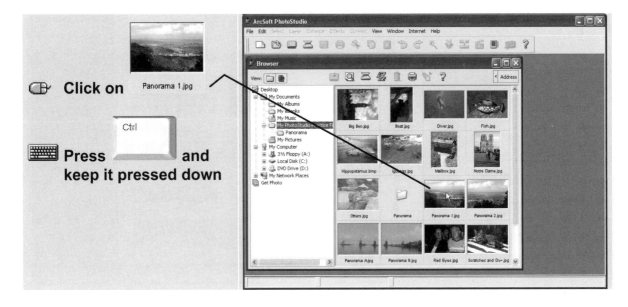

Click on   panorama 2.jpg

Click on   panorama A.jpg

Click on   panorama B.jpg

Now you've selected all the files you need:

Ctrl

Release

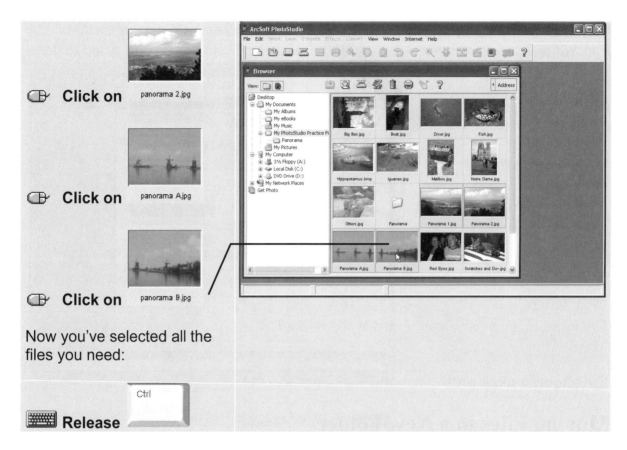

You can drag all four files to the new folder at the same time.

Place the mouse

pointer on   panorama 1.jpg

Press the left mouse button and keep it pressed down

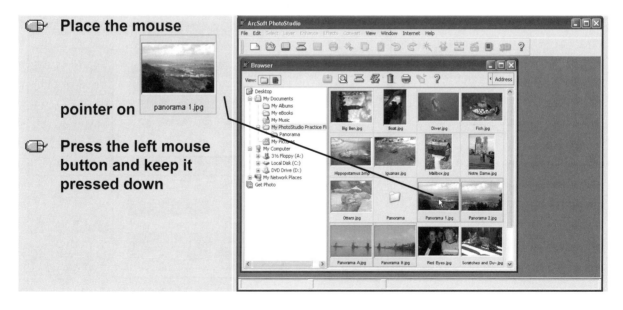

Drag the photos to the folder 🗀 Panorama

The folder name turns blue. A rectangle appears under the mouse pointer.

Release the mouse button

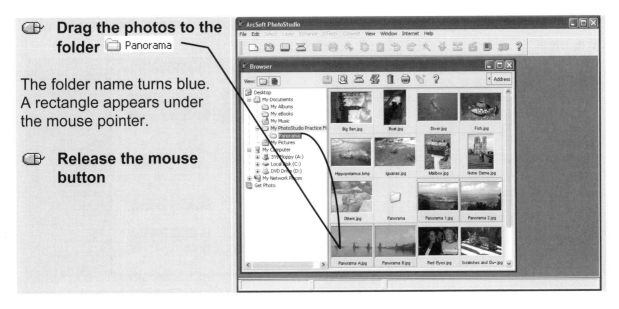

The four photos have been moved to the folder *Panorama.* You can check to make sure.

Double-click on

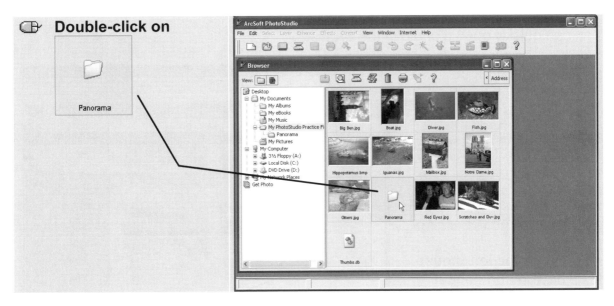

The four photos are in their own folder:

Now you can go back to the other practice photos.

☞ **Click on**

📁 My PhotoStudio Practice Files

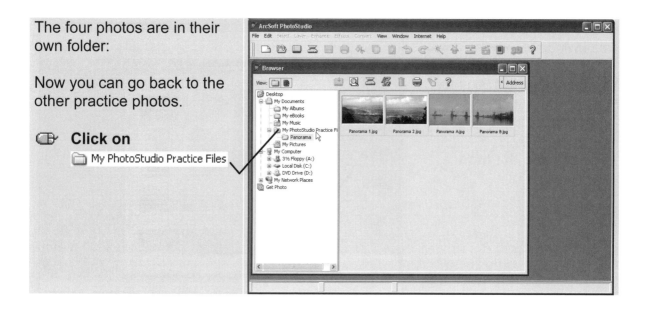

Opening a Photo

You can quickly open a photo in the *Browser*.

☞ **Double-click on**

Big Ben.jpg

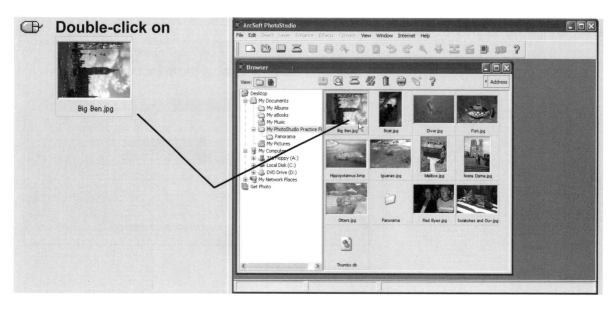

The photo appears inside a small window:

You can close the *Browser* now.

👉 **Click on** ❌

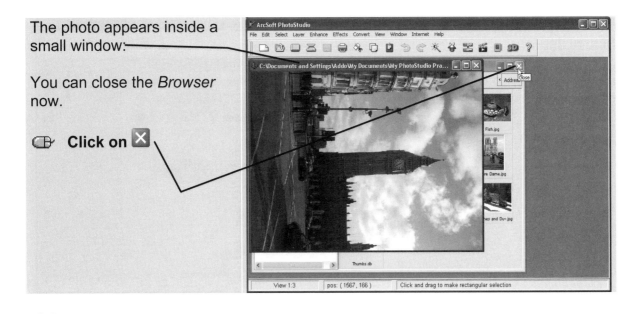

🪡 HELP! I don't see the *Browser*.

If you can't see the *Browser*:

☞ **Drag the window containing the photo away**
☞ **Close the *Browser***
☞ **Drag the photo window back**

You can display the photo at its largest size by maximizing the window.

👉 **Click on** ☐

Now the photo is in the center of the window:

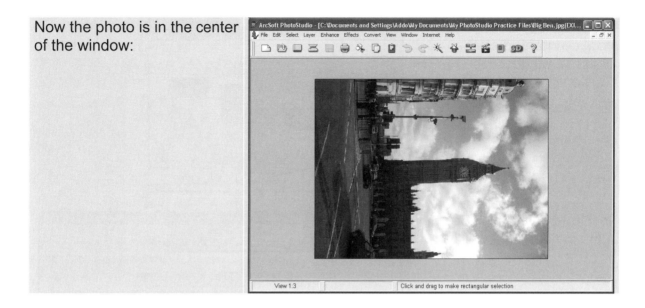

Rotating a Photo

Photos from your digital camera or scanner may frequently be displayed in the wrong orientation. This is an easy problem to solve.

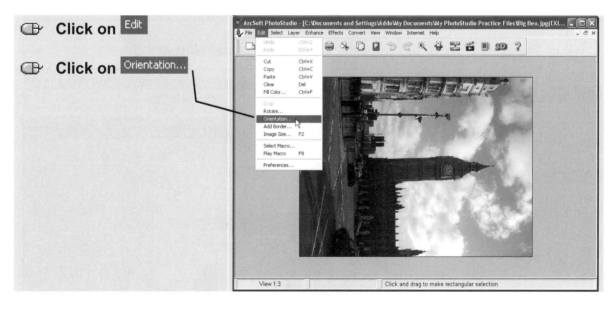

In the *Orientation* window, you can choose from four orientations for the photo: rotated 0, 90, 180, or 270 degrees. *PhotoStudio* automatically selects a rotation of 90 degrees.

You see that the photo is properly oriented after rotating it 90 degrees:

👉 **Click on** OK

Now the photo of Big Ben is right-side up:

You have enough room in this window to display the *Tools Palette*.

👉 **Click on** View

👉 **Click on** Show Tools Palette

The *Tools Palette* reappears.

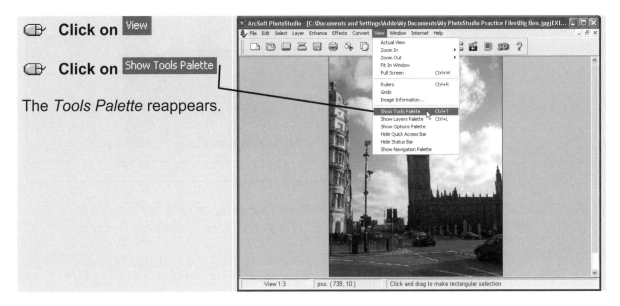

In the next section, you'll take a closer look at this photo.

Zooming In and Out

You can use the magnifying glass to zoom in on the photo. Then you can see what the photo is made of.

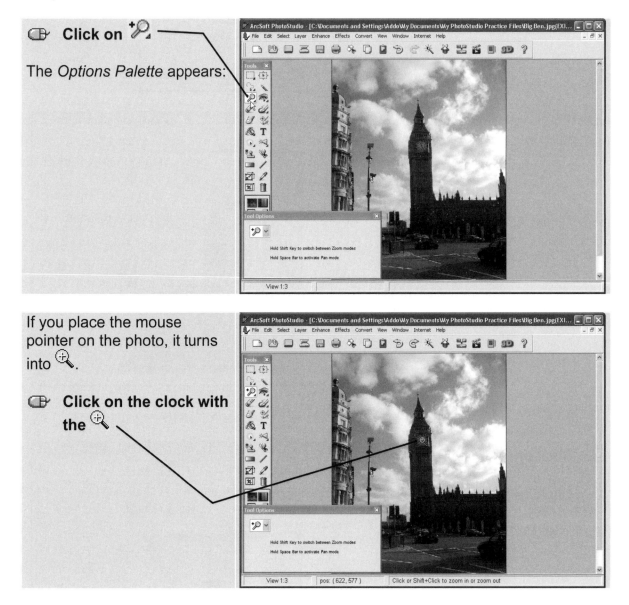

☞ **Click on** 🔍

The *Options Palette* appears:

If you place the mouse pointer on the photo, it turns into 🔍.

☞ **Click on the clock with the** 🔍

🖱️ **Click four more times on the clock** ─────

You see that you're zooming in more and more on the clock.

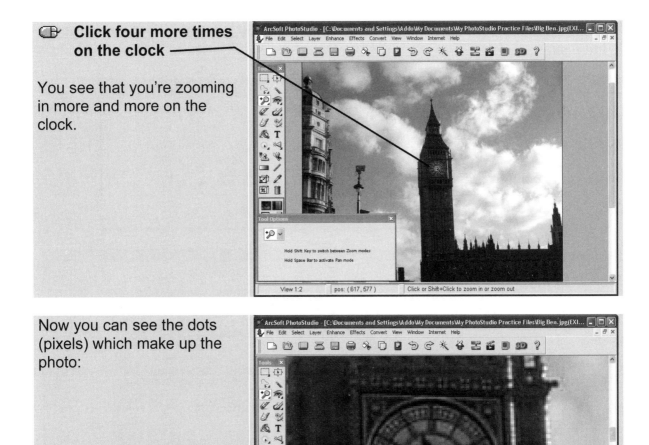

Now you can see the dots (pixels) which make up the photo:

You can zoom out now to a handier size. You do that by choosing the *Zoom Out* tool in the *Options Palette*.

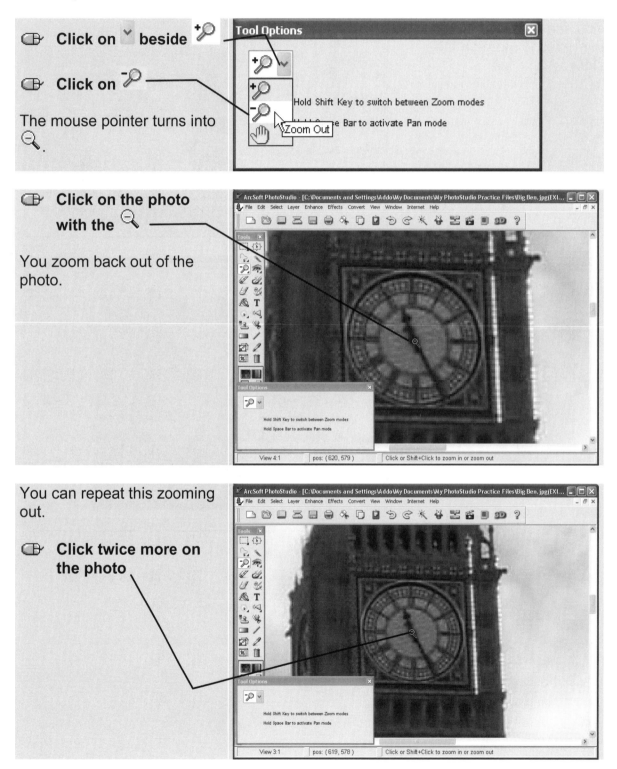

Click on ∨ beside 🔍

Click on 🔍

The mouse pointer turns into 🔍.

Click on the photo with the 🔍

You zoom back out of the photo.

You can repeat this zooming out.

Click twice more on the photo

⇨ **Please note:**

Zooming in and out doesn't change anything in the photo itself. You're just looking at the photo from closer by or farther away. That means this is <u>not</u> an enlargement you can save.

When you're editing a photo, it's useful to see the entire image. Here's how you can zoom out to full window size all at once:

☞ **Click on** View

☞ **Click on** Fit In Window

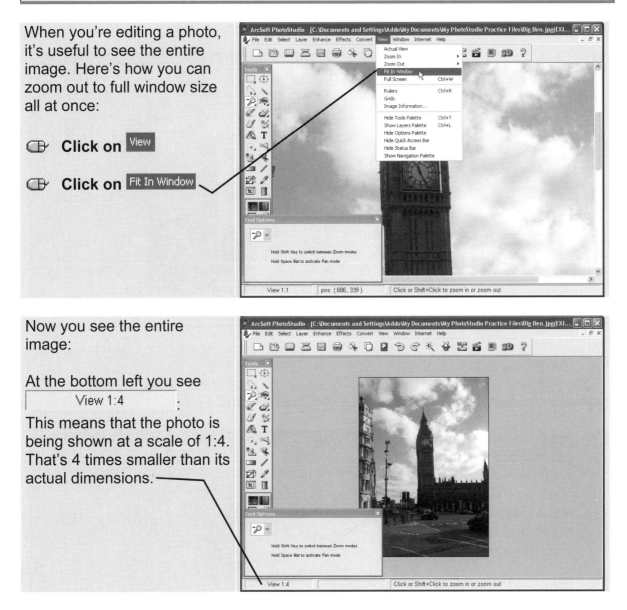

Now you see the entire image:

At the bottom left you see

View 1:4

This means that the photo is being shown at a scale of 1:4. That's 4 times smaller than its actual dimensions.

⇨ **Please note:**

The scale might be different for you. It depends upon the size of your window and your screen resolution. This won't affect further operations.

Cropping a Photo

Photos often contain irrelevant parts no one really looks at. For example, the building on the left and the pavement distract the viewer from the subject of this photo: Big Ben and the Parliament buildings in London. In *PhotoStudio* you can easily crop (cut out part of) a photo.

Click on ⬚

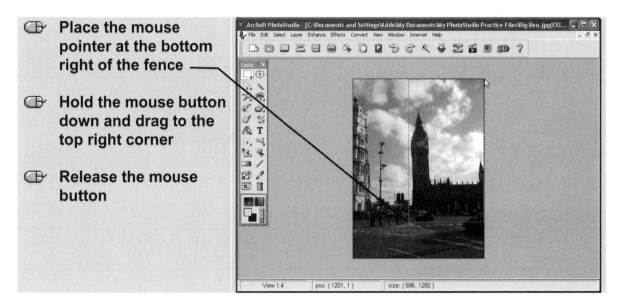

☞ Hide the *Options Palette* ✐1

Now you can select the part of the photo that's of interest.

Place the mouse pointer at the bottom right of the fence

Hold the mouse button down and drag to the top right corner

Release the mouse button

The blinking dotted line encloses the part of the photo you've selected:

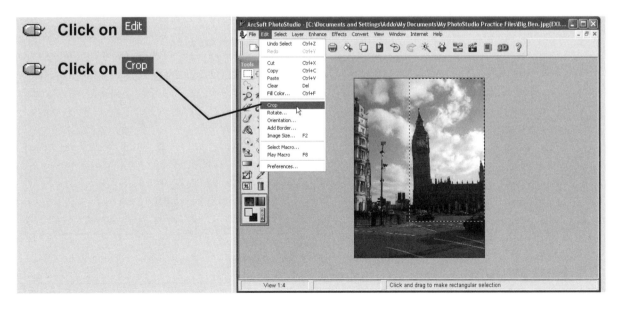

✖ HELP! I selected the wrong thing.

You might decide that you didn't select exactly the part of the photo you'd like. In that case, you can remove the selection and start over again.

👆 **Click on** Select
👆 **Click on** None
☞ **Select the part you want**

Here's how you cut out just this selection:

👆 **Click on** Edit

👆 **Click on** Crop

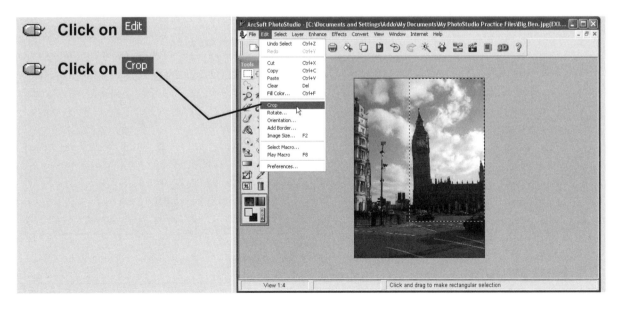

The photo is quite a bit smaller now. You can display it at a larger size.

Click on View

Click on Fit In Window

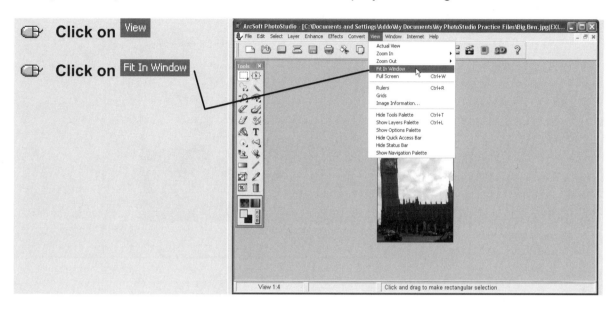

The Photo's Dimensions

The dimensions of a photo are expressed in *pixels*, *inches*, or *centimeters*.
You can take a look at the size of the photo you've just cropped.

Click on View

Click on Image Information...

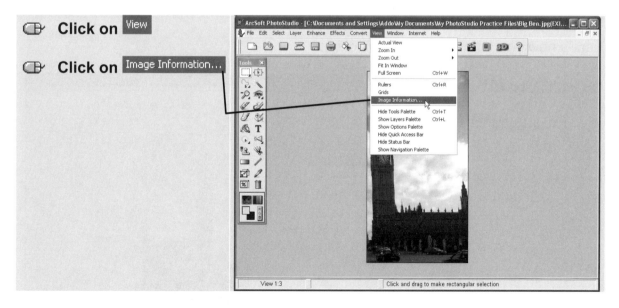

⇨ **Please note:**

The dimensions in the *Image Information* window won't be exactly the same for you as in the picture below. These numbers depend on the size of the selection you made.

The photo is 696 pixels wide
and 1280 pixels high:

☞ **Click on the radio
button ○ beside** Inch

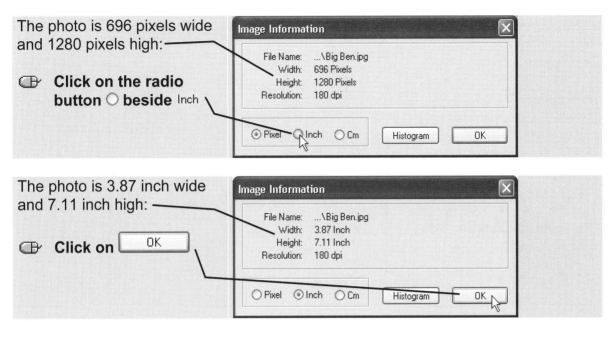

The photo is 3.87 inch wide
and 7.11 inch high:

☞ **Click on** OK

The photo is very tall and narrow. In *PhotoStudio* you can enlarge or shrink the photo
to any desired size. You'll find out how to do that in the following sections.

Shrinking a Photo

Every photo-editing program can enlarge or shrink a photo. These changes are
sometimes necessary to fit a photo into a document at a particular place, or if you
want to send a photo by e-mail.

☞ **Click on** Edit

☞ **Click on** Image Size...

In the *Image Size* window, the photo size is only displayed in pixels:

The option ☑ Keep Aspect Ratio is selected. This means that if you change the width of the image, the height will automatically change along with it: ────────

The width and height of the photo are set to 100%:

Image Size   ☒

> Width: 696   Pixels
> Height: 1280   Pixels
> Resolution: 180   dpi

☑ Keep Aspect Ratio

> Width: 696   Pixels   WScale: 100 %
> Height: 1280   Pixels   HScale: 100 %
> Resolution: 180   dpi

Quality
○ Good
◉ Best

OK   Cancel

Now you can shrink the photo to, say, 25%.

⌨ **Type:** 25 **beside** WScale:

You see that the numbers beside Width:, Height: and HScale: automatically change:

☞ **Click on** OK

Image Size   ☒

> Width: 696   Pixels
> Height: 1280   Pixels
> Resolution: 180   dpi

☑ Keep Aspect Ratio

> Width: 174   Pixels   WScale: 25   %
> Height: 320   Pixels   HScale: 25   %
> Resolution: 180   dpi

Quality
○ Good
◉ Best

OK   Cancel

The photo's quite a bit smaller now:

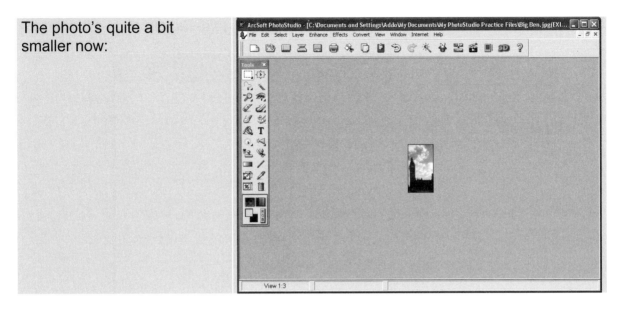

Of course, you can also enlarge a photo. In the next section, you'll see what effect that has.

Enlarging a Photo

You can enlarge a photo in the same window you just used to shrink the photo of Big Ben.

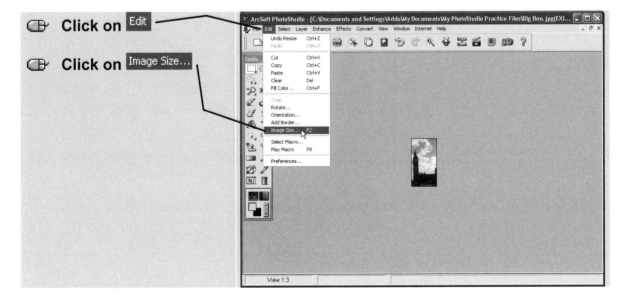

Now you can make the photo 15 times (1500%) larger, for example.

⌨ **Type:** 1500 **beside**
WScale:

🖰 **Click on** ⌷ OK ⌷

The program needs a little time to calculate the new size.

You see that the photo has become very grainy and blurry:

The reason for this is that the program can't change the size of a pixel. A pixel is a pixel. In order to enlarge the photo, the program adds pixels of the same color next to each existing pixel. This makes the photo grainy, and you almost see blocks instead of dots.

You can easily see this in this example because we've made an extreme enlargement from a photo that was shrunk first.

Digital enlarging can, therefore, give an unimpressive result due to the limited number of pixels. It certainly can't be compared with enlargements made in traditional photography. This disadvantage is eliminated, however, if you use a more professional digital camera. These cameras take photos containing tens of millions of pixels.

Undo

The result from the last action isn't too attractive. You could, of course, shrink the enlarged photo back down, but you won't get the same quality—after all, you'd be shrinking an ugly photo. By undoing the last action, however, you will get the original small photo back.

Click on Edit

Click on Undo Resize

Now you have the small photo back:

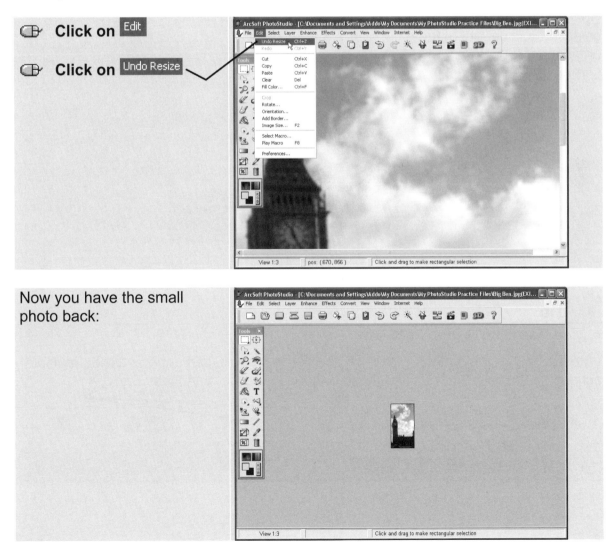

You can repeat this, undoing additional actions. Give it a try:

👆 **Click on** Edit

🖱 **Click on** Undo Resize

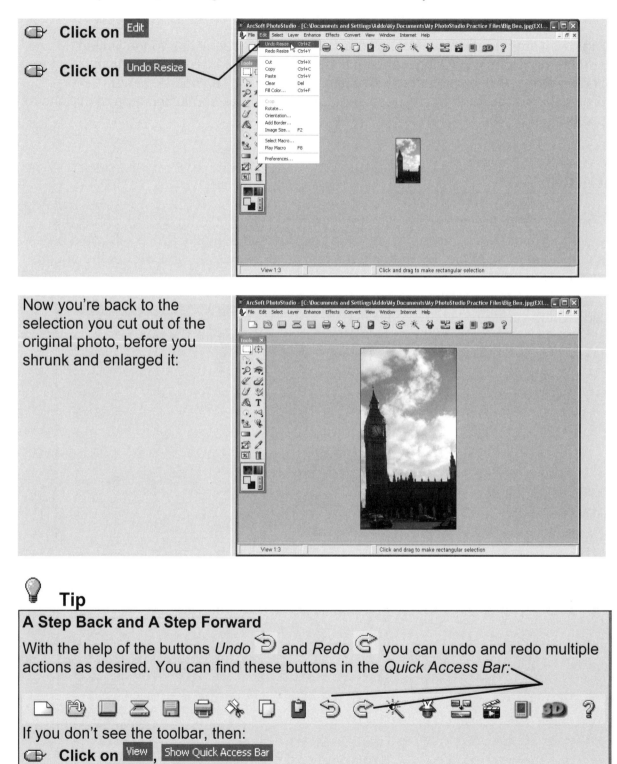

Now you're back to the selection you cut out of the original photo, before you shrunk and enlarged it:

💡 **Tip**

A Step Back and A Step Forward

With the help of the buttons *Undo* 🔙 and *Redo* 🔜 you can undo and redo multiple actions as desired. You can find these buttons in the *Quick Access Bar:*

If you don't see the toolbar, then:
👆 **Click on** View , Show Quick Access Bar

In *PhotoStudio* you can specify the maximum number of actions you want to be able to undo. You can change this setting in the *Preferences* window.

☞ **Click on** Edit

☞ **Click on** Preferences...

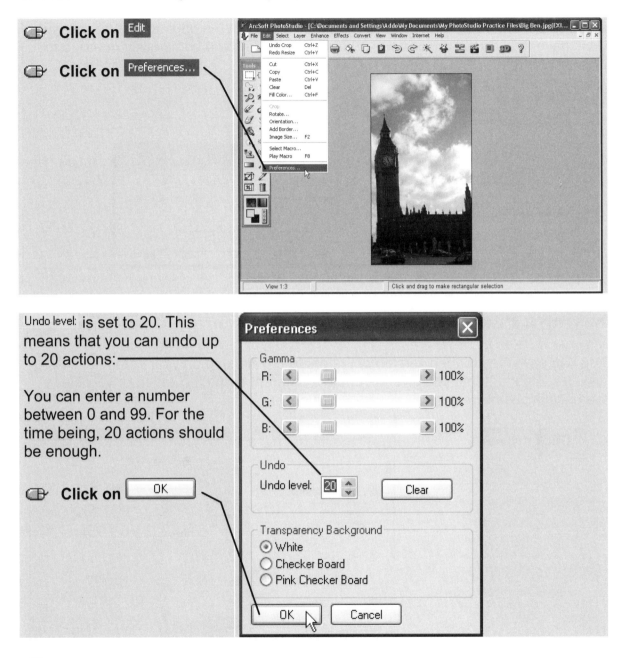

Undo level: is set to 20. This means that you can undo up to 20 actions:

You can enter a number between 0 and 99. For the time being, 20 actions should be enough.

☞ **Click on** OK

Tip

Since you can always undo your last actions, you have the freedom to experiment with your photos in different ways. You immediately see what the result of a particular action is. If you don't like the effect, just undo the action.

Tip

Restoring a Photo
If you've performed several actions and you want to get the original photo back, you
don't have to undo the actions one by one. Here's how you can quickly return to the
original photo:

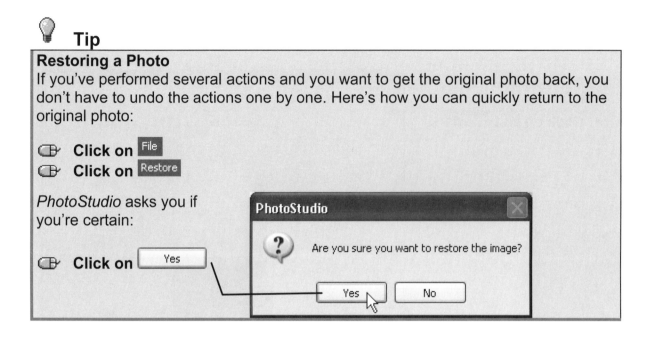

☞ **Click on** File
☞ **Click on** Restore

PhotoStudio asks you if
you're certain:

☞ **Click on** Yes

Saving a Photo

You can save the cropped version of the photo *Big Ben.jpg* on your computer's hard
disk. It's important that you give the photo a different name, however, or you'll lose
the original photo. Here's how you save the photo:

☞ **Click on** File

☞ **Click on** Save As...

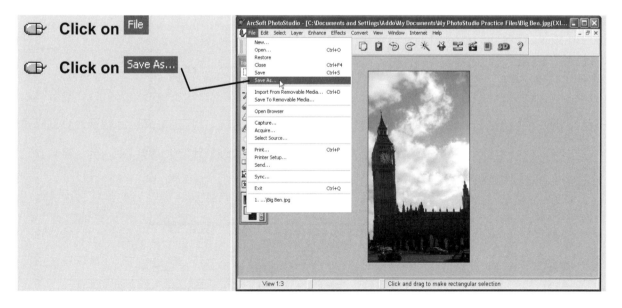

You see the *Save As* window.

PhotoStudio has already
opened the practice files
folder:

Now you can give the cropped photo a new name.

⌨ **Type beside** File name: :
Cropped Picture
Big Ben

🖰 **Click on** Save

The photo has been saved.
At the top of the window you
see the photo's new name:

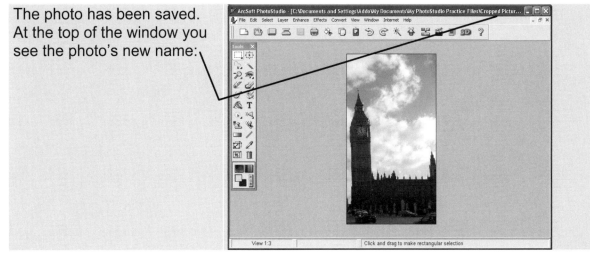

Closing PhotoStudio

You can close the *PhotoStudio* program as follows:

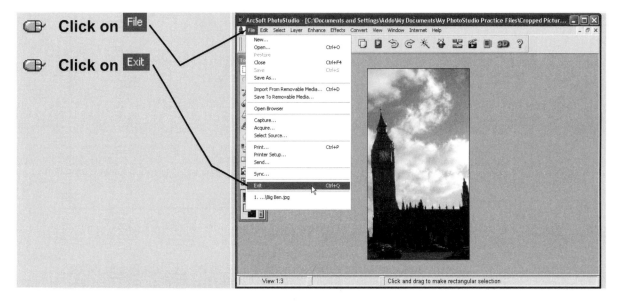

PhotoStudio has now been closed.

Exercises

The following exercises will help you master what you've just learned. Have you forgotten how to perform a particular action? Use the number beside the footsteps to look it up in the appendix *How Do I Do That Again?*

Exercise: Working with the Browser

In this exercise, you'll practice working with the *Browser*.

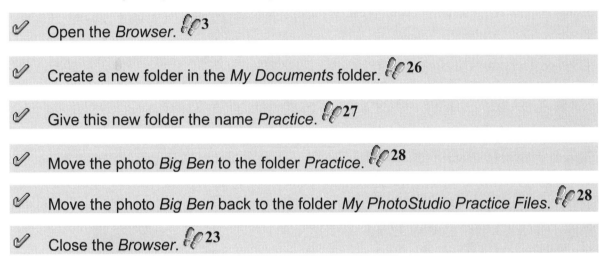

☑ Open the *Browser*. $\ell\ell^3$

☑ Create a new folder in the *My Documents* folder. $\ell\ell^{26}$

☑ Give this new folder the name *Practice*. $\ell\ell^{27}$

☑ Move the photo *Big Ben* to the folder *Practice*. $\ell\ell^{28}$

☑ Move the photo *Big Ben* back to the folder *My PhotoStudio Practice Files*. $\ell\ell^{28}$

☑ Close the *Browser*. $\ell\ell^{23}$

Exercise: Opening a Photo Using the Browser

In this exercise, you'll practice opening and editing a photo in the *Browser*.

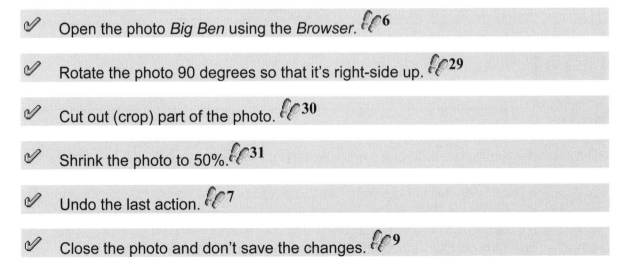

☑ Open the photo *Big Ben* using the *Browser*. $\ell\ell^6$

☑ Rotate the photo 90 degrees so that it's right-side up. $\ell\ell^{29}$

☑ Cut out (crop) part of the photo. $\ell\ell^{30}$

☑ Shrink the photo to 50%. $\ell\ell^{31}$

☑ Undo the last action. $\ell\ell^7$

☑ Close the photo and don't save the changes. $\ell\ell^9$

Background Information

What Is Digital Photography?

Digital photography is a method for taking photos using a light-sensitive chip, and saving and displaying them electronically.

A digital camera is actually just like an old-fashioned camera, except the film roll has been replaced by a CCD (*Charge Coupled Device*), a chip which captures the image in pixels. Then the digital photo is stored in a memory device.

One of the most striking differences between traditional and digital photography is the way in which the photo is taken. Like regular cameras, most digital cameras have a viewfinder you can hold up to your eye. However, many people use the LCD screen on the back of the digital camera much more often when taking photos. In that case, the photographer holds the camera a little bit in front of her:

Memory

The memory in many digital cameras is in the form of a *memory card*. This memory card is a little like an old-fashioned film roll: when the memory card is full, it has to be replaced with an empty memory card in order to take more pictures. You can transfer the photos on the full memory card to your computer, after which you can erase the memory card. This means you can reuse your memory cards over and over again, in contrast to the old-fashioned film roll. Some (less expensive) digital cameras don't use memory cards: they have only a small internal memory.

Switch to a Digital Camera, or Stick with the Trusty Film Roll?

Digital cameras have both advantages and disadvantages compared with regular cameras.

Advantages

The most obvious advantage of a digital camera is that you no longer have to buy rolls of film.
Nor do you have to wait for your photos to be developed and printed. You can immediately view the photos you take on the LCD screen on the back of the camera. You can see right away if the photo turned out well, and you can delete a bad photo on the spot.

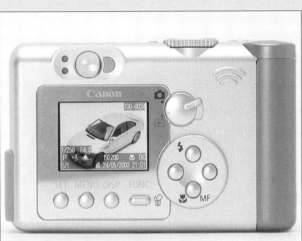

Camera with LCD screen

In addition, you can often take many more photos with a digital camera than the 36 maximum on a roll of film. Another advantage is that you can easily connect the camera to your computer. You can quickly send your photos to family and friends by e-mail. You can also edit your photos with a photo-editing program such as *PhotoStudio*.

Disadvantages

Of course, a digital camera also has its disadvantages. Although prices continue to drop, digital cameras are still more expensive than standard 35-mm cameras. Price differences among digital cameras can be great. These differences are related to the features offered by the camera, and its *resolution*. If you want to use your camera to take photos for your website, you can choose a camera with a low resolution. If you want to print enlargements of your photos, however, you'll need a more expensive camera with a higher resolution.

The higher the photo resolution, the more memory you need for the photo files. The price of memory cards for the camera increases as the storage capacity increases. Some digital cameras suffer from a bothersome delay between the moment you press the button and the moment the photo is actually taken. This can lead to unsuccessful photos of moving objects in particular, because the right moment has already passed. More expensive cameras have less to no delay.
Some LCD screens reflect (sun)light, which can make it difficult for you to see what's on the screen when taking or viewing photos.

What Does Resolution Mean?

All types of computer images (drawings and photos) are made up of thousands of small dots. These dots are called *pixels*. The quality of the photo depends on the number of dots it contains. If the photo contains many pixels, it will be sharp and clear. If the photo contains fewer pixels, it will be grainy or blurry. The number of pixels in the image is called the *resolution*.

Take a look at the examples below:

If you enlarge a photo significantly, you can see the pixels:

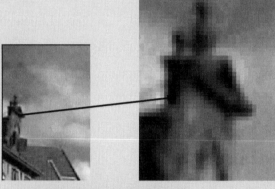

Here you see part of a low-resolution photo:

This photo was taken at a resolution of 640 pixels wide and 480 pixels high.

This is the same photo, but taken with a high-resolution camera:

This photo was taken at a resolution of 2048 pixels wide and 1536 high.

Megapixels

The term *megapixel* is often used to describe the resolution.

The number of megapixels is usually stated right on the camera:

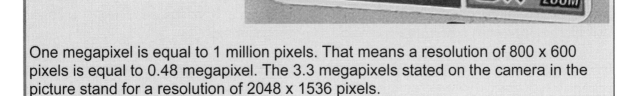

One megapixel is equal to 1 million pixels. That means a resolution of 800 x 600 pixels is equal to 0.48 megapixel. The 3.3 megapixels stated on the camera in the picture stand for a resolution of 2048 x 1536 pixels.

Color Depth

In addition to resolution, the number of colors used in a photo helps determine the quality of the photo. The number of available colors is called the *color depth*. Each pixel can take on a different color. The more colors that are used, the more information there is in the photo.

More colors produce a more realistic photo. At present, 16 million colors is a common number on a standard computer. Professional photos use even higher numbers, however.

What Should You Look For When Buying a Digital Camera?

The Resolution:

If you want to enlarge and print your photos, you'll need a camera with a high resolution. If you just want to use your photos on a website, a lower-resolution camera will be sufficient.

The Memory:

A camera that only has internal memory isn't very flexible. You can easily expand the available memory on a camera that uses memory cards by buying another memory card with greater capacity.

The Viewfinder:

The best option is a combination of the old-fashioned viewfinder and an LCD screen—particularly if you want to take photos at the beach, in the snow, or in the dark. In these situations, the image on the LCD screen is hard to see. Then you can use the viewfinder to better see what you're photographing.

The Energy Source:

It's a good idea to choose a camera that uses either rechargeable AA batteries or a proprietary battery that can be charged away from the camera. Otherwise you can never take photos and charge the battery at the same time. This way, you'll also always have reserve batteries on hand.

The Zoom Ratio:

Most digital cameras don't have exchangeable lenses like standard cameras do. That means you can't put a different lens on the camera in order to zoom way in and bring an image closer by. Digital cameras generally do have a small built-in zoom lens.

Optical or Digital Zoom:

There are two kinds of zoom: *optical* and *digital*. Digital zoom "blows up" the photo electronically, so to speak. As a result, the photo loses some of its sharpness. Digital zoom limits the file size, thereby decreasing the memory necessary to store the photo. Digitally zoomed photos are of poorer quality than unzoomed or optically zoomed photos.

Optical zoom works the same way as the zoom lens on your regular 35-mm camera. This zoom method preserves optimal quality, even after enlargement. This is because optical zoom alters the angle of view. At every zoom ratio, the camera uses the full resolution. The quality of the photo remains the same. For this reason, a camera with optical zoom is preferable.

Ease of Use:

Some types of cameras have several functions you might never (want to) use. Moreover, not every camera is a model of user friendliness. Be sure to inquire thoroughly about a camera's features and operation when you're thinking about buying it. You'll quickly see if the camera meets your desires in terms of ease of use.

Tips

💡 Tip

Extra Buttons in the Browser
At the top of the *Browser* in the program *PhotoStudio* you'll see a number of useful buttons:

With the button 🔍 you can search for a photo file on your computer's hard drive.

With the button 🗁 you can start your scanner program.

With the button ⚡ you can sort your photo files by name, type, size, or date.

With the button 🗑 you can delete a selected file. Before the file is deleted, *PhotoStudio* will ask you if you really want to remove it.

With the button 🖨 you can print the thumbnails you see in the *Browser*.

With the button ❓ you can start the Help function in *PhotoStudio*.

💡 Tip

Opening a Photo with the Shortcut Menu
You can also open a photo in the *Browser* using a shortcut menu:

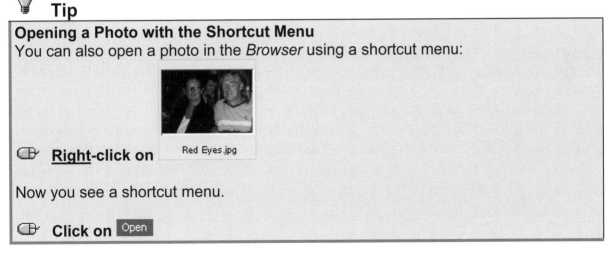

Red Eyes.jpg

👉 **Right**-click on

Now you see a shortcut menu.

👉 **Click on** Open

3. Improving Photos

You'll often want to improve a photo. The photo might be too light, or conversely too dark. Improperly lighted photos often occur when you use the flash. As you'll see in this chapter, you can do a lot to improve these kinds of photos.
Poor color is another common problem in photos. You can adjust these photos, too. Digital photos taken from far away are often not completely sharp. This is the result of the conversion of the image into pixels, and the camera-to-subject distance. With *PhotoStudio*, you can make these photos look better in a snap.

In this chapter, you'll learn how to:

- use the *Auto Enhance* function
- use the *Equalization* function
- manually adjust over- and underexposure
- use the *Color Balance* window
- make a photo sharper
- blur a photo

Auto Enhance

Sometimes photos are too dark; sometimes they're too light. Too-dark photos occur when you take a picture with too little light, or when the subject is backlit and you don't use the flash. Then the subject is underexposed. In *PhotoStudio* you can improve these photos in no time.

☞ **Start *PhotoStudio*** 2

☞ **Open the *Browser*** 3

☞ **Double-click on**

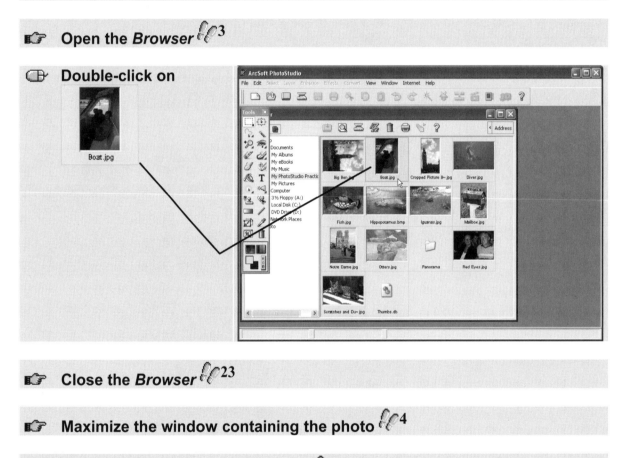

Boat.jpg

☞ **Close the *Browser*** 23

☞ **Maximize the window containing the photo** 4

☞ **Fit the photo to the whole window** 5

Now you see this photo of three people in a boat:

The light coming through the window caused the foreground of the photo to be much too dark.

See the color supplement, plate 1

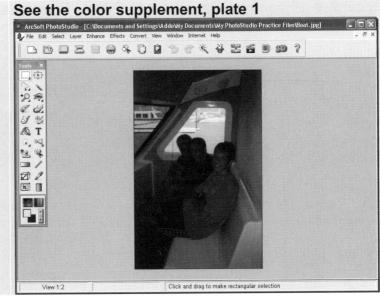

You can quickly improve this underexposed photo with the *Auto Enhance* function.

Click on `Enhance`

Click on `Auto Enhance...`

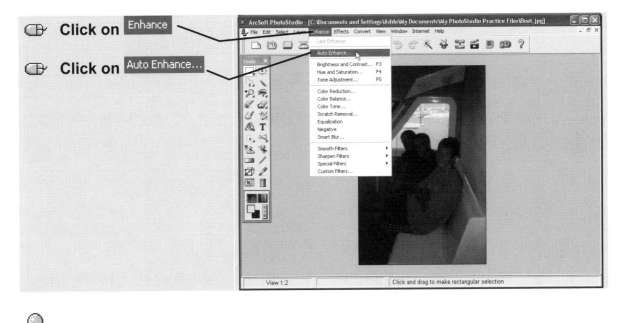

Tip

Quick Access

You can also start the *Auto Enhance* function with the button on the *Quick Access Bar*.

If you don't see this toolbar, then:

Click on `View`, `Show Quick Access Bar`

In the *Auto Enhance* window you can choose from several examples of adjustments to the photo. In these examples the original photo has been darkened as well as lightened. Go ahead and choose the lightest possible setting for the photo.

Click on the bottom right example

Click on OK

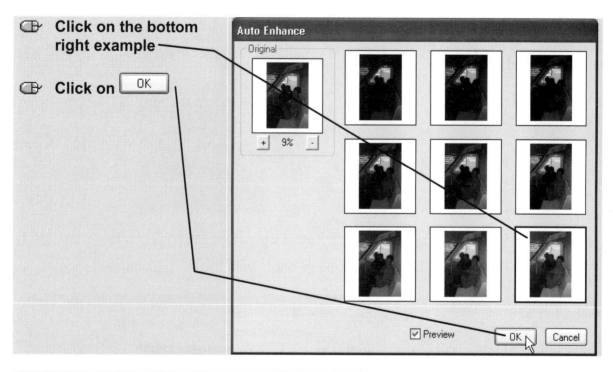

You see that the photo has gotten lighter. You can see the people somewhat better:

See the color supplement, plate 2

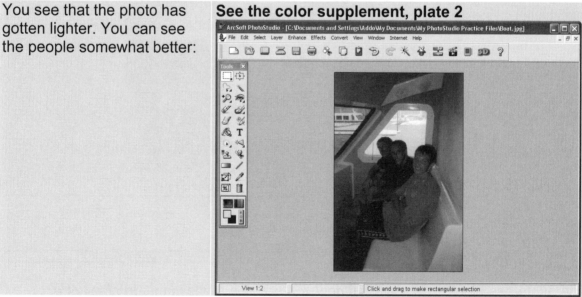

The photo has been improved. In order to see the people even more clearly, however, you'd have to repeat this action several times. You can correct the photo more quickly using another handy feature in *PhotoStudio*.

Equalization

The *Equalization* function vigorously adjusts the photo's brightness and contrast all at once. Go ahead and give it a try.

Click on Enhance

Click on Equalization

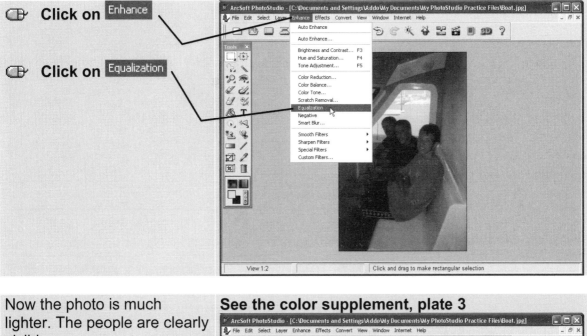

Now the photo is much lighter. The people are clearly visible:

See the color supplement, plate 3

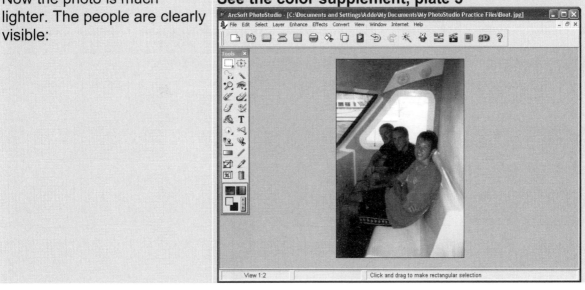

The photo has been improved. But now you can see spots in the photo all of a sudden. You can't do much about that. The spots are in the original photo, but they weren't visible because the photo was too dark. You can see them now because of the extensive corrrection that's been applied to the photo. Correcting a poor image won't always result in a perfect photo!

You can close the photo of the boat now.

Click on File

Click on Close

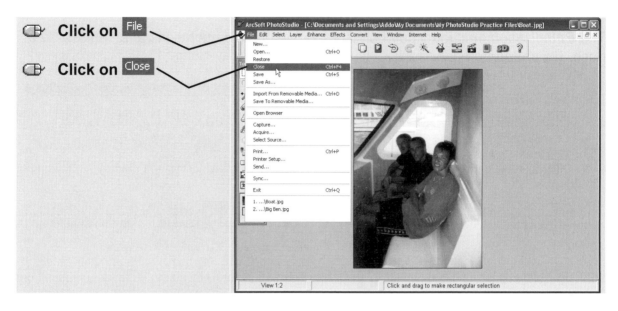

You can save the changes you've made.

Click on Yes

In the next section, you're going to adjust an overexposed photo.

Overexposed Photos

Photos that are too light occur when the flash is too close to the subject. A photo can also be overexposed if the subject is standing in strong sunlight. With *PhotoStudio* it is easy to take care of this common problem.

☞ **Open the photo *Otters* in the folder *My PhotoStudio Practice Files*** 𝓁𝓁⁶

☞ **Maximize the window containing the photo** 𝓁𝓁⁴

Now you see this photo of two otters in the zoo:

This photo is much too light, and the colors are washed out.

See the color supplement, plate 4

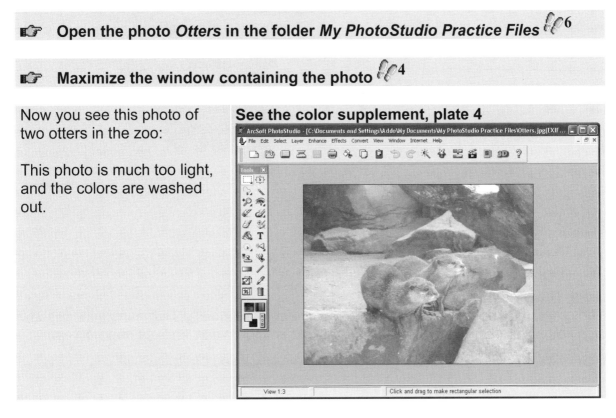

Let's give the *Equalization* function a try first.

🖱 **Click on** Enhance

🖱 **Click on** Equalization

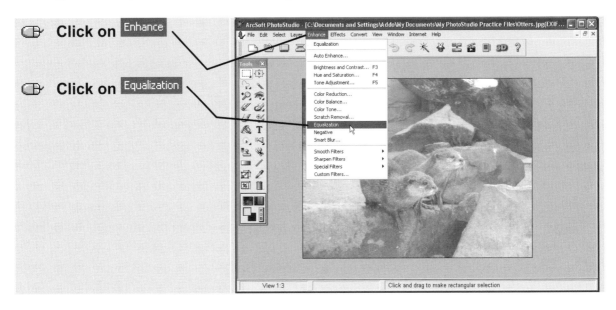

Although the photo has gotten darker, some parts of the photo are still very light. You can see this well if you look at the otters' snouts:

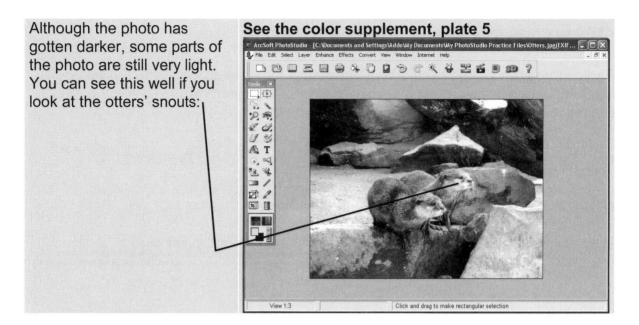

See the color supplement, plate 5

☞ **Undo the last action** 𝒻𝒸7

💡 **Tip**

Do-It-Yourself Improvements
The program performs the *Equalization* function automatically. Sometimes the result won't be what you were hoping for. In the next section, you'll find out how you can make additional improvements by hand.

The Brightness and Contrast Window

You can adjust the lighting in the photo even more with the help of the *Brightness and Contrast* window. In this window you have more control over the changes applied to the photo than you do with the *Equalization* function. Here's how you open the *Brightness and Contrast* window:

👉 **Click on** Enhance

👉 **Click on**
Brightness and Contrast...

In this window you can increase or decrease the brightness with the first slider:

When the check box beside ☑ Preview is checked, you immediately see what the effect on the original photo will be:

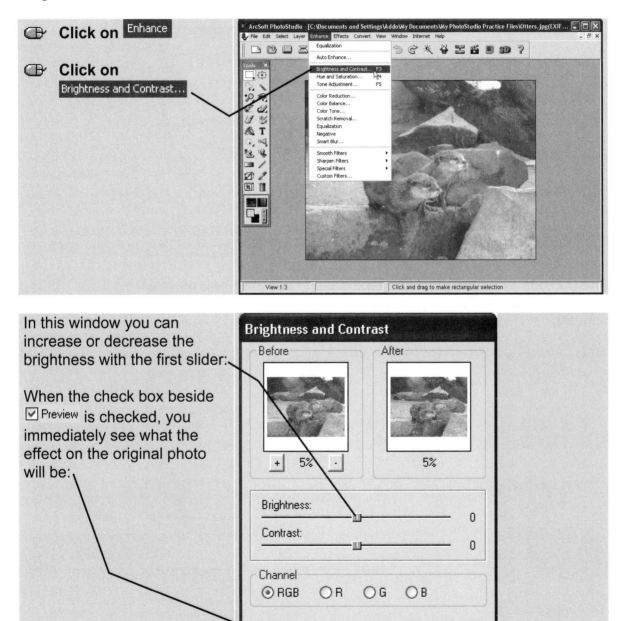

The photo of the otters is too bright, so you're going to decrease the brightness.

Drag the slider ▯ for
Brightness: **to the left until**
-20

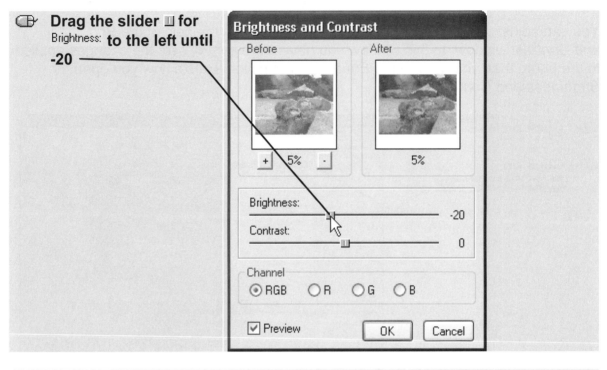

The photo has gotten a little darker, but not yet dark enough:

See the color supplement, plate 6

💡 **Tip**

Moving the Window
If the *Brightness and Contrast* window is in the way, you can move it:
- **Place the mouse pointer on the window's title bar**
- **Hold the mouse button down**
- **Drag the window to the desired location**

👆 **Drag the slider ▣ for**
Brightness: **to the left until**
-50

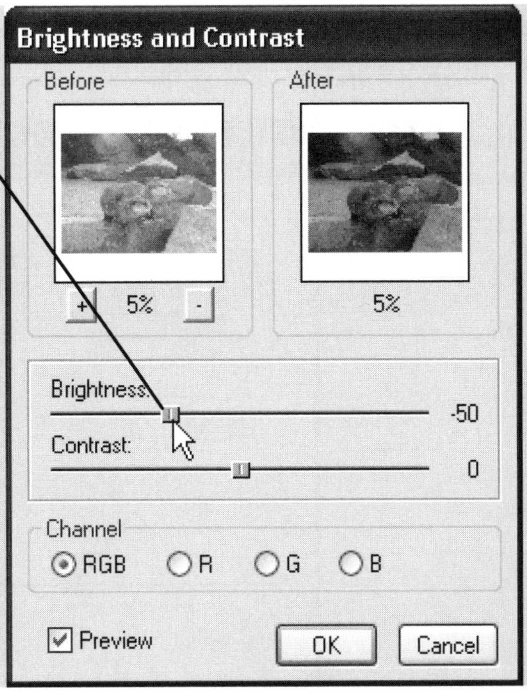

Brightness and Contrast

Before

After

+	5%	-

5%

Brightness: -50

Contrast: 0

Channel

⊙ RGB   ○ R   ○ G   ○ B

☑ Preview   [OK]   [Cancel]

Now the photo is dark enough, but it still looks a little hazy:

See the color supplement, plate 7

By increasing the photo's contrast, you decrease the degree to which the colors run together. This will make the photo look "harsher".

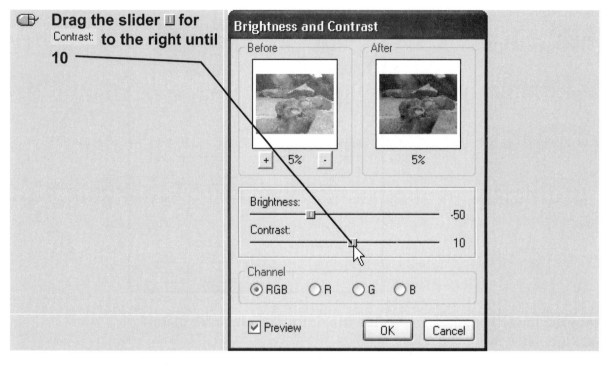

Drag the slider ▯ for Contrast: **to the right until 10**

The brightness and contrast have been sufficiently altered:

Click on ▭ OK

See the color supplement, plate 8

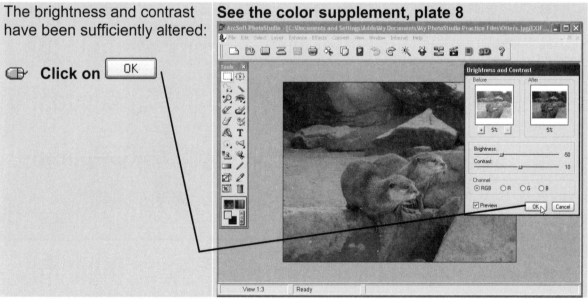

☞ **Close the photo *Otters* and save the changes** $\textit{l}\textit{l}^8$

Color Balance

Sometimes a photo seems to be covered by a film of color. The photo might be too red, too green, or too blue. In *PhotoStudio* you can adjust the color balance in a photo.

☞ **Open the photo *Red Eyes* in the folder *My PhotoStudio Practice Files* ℓℓ⁶**

☞ **Maximize the window containing the photo ℓℓ⁴**

This photo is clearly too red. You can see this if you look at the faces of the people in the photo:

See the color supplement, plate 9

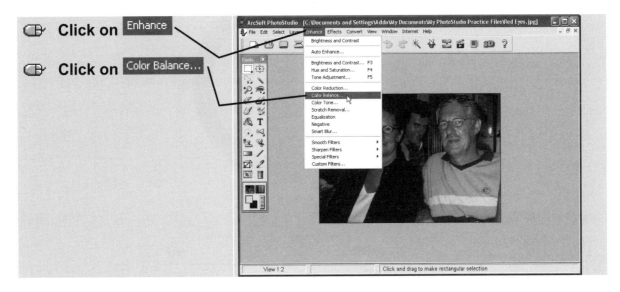

You can easily adjust this photo in the *Color Balance* window. You open this window as follows:

☞ **Click on** Enhance

☞ **Click on** Color Balance...

In the *Color Balance* window, you first specify that you want to adjust the *Midtones*.

☞ **Click on the radio button ○ beside** Midtones

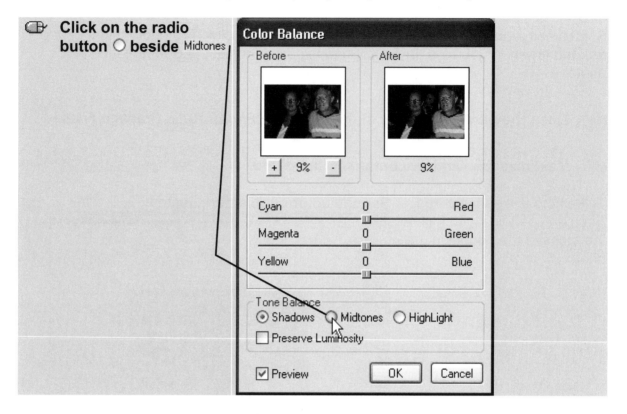

Now you can adjust the three complementary color pairs: cyan-red, magenta-green, and yellow-blue. You can create every possible color using these colors and black and white.

You can see this in the *color wheel*:

See the color supplement, plate 10

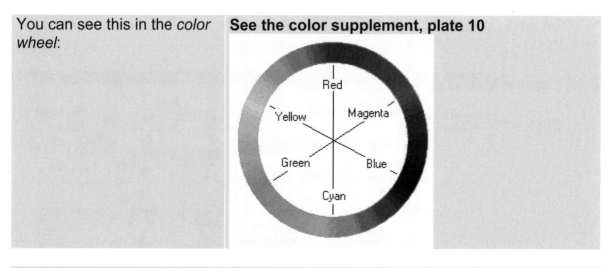

In the *Color Balance* window, you see sliding bars for these complementary color pairs:

You can correct the too-red photo now by taking out some red. Because red and cyan are complementary colors, you achieve the same effect by adding cyan.

☞ **Drag the slider ⬜ for** ^{Cyan} **to the left until -50**

☞ **Click on** OK

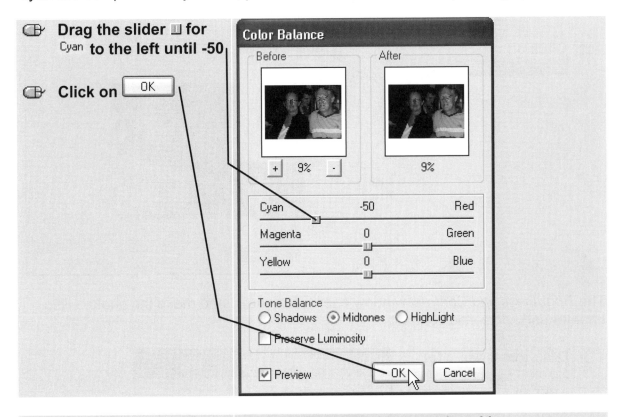

Now you see the altered photo. The photo is a little less red now. Because the photo is fairly dark, the suntanned faces still look a little red:

See the color supplement, plate 11

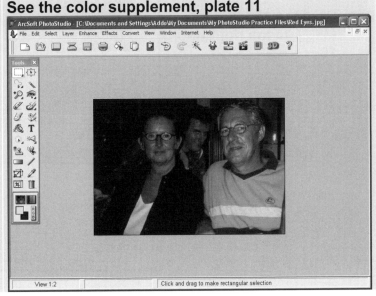

The photo will look even better if you make it a little lighter.

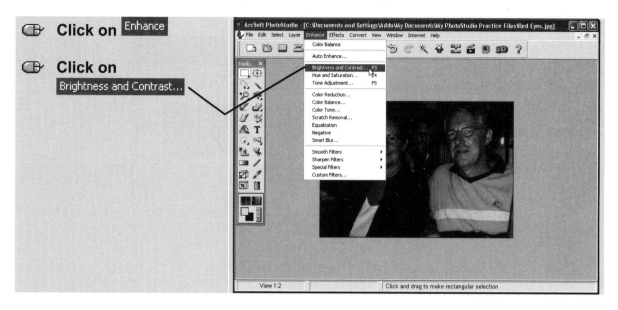

Click on Enhance

Click on
Brightness and Contrast...

The *Brightness and Contrast* window opens. Go ahead and make the photo a little brighter and add a little contrast.

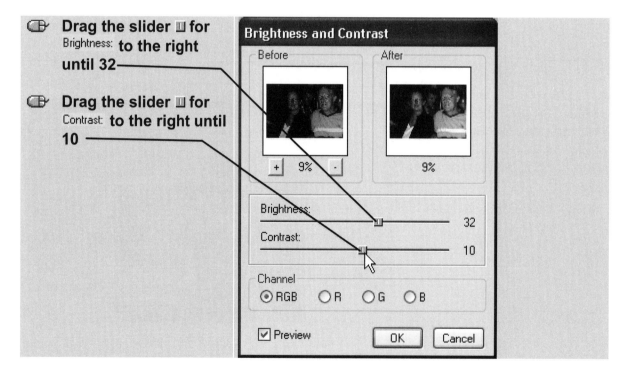

Drag the slider ▥ for Brightness: **to the right until 32**

Drag the slider ▥ for Contrast: **to the right until 10**

Now the photo has been sufficiently adjusted:

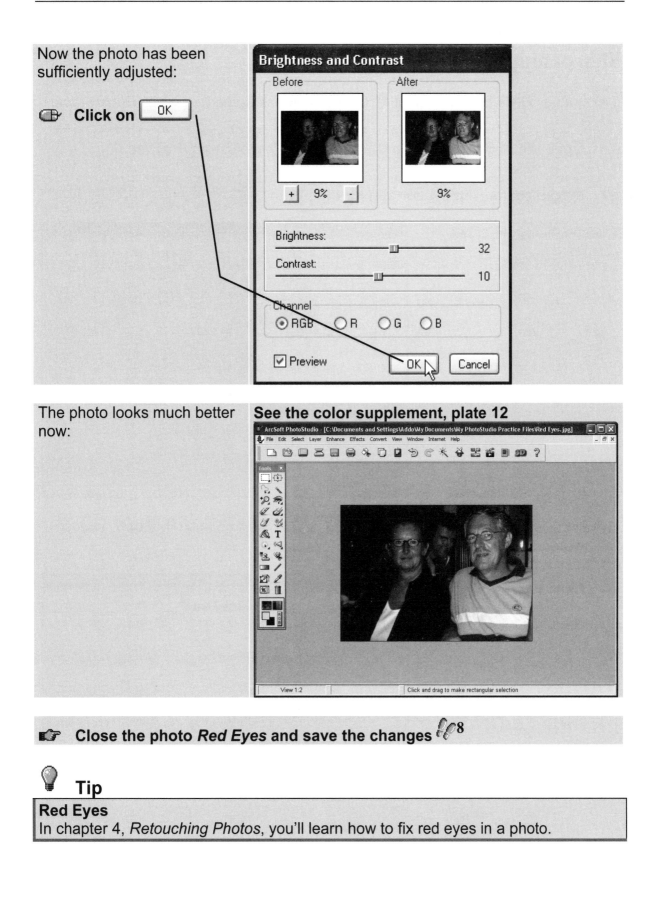

👆 **Click on** OK

The photo looks much better now:

See the color supplement, plate 12

☞ **Close the photo *Red Eyes* and save the changes** 👣⁸

💡 **Tip**

Red Eyes
In chapter 4, *Retouching Photos*, you'll learn how to fix red eyes in a photo.

Sharpening a Photo

If a photo is a little blurry or out of focus, you can easily sharpen it with *PhotoStudio*.

☞ **Open the photo *Iguanas* in the folder *My PhotoStudio Practice Files* 🐾⁶**

☞ **Maximize the window containing the photo 🐾⁴**

You see this photo of two iguanas:

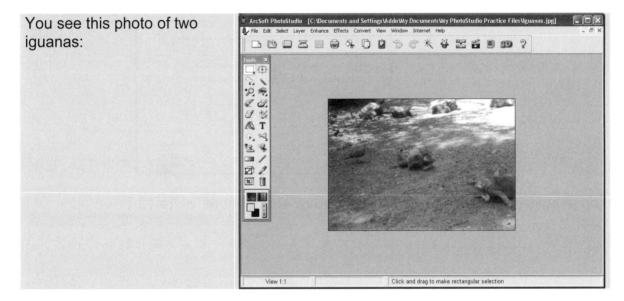

This photo was taken from a distance and therefore isn't completely sharp. You can see this more clearly if you view the photo closer up.

👆 **Click on** View

👆 **Click on** Zoom In

👆 **Click on** 2:1

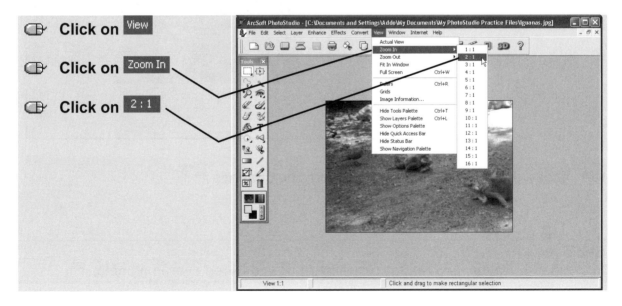

You see clearly that the photo isn't completely sharp:

See the color supplement, plate 13

You can sharpen this photo with the help of the *Sharpen Filters*. Here's how you do it:

Click on Enhance

Click on Sharpen Filters

Click on Sharpen Heavily

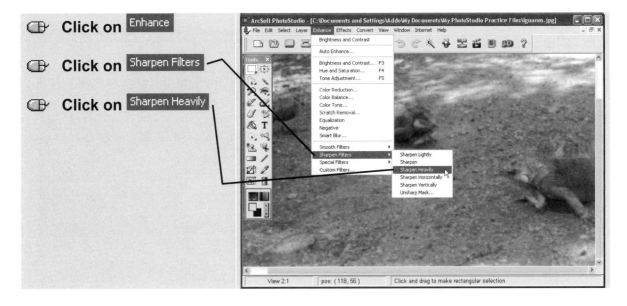

This correction is much too strong. The photo's become very splotchy.

You can undo this action:

☞ **Click on** ↩

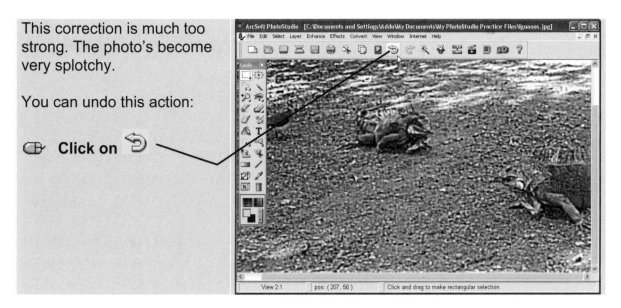

The *Sharpen Filters* work by increasing the contrast between neighboring pixels. If this is carried too far, the excessive contrast makes the image splotchy. Let's try it again, this time with a lighter correction.

☞ **Click on** `Enhance`

☞ **Click on** `Sharpen Filters`

☞ **Click on** `Sharpen Lightly`

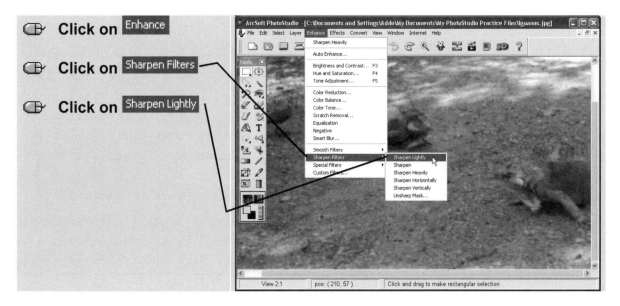

The iguanas are in better focus now, so that you can see more details:

See the color supplement, plate 14

  Tip

Another Use
You'll also get good results with the *Sharpen Filters* on photos that are blurry because the subject moved or the photo was taken too quickly.

  Tip

A Good Look at the Effects
If you undo the last action, you'll get the old, blurry photo back:

⊂⊟ **Click on** ↶

If you now redo the last action, the filter is applied again:

⊂⊟ **Click on** ↷

This lets you see clearly how the photo's been changed, in two consecutive images.

☞ **Close the photo *Iguanas* and save the changes** *ℓℓ*[8]

Blurring a Photo

You can also deliberately blur a photo with the *soft-focus* effect.

☞ **Open the photo *Fish* in the folder *My PhotoStudio Practice Files*** 🦶⁶

☞ **Maximize the window containing the photo** 🦶⁴

The photo of this fish is razor-sharp in the foreground and a little less sharp in the background:

See the color supplement, plate 15

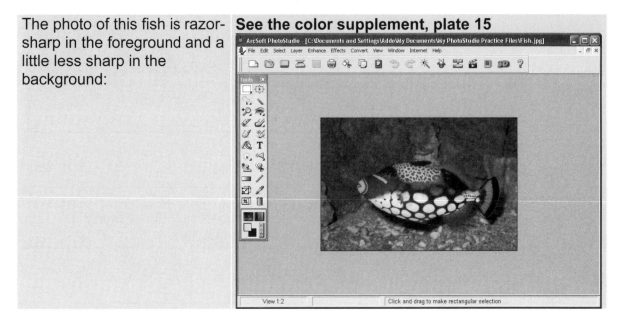

You can blur this photo with the help of a filter.

🖱 **Click on** Enhance

🖱 **Click on** Smooth Filters

🖱 **Click on** Blur Heavily

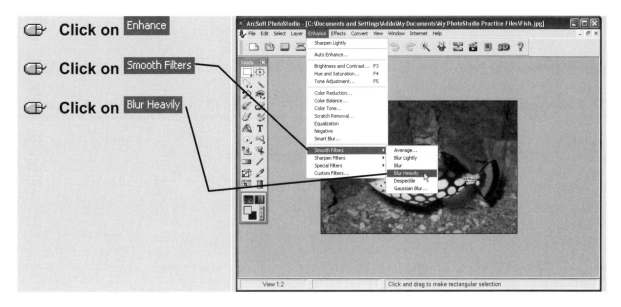

The photo's become quite a bit softer now. As a result, fewer details are visible on the fish, and it blends more into the background:

See the color supplement, plate 16

☞ **Close the photo *Fish* and <u>don't</u> save the changes** *ℓℓ*⁹

In this chapter, you've seen how you can improve photos. Now you can close *PhotoStudio.*

☞ **Close *PhotoStudio*** *ℓℓ*¹⁰

Exercises

The following exercise will help you master what you've just learned. Have you forgotten how to perform a particular action? Use the number beside the footsteps to look it up in the appendix *How Do I Do That Again?*

Exercise: Improving a Photo

In this exercise, you'll practice improving a photo by applying various functions.

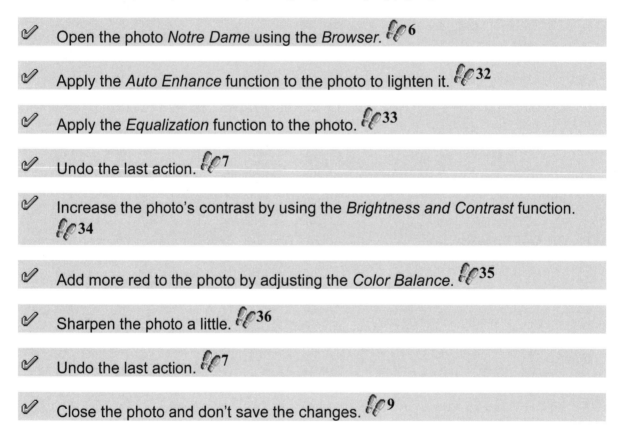

☑ Open the photo *Notre Dame* using the *Browser*. 𝓁𝓁6

☑ Apply the *Auto Enhance* function to the photo to lighten it. 𝓁𝓁32

☑ Apply the *Equalization* function to the photo. 𝓁𝓁33

☑ Undo the last action. 𝓁𝓁7

☑ Increase the photo's contrast by using the *Brightness and Contrast* function. 𝓁𝓁34

☑ Add more red to the photo by adjusting the *Color Balance*. 𝓁𝓁35

☑ Sharpen the photo a little. 𝓁𝓁36

☑ Undo the last action. 𝓁𝓁7

☑ Close the photo and don't save the changes. 𝓁𝓁9

Background Information

Digital Photography: Points to Consider

You'll usually get good results with a digital camera when lighting conditions are good. However, digital shots may give disappointing results in bad weather or weak lighting indoors.

Pay attention to the following points when taking photos with a digital camera:

- Make sure there's sufficient light.
- Avoid shots in which objects are strongly lit. This usually causes the rest of the photo to be underexposed.
- Avoid backlighting. When necessary, use the flash or the backlight setting on your camera. Consult your camera's manual to learn more.

- Don't take photos too quickly after one another. The camera needs a little time to activate and become light sensitive.

Light Sensitivity

Digital cameras have variable light sensitivity. You can adjust this setting on many cameras. Some digital camera brands express light sensitivity in **ISO** values, just as for standard cameras. (You may be more familiar with ASA, the old name for ISO.) Different ISO values apply to different circumstances.

- 100: outdoor shots in good weather, and to a limited degree indoor shots with flash
- 200: outdoor shots and indoor shots with flash
- 400: outdoor shots in bad weather and indoor shots (with flash)
- 1600: poor lighting conditions (indoors, pop concerts) and situations requiring a fast shutter speed (sports)

Lighting
Almost all digital cameras are equipped with automatic lighting. A light meter measures the quantity of light and then automatically sets the lighting for you. Usually you have to press the camera button slightly to allow the camera to measure the light in the scene. After a sound or light signal, you can press all the way down and take the photo.

Various Light Measurement Methods
Digital cameras use various methods for measuring the light in a scene. You can set the camera to use one of the following methods:

- **Matrix metering** is the standard setting for the automatic light meter. This method measures the light in the entire frame and chooses the best lighting.
- You can use **center-weighted metering** when the object is in the center of the shot and has an average gray value (18%).
- **Spot metering** measures only the light in a small area in the middle of the frame shown in the viewfinder. This is a good method when the background is much lighter than the subject.

The Flash
Most digital cameras have a built-in flash. When your camera is on the automatic setting, it will first calculate the lighting level and then decide whether or not to flash. The camera usually won't flash automatically when the subject is backlit: if the backlighting is strong enough, it will seem to the camera that there's enough light for the photo. Then the subject of the photo will be underexposed. Most cameras have a backlight setting. If you turn it on, the camera will go ahead and flash in that situation.

When you take pictures using the flash, there's a chance you'll end up with the *red- eye effect*. As a result of the light from the flash, the eyes of the person you're photographing take on an unnatural red color.

A special flash function can reduce this phenomenon. The flash gives off a series of preparatory flashes, allowing the pupils of the person being photographed to adjust to the bright light of the flash. The pupils contract, and the effect of the reflected light is less noticeable.

The Parts of the Digital Camera
Though digital cameras come in many shapes and sizes, several parts are common to all.

Camera Front:

Shutter release:

Flash:

Sensor:

Viewfinder:

Lens:

The available settings and number of buttons differ greatly among cameras. Some cameras have only a few settings, which you can usually access on the LCD screen on the back.

Camera Back:

Primary settings, such as shooting and displaying:

Viewfinder:

A selector switch for e.g. the flash:

The LCD screen:

The zoom button:

There's a compartment on the side for the memory card and a rechargeable battery:

In addition, many cameras have a port for a USB cable, so that you can connect the camera directly to your computer and upload the photos.

Batteries
Digital cameras devour batteries. It isn't much fun to find out the battery's dead right at the moment you want to take a good picture.

Capacity
Battery capacity is expressed in mAh (milliamp hour). This unit states the maximum current that can be provided for one hour. (If the current is half that amount, the battery will last two hours, and so on.)

Different kinds of batteries

Different Kinds of Batteries
- **Nickel Metal Hydride** (NiMH) is the type of rechargeable battery most suitable for use with digital cameras. One disadvantage of NiMH batteries is that they lose their charge: per day, they lose a little more than 1%. These batteries can be fully charged in 30 to 60 minutes using a special rapid charger. That means you quickly have full power at your disposal again. These batteries can be recharged up to 1,000 times.
- **Nickel Cadmium** (NiCd) rechargeable batteries have greater disadvantages. This type is more destructive for the environment because it contains cadmium, retains its electric charge for a shorter period, and has a shorter lifetime. In addition, these batteries permanently lose capacity if they are repeatedly recharged before they're completely empty. NiMH batteries are definitely the first choice!
- **Lithium** is an expensive, non-rechargeable battery. The advantage of lithium batteries is that they can be stored for up to 10 years without losing their charge. That makes them ideal reserve batteries for a digital camera.
- **Alkaline** is the most widely sold and least expensive non-rechargeable battery. These batteries keep for up to 3 years. Alkaline batteries can be bought anywhere in the world and are therefore very useful in an emergency. This kind of battery doesn't last long in a digital camera-less than half an hour of continuous use!

Characteristics of AA Batteries

Type	NiMH	Lithium	Alkaline
Capacity (mAh)	1,800	2,100	2,800
Life (hours)	2.0	2.0	0.4
Rechargeable?	Yes	No	No
Charged storage (months)	1	120	36

You can also buy more expensive rechargeable NiMH batteries with greater capacity. The capacity can reach 2,300 mAh.

How To Extend the Life of Your Batteries

- Remove the batteries if you won't be using the camera for an extended period. This prevents damage from leaking batteries.
- New rechargeable batteries don't reach their full capacity until they've been fully loaded and discharged several times.
- Turn off your camera's LCD screen, or set its brightness as low as possible.
- If possible, turn off the continuous auto-focus feature; this will save a lot of energy.
- It's a lot of fun to view the photos you've made over and over on the LCD screen. Just remember that viewing and paging through the photos with this LCD screen uses a lot of energy!

Memory Cards

Most cameras store photos on memory cards. These cards usually have 16 to 256 MB of memory and can therefore store many photos. The most commonly used types of cards are:

SmartMedia

Memory Stick

CompactFlash

Tips

🔅 Tip

Repeating the Same Action with a Macro

If you need to perform the same action on several photos, a *Macro* can save you a lot of time. You can save a series of commands in a macro and then apply them to the next photo(s) with a single mouse click.

For example, you can create a macro to shrink a photo by 25% and add a white border. It's very easy to record this macro: first, you carry out the actions just the way you want to save them in the macro.

☞ **Open a photo**

🖰 **Click on** Edit

🖰 **Click on** Image Size...

Shrink the photo to 75% of its current size:

⌨ **Type:** 75 **beside** WScale:

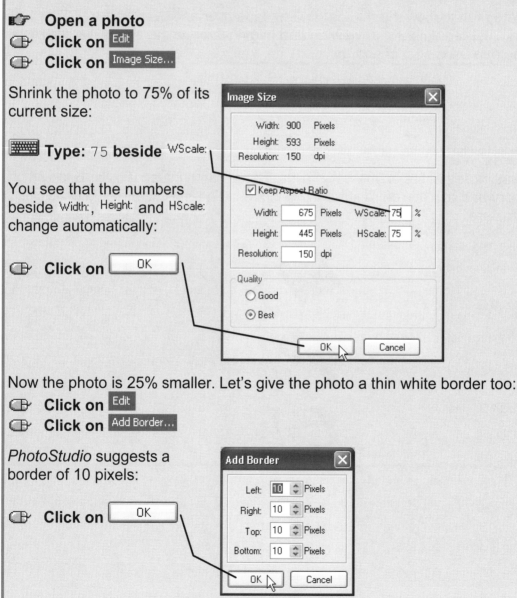

You see that the numbers beside Width:, Height: and HScale: change automatically:

🖰 **Click on** OK

Now the photo is 25% smaller. Let's give the photo a thin white border too:

🖰 **Click on** Edit

🖰 **Click on** Add Border...

PhotoStudio suggests a border of 10 pixels:

🖰 **Click on** OK

-Continue reading on the next page

Here's how the photo looks now:

You can save the changes you've just applied to the photo as a macro. You do this as follows:

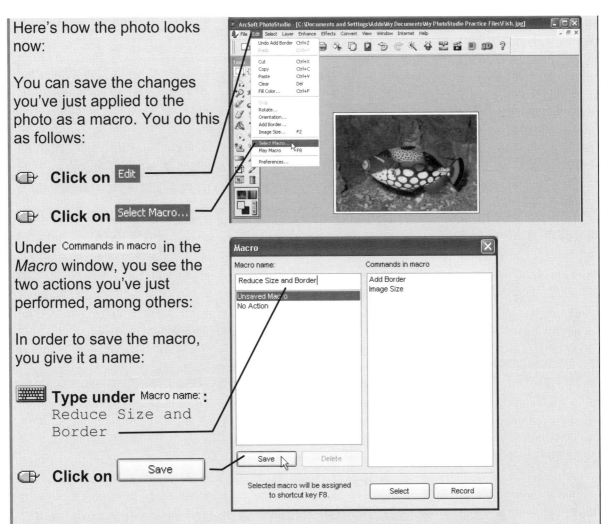

☞ **Click on** Edit

☞ **Click on** Select Macro...

Under Commands in macro in the *Macro* window, you see the two actions you've just performed, among others:

In order to save the macro, you give it a name:

⌨ **Type under** Macro name: :
  Reduce Size and
  Border

☞ **Click on** Save

The macro has now been saved. If you select this macro, you can apply it to another photo.

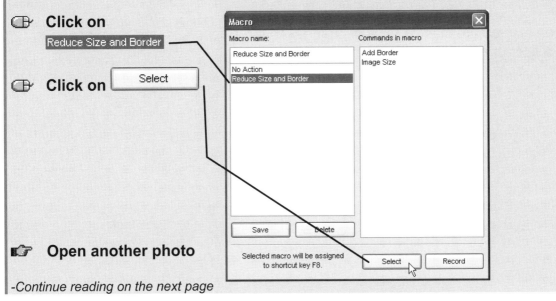

☞ **Click on**
  Reduce Size and Border

☞ **Click on** Select

☞ **Open another photo**

-Continue reading on the next page

Now you can quickly apply the macro using a button on the *Quick Access Bar*:

👆 **Click on**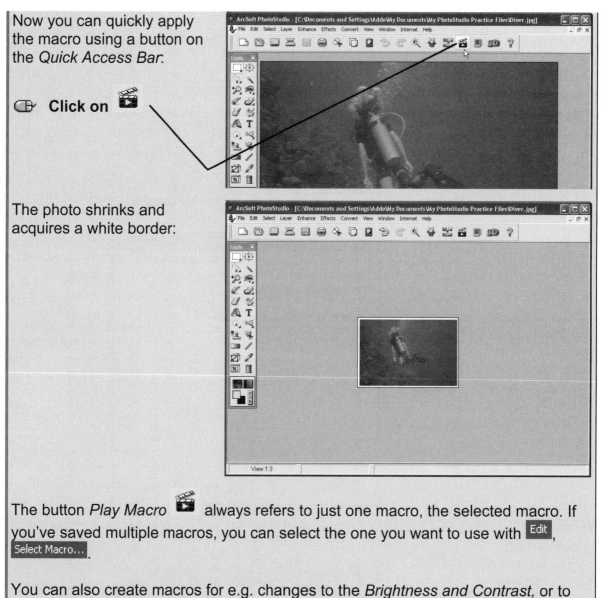

The photo shrinks and acquires a white border:

The button *Play Macro* 🎬 always refers to just one macro, the selected macro. If you've saved multiple macros, you can select the one you want to use with `Edit`, `Select Macro...`

You can also create macros for e.g. changes to the *Brightness and Contrast,* or to apply a filter or effect to the photo.

4. Retouching Photos

Photo-editing programs like *PhotoStudio* have many tools for touching up photos. Before, you could only touch up photos by hand; these days, there are electronic resources at our disposal. You can use them to rub out mistakes in a photo right on your computer screen. This is called *retouching*. For example, you can remove dust and small scratches with the help of a special filter. For larger scratches and other things that you don't want to see in the photo, you can use the *Clone* tool. This tool lets you replace part of a photo with something from elsewhere in the photo.
These skills will come in particularly handy when you scan in old photos or slides. But mistakes in photos also occur with modern digital cameras. Just think about the annoying phenomenon red eyes, resulting from the flash. *PhotoStudio* contains special functions for getting rid of these red eyes.
The program also provides professional exposure and focus tools. This puts resources at your disposal that were previously available only to professional photographers in darkrooms.

In this chapter, you'll learn how to:

- remove red eyes
- use the exposure tools *Lighten* and *Darken*
- remove spots with the *Clone* tool
- use the focus tools *Sharpen* and *Blur*
- select an entire photo
- remove small scratches and dust
- remove larger scratches

Removing Red Eyes

The red eyes that result from using the flash are one of the most common "mistakes" in photos. *PhotoStudio* contains a tool you can use to remove these red eyes.

☞ **Start *PhotoStudio*** 𝓮𝓮²

☞ **Open the photo *Red Eyes* in the folder *My PhotoStudio Practice Files*** 𝓮𝓮⁶

☞ **Maximize the window containing the photo** 𝓮𝓮⁴

You see the photo in which you previously adjusted the colors. The couple's eyes are clearly too red:	**See the color supplement, plate 17**

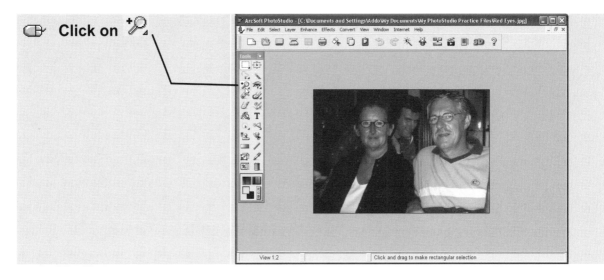

When you're going to fix red eyes, it's a good idea to zoom way in on the eyes.

🖱 **Click on** ⁺🔍

Go ahead and zoom in on the man using the magnifying glass.

Click four times with the 🔍 between the man's eyes

Now you see a good close-up of the eyes:

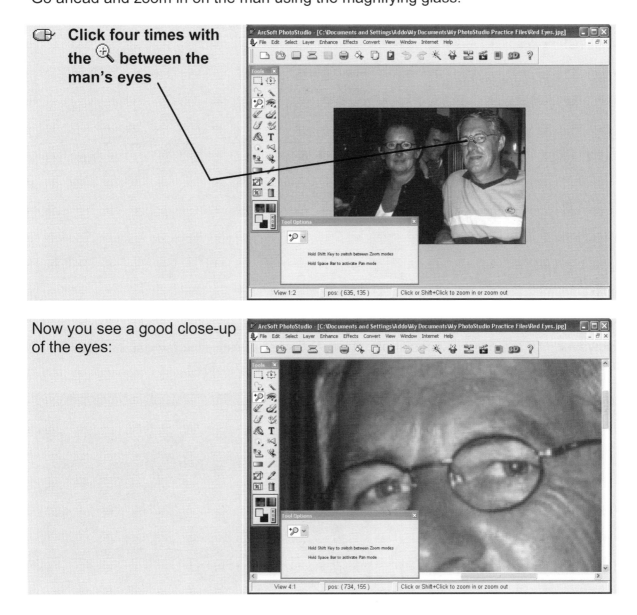

The *Auto Red-eye Removal* tool is in the *Tools Palette*.

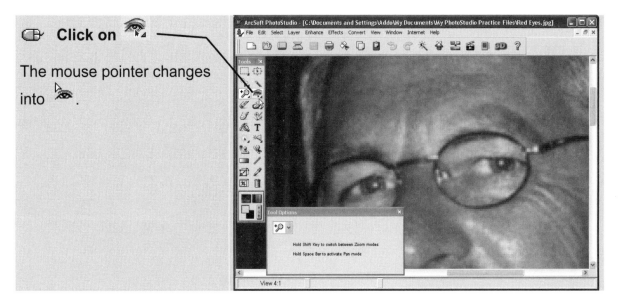

If the eye is red enough, this tool will touch up the entire red area in one go. Often, however, the red eye will consist of different shades of red, which means it can't be automatically fixed. Go ahead and give it a try on the right eye.

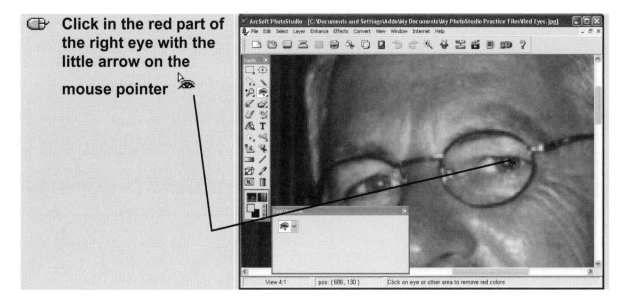

The tool doesn't recognize the red eye, so it can't automatically touch it up. *PhotoStudio* asks if you'd like to continue in *Manual* mode.

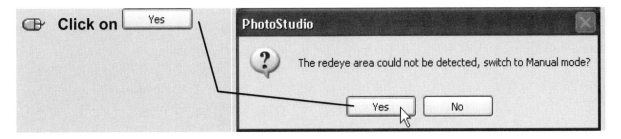

Click on Yes

Now you see the setting for the *Manual Red-eye Removal* tool in the *Options Palette*.

The *Brush Size* indicates how large an area will be affected with one mouse click:

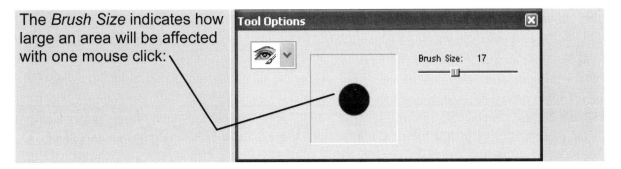

It's a good idea to choose a brush size that matches the size of the red eye. The current size is good for the left eye.

Click in the center of the left eye with the little arrow on the mouse pointer

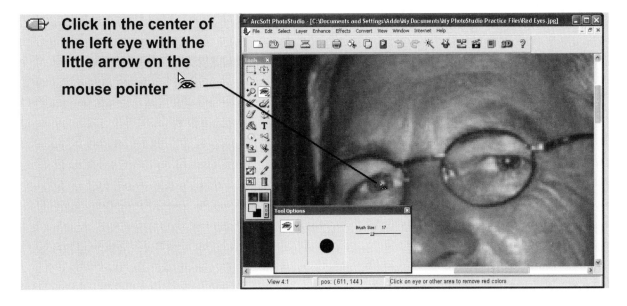

You see that the pixels surrounding the spot where you clicked immediately change color. The eye looks much better now:

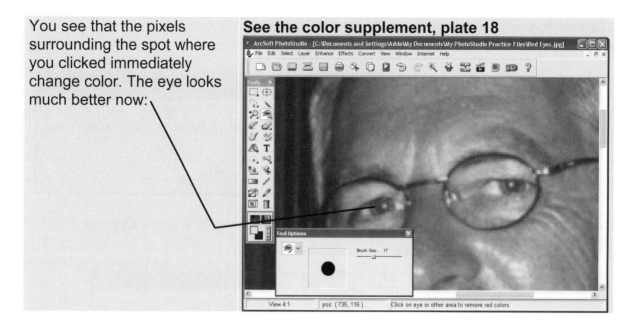

See the color supplement, plate 18

💡 **Tip**

Brush Size

If the person in the photo has a pinkish skin, the *Manual Red-eye Removal* tool can't distinguish between the red eye and the rest of the face. That means a section of the eyelid, for example, may change color if it falls within the brush size. For this reason, always choose the brush size that best matches the size of the red eye.

You can apply the same correction to the right eye now. The red part of this eye is somewhat smaller, so you can adjust the brush size.

👆 **Drag the slider ▯ for** Brush Size: **to the left until** **13**

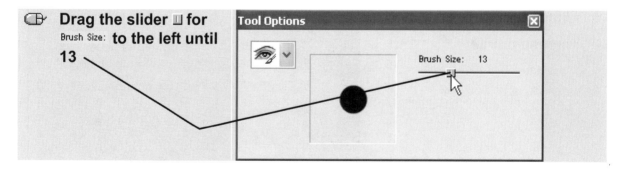

Click in the center of the right eye with the little arrow on the mouse pointer

Both eyes look much more natural now:

See the color supplement, plate 19

Now you can touch up the woman's eyes.

Drag the right and bottom scrollbars until you see the woman's eyes

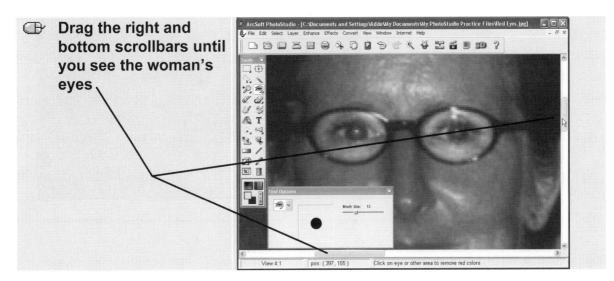

Go ahead and increase the brush size for these eyes.

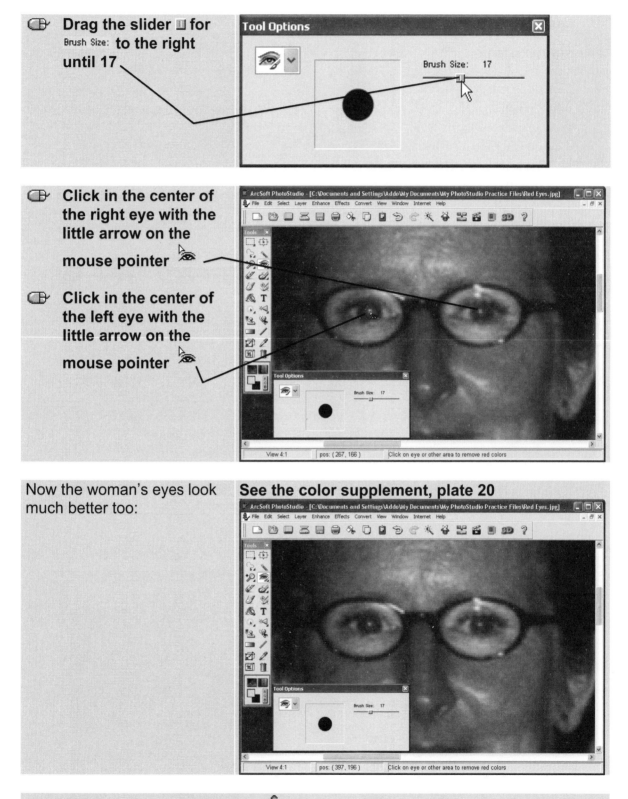

☞ **Drag the slider ▯ for** Brush Size: **to the right until 17**

☞ **Click in the center of the right eye with the little arrow on the mouse pointer** 👁

☞ **Click in the center of the left eye with the little arrow on the mouse pointer** 👁

Now the woman's eyes look much better too:

See the color supplement, plate 20

☞ **Fit the photo to the window** 👆⁵

☞ **Hide the *Options Palette* 🖌1**

You see that the photo looks much better and the red-eye effect is gone:

See the color supplement, plate 21

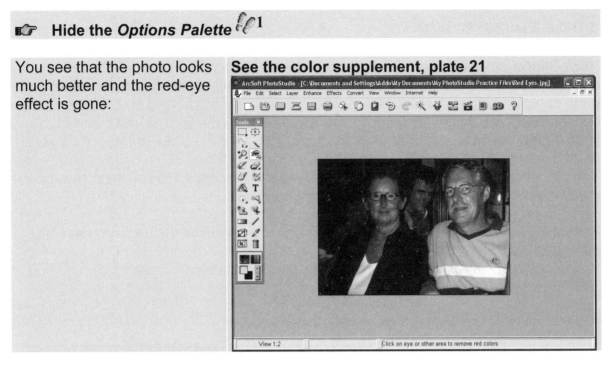

Let's work on this photo a little more. To be on the safe side, you can go ahead and save the changes you've already made.

👆 **Click on** `File`

👆 **Click on** `Save`

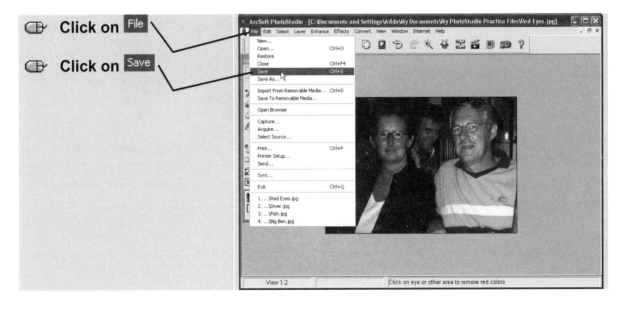

The Exposure Tools

PhotoStudio provides two special exposure tools: *Lighten* and *Darken*. These tools are based on two old darkroom techniques, *dodging* and *burning*, in which certain parts of the photo paper are under- or overexposed during printing so that they become lighter or darker. Photographers avoid (dodge) the light to make part of a photo lighter, or expose part of a photo to the light longer in order to make it darker (burn it in).
You can use the *Lighten* tool to make details in shadow easier to see. You can use the *Darken* tool to make details in bright light clearer.

Behind the woman in the photo, you can see a young man who's eager to have his picture taken.
You're going to make this young man's face somewhat easier to see.

☞ **Select the *Zoom In* tool** 🖐11

☞ **Click twice on the young man's face with the** 🔍

You can lighten the face with the *Lighten* tool. First, select the right tool:

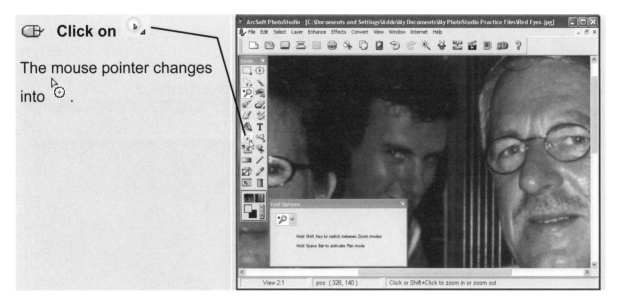

Click on

The mouse pointer changes into ⊘ .

Now change the brush size for the *Lighten* tool in the *Options Palette*.

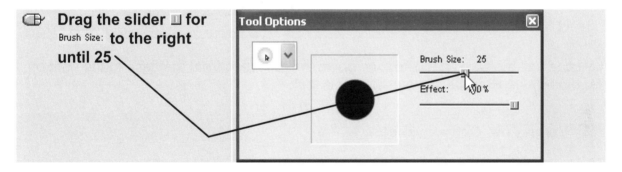

Drag the slider □ for Brush Size: **to the right until 25**

Adjust the strength of the effect next. It's a good idea to use a low value here, so the correction won't be too strong.

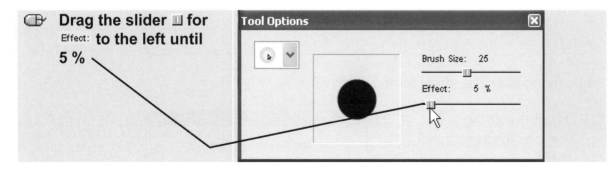

Drag the slider □ for Effect: **to the left until 5 %**

The palettes are covering the photo and are in the way; go ahead and close them.

☞ **Hide the *Tools Palette*** ✎12

☞ Hide the *Options Palette* ✍¹

By dragging over the area you want to correct, you can gradually adjust the exposure.

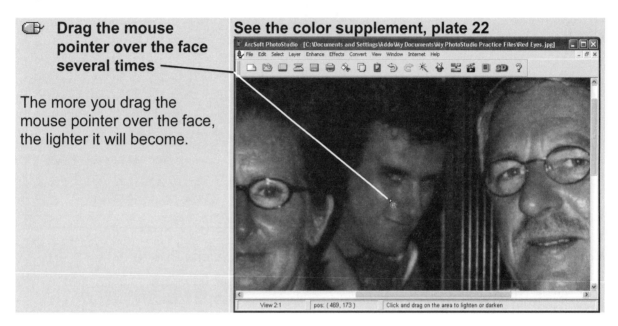

☞ **Drag the mouse pointer over the face several times**

The more you drag the mouse pointer over the face, the lighter it will become.

See the color supplement, plate 22

You can use the *Darken* tool to tone down the reflection from the flash to the right of the older man. Here's how you select this tool:

☞ **Display the *Options Palette* ✍¹³**

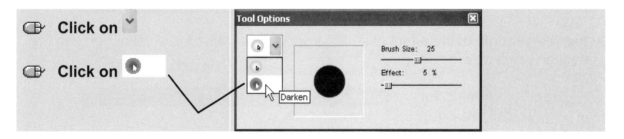

☞ **Click on** ⌄

☞ **Click on** ●

You can increase the effect for this tool:

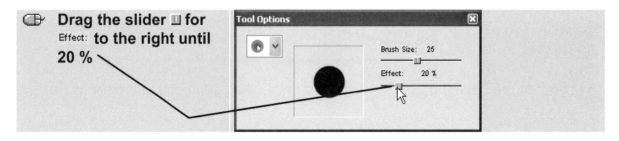

☞ **Drag the slider ▯ for** Effect: **to the right until 20 %**

🖱️ **Drag the scrollbars at the right and the bottom until you see the reflection on the right-hand side of the man**

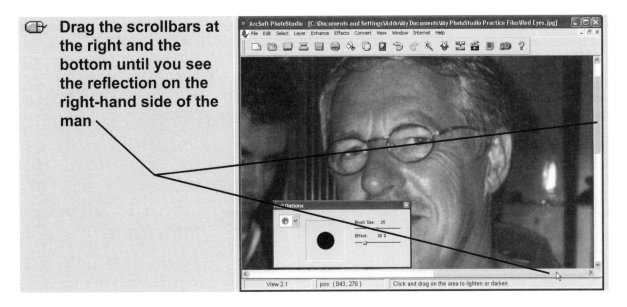

Now you can adjust the exposure.

🖱️ **Drag the mouse pointer over the light spot several times**

The more you drag the mouse pointer over this spot, the darker it will become. Keep going until this spot is no longer noticeable.

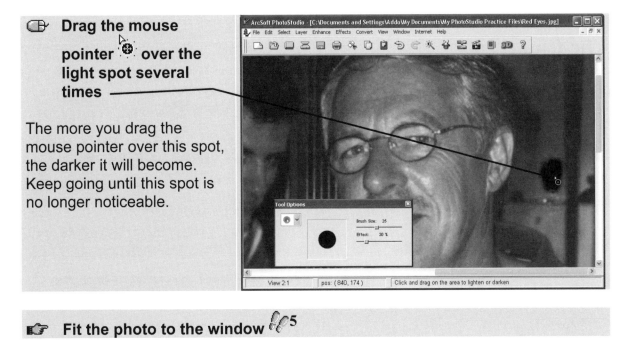

👉 **Fit the photo to the window** ✍️5

👉 **Hide the *Options Palette*** ✍️1

Now the photo's been adjusted well enough: the reflection from the flash is gone, and the young man in the middle is more clearly visible.

See the color supplement, plate 23

☞ **Close the photo and save the changes** ✍8

The Clone Tool

Sometimes you'll want to remove irregularities or spots in a photo in order to make the photo more attractive. You can do this by using the *Clone* tool.

☞ **Open the photo *Mailbox* in the folder *My PhotoStudio Practice Files*** ✍6

☞ **Maximize the window containing the photo** ✍4

☞ **Display the *Tools Palette*** ✍14

You see a photo of a mailbox. The white pole is a bit damaged:

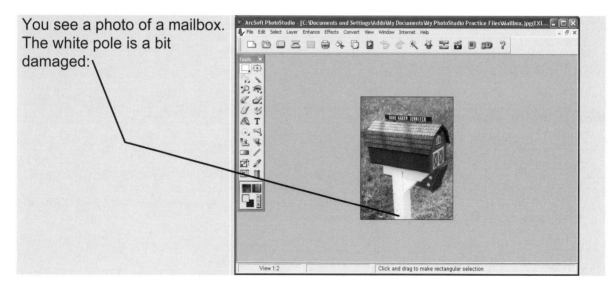

First, zoom in on the area you want to fix.

☞ **Select the *Zoom In* tool** 👆11

☞ **Hide the *Options Palette*** 👆1

Click twice on the bottom of the pole with the 🔍

Now the problem area is clearly in view:

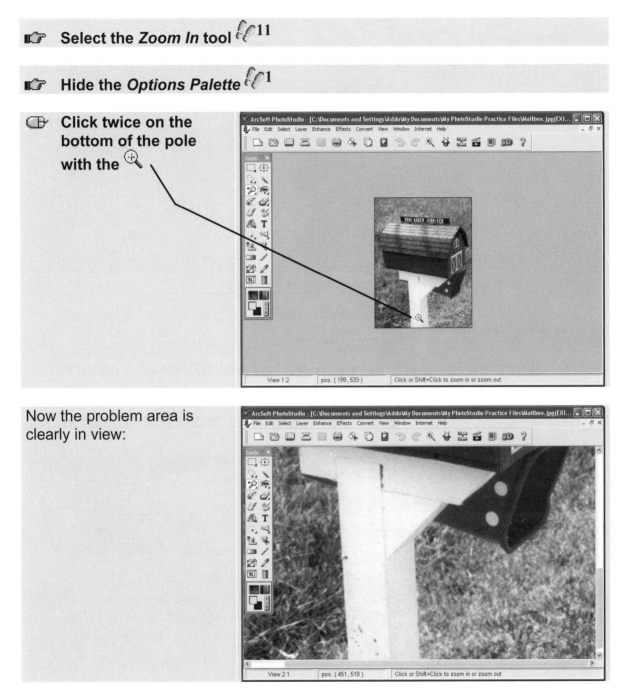

The *Clone* tool allows you to duplicate one area of the photo and paste it onto another. You can use this technique to cover the damaged area on the pole with the white color from an area on the rest of the pole.

First, select the *Clone* tool.

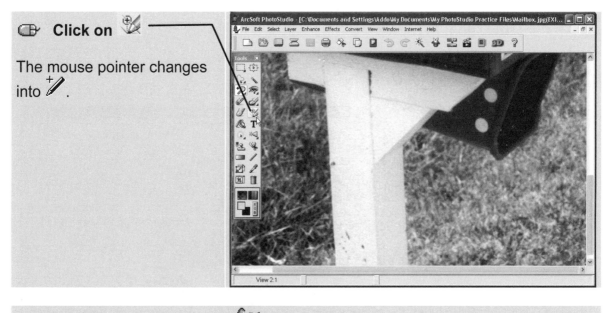

☞ **Hide the *Options Palette* ** 1

First, select the area you want to clone onto the ugly spots. This area is called the *cloning source*. Here's how you specify a point source:

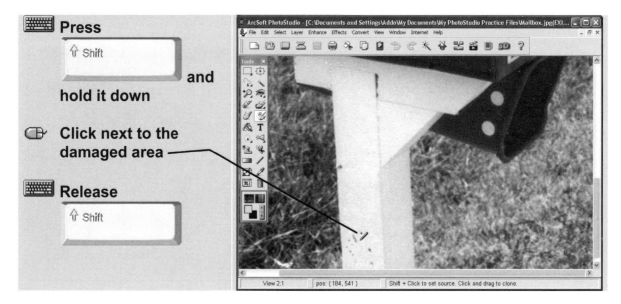

HELP! I see an error message.

If you see the error message below, then you've clicked on the image without first selecting a clone source.

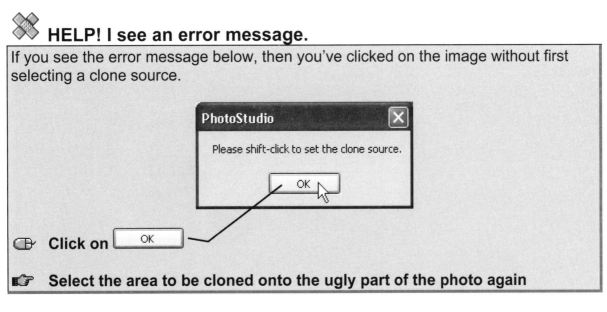

☞ **Click on** OK

☞ **Select the area to be cloned onto the ugly part of the photo again**

Now you can clone out the ugly spots on the pole.

☞ **Click on the ugly areas several times**

The dark spots are replaced.

While you're clicking, you'll see a ┼ beside the mouse pointer. This is the exact point on the photo that is being cloned out: ───

☞ **Repeat this action until the dark spots are gone**

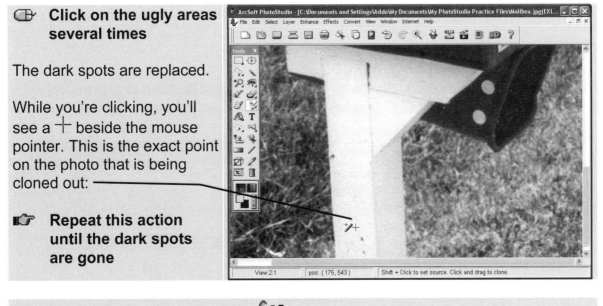

☞ **Fit the photo to the window** *e e*5

It takes some practice to get good at using the clone tool, but the results can be very rewarding:

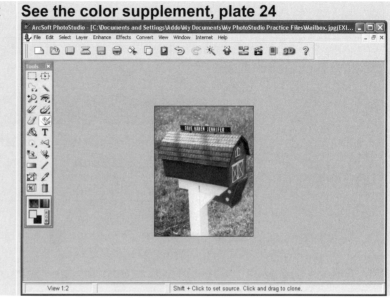

In the following section, you're going to work on this photo a little more.

The Focus Tools

In addition to the exposure tools you've already used, *PhotoStudio* also provides focus tools: *Sharpen* and *Blur*. You use *Blur* to soften hard edges in an image, so that some details are lost.
The *Sharpen* tool does just the opposite: it sharpens soft edges. The names on the mailbox aren't completely in focus. You can see this better if you zoom in on them.

☞ **Select the *Zoom In* tool** *ᵉᵉ*11

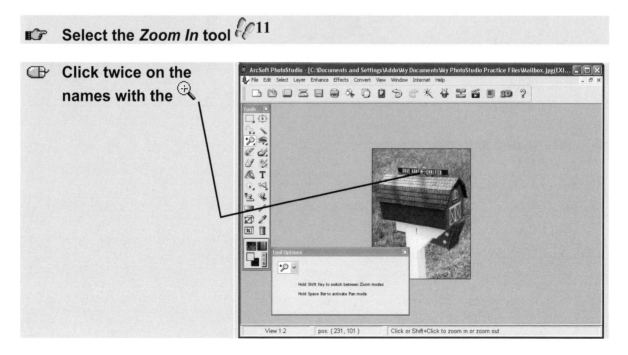

👆 **Click twice on the names with the** 🔍

The names are easier to see. Now you can select the *Sharpen* tool.

Click on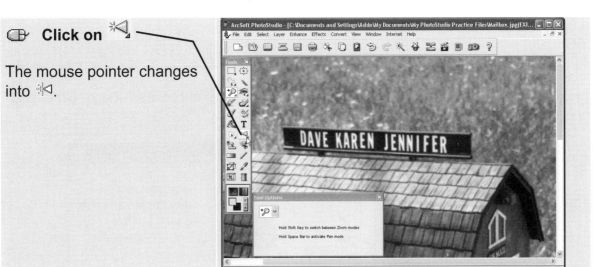

The mouse pointer changes
into .

Let's change the settings for this tool in the *Options Palette*.

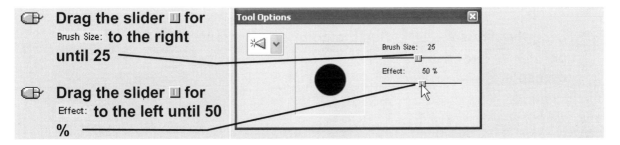

Drag the slider for
Brush Size: **to the right**
until 25

Drag the slider for
Effect: **to the left until 50**
%

The tool's effect has now been reduced and the brush is somewhat thicker. You can
sharpen the whole nameplate in one stroke with this thicker brush.

Drag the mouse
pointer from left to
right over the middle
of the letters

The more you drag across
the nameplate, the sharper
the letters become.

See the color supplement, plate 25

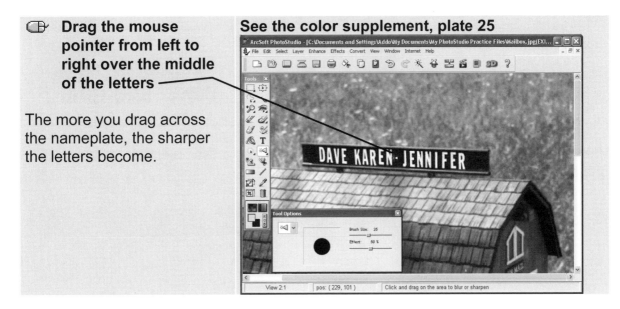

💡 Tip

If you drag over the letters too many times, they'll become splotchy. You can undo your last few actions with the help of the ↺ button.

In contrast, you can use the *Blur* tool to make part of the photo less sharp. Go ahead and select this tool in the *Options Palette*.

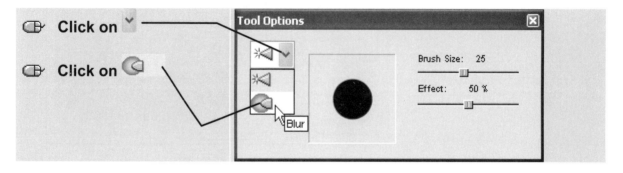

☞ Click on ˅ ────────

☞ Click on ◔

Now you can blur the letters on the mailbox a little.

☞ **Drag the mouse pointer ◔ over the nameplate** ──────

The more you drag over the nameplate, the fuzzier the letters become:

See the color supplement, plate 26

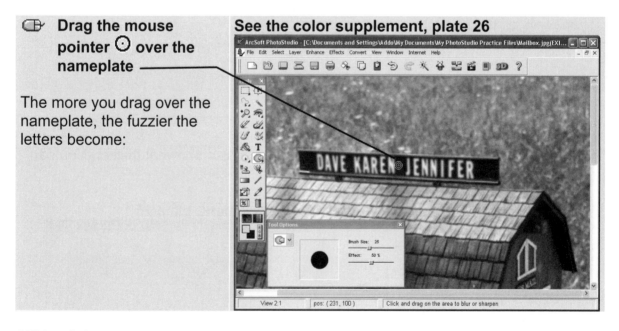

With a little practice, you can use these tools to add an artistic element to your photos.

☞ **Close the photo and <u>don't</u> save the changes** 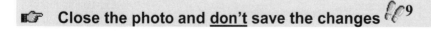⁹

Removing Scratches and Dust

There may be scratches and dust on printed photos that you have scanned. In *PhotoStudio*, you can quickly make these photos look better with the help of a filter.

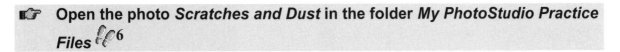

☞ **Open the photo *Scratches and Dust* in the folder *My PhotoStudio Practice Files* ℓ℘6**

☞ **Maximize the window containing the photo ℓ℘4**

☞ **Hide the *Options Palette* ℓ℘1**

You see this damaged photo with a long scratch and a number of smaller scratches and bits of dust:

See the color supplement, plate 27

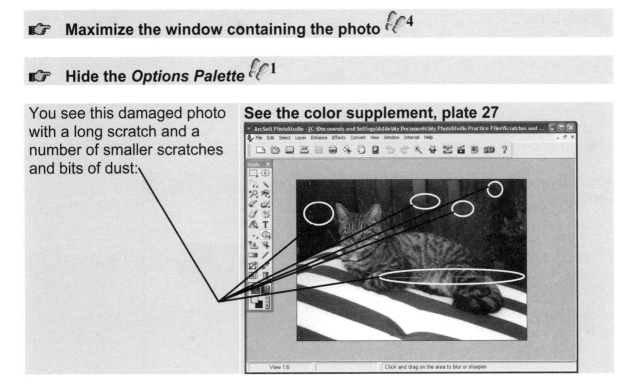

You're going to try to remove these blemishes with the *Scratch Removal* filter. First, select the entire photo.

⊕ **Click on** Select

⊕ **Click on** All

A blinking dotted line appears around the photo.

☞ **Click on** Enhance

☞ **Click on** Scratch Removal...

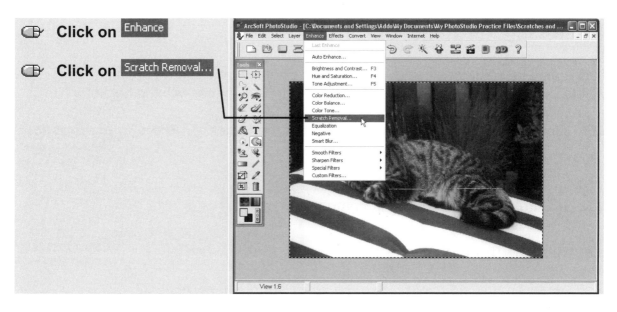

The *Scratch Removal* window appears.

The *Before* and *After* images in this window are very small.

If the box beside ☑ Preview is checked, you can also see the effect of the filter right away in the underlying photo:

The *Scratch Removal* filter changes pixels in the photo that differ greatly from the surrounding pixels, so that small scratches and dust particles disappear.
The *Threshold* determines how large the difference between adjacent pixels must be for the filter to be applied. The *Radius* determines how many pixels around an offending pixel will be altered.

You see that the default setting (Threshold:=0 and Radius:=3) makes the original photo very blurry:

You can sharpen the photo by raising the *Threshold*. The higher you set the threshold, the fewer pixels there will be to trigger the filter.

☞ **Drag the slider ▥ for** Threshold: **to the right until** 100

Now the photo's sharp again:

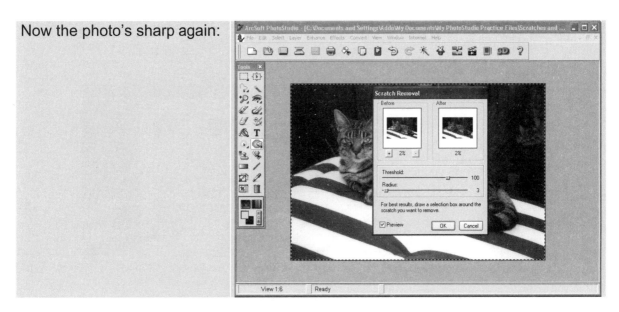

To remove slightly larger specks, increase the radius by 1 pixel.

☞ **Drag the slider ▯ for** Radius: **a little to the right until** [4]

The small scratches and dust are practically gone.

☞ **Click on** `OK`

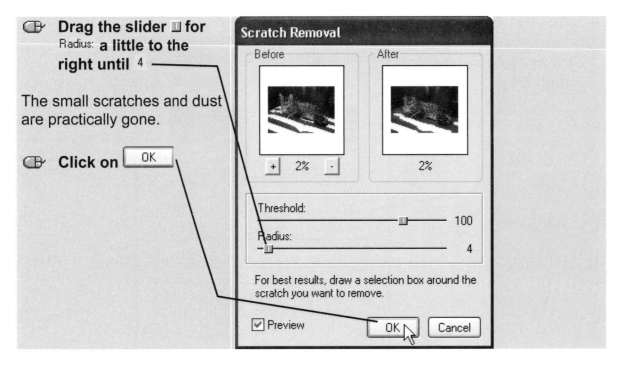

Now the program is busy processing the changes to the photo.

You can see that the small spots are nearly all gone now. Only the large scratch along the cat's belly is still partially visible:

See the color supplement, plate 28

💡 **Tip**

Experiment
Try different combinations for the radius and threshold settings until you find the combination that removes the scratches while keeping the photo as sharp as possible.

Here's how you hide the selection boundary around the photo:

👆 **Click on** Select

👆 **Click on** None

If you were to apply a stronger filter to remove the large scratch, the photo would become blurry. It's better to remove this scratch with the help of the *Clone* tool.

Cloning Out a Large Scratch

Before you start cloning, zoom way in on the scratch first.

☞ **Select the *Zoom In* tool** 👓⁻¹¹

| ⬇ | **Click on the scratch five times with the** 🔍 |

Then you can select the clone tool.

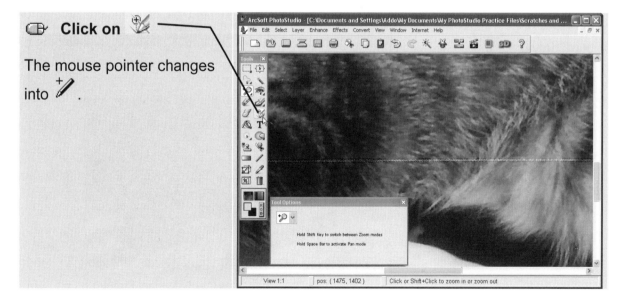

| ⬇ | **Click on** ✒ |

The mouse pointer changes into ✏ .

When you need to clone out a narrow area like this scratch, it's a good idea to use a smaller brush. You can set the brush size in the *Options Palette*.

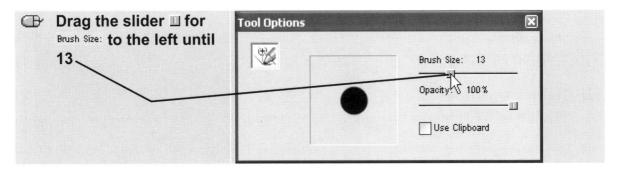

Drag the slider 🖳 for Brush Size: **to the left until 13.**

Now you can specify the cloning source, the area that should fill in the scratch.

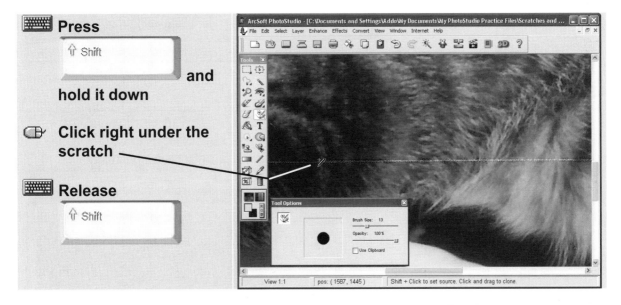

Press

⇧ Shift

and hold it down

Click right under the scratch

Release

⇧ Shift

The cat's fur consists of many different colors. That makes it hard to choose a cloning source that can fill the entire scratch. *PhotoStudio* has a solution for that. If, instead of clicking, you drag with the mouse while cloning, the cloning source will move along with the mouse. The position and the distance from the cloning source to the mouse pointer remain the same while you're cloning something out. This is very useful when you want to remove a scratch or tear in a photo.

Now you're ready to clone out the first part of the scratch.

☞ **Place the mouse pointer on the scratch right above the cloning source**

☞ **Hold down the left mouse button and drag along a section of the scratch**

The scratch is filled with the pattern the cloning source encounters during the dragging.

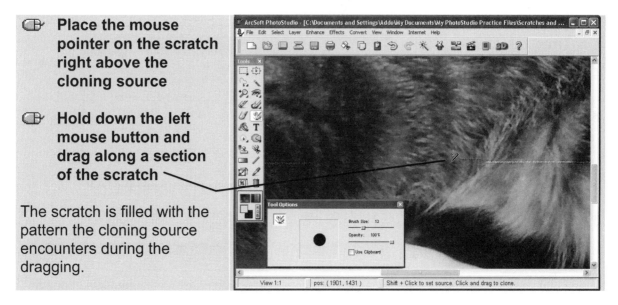

⇨ **Please note:**

As soon as you stop dragging and release the mouse button, the cloning source resets to the spot where you first selected it. When you start dragging again, the wrong color will appear. In that case, you should select a new cloning source.

☞ **Choose a new cloning source**

☞ **Place the mouse pointer on the scratch right above the new cloning source**

☞ **Hold down the left mouse button and drag along the scratch**

☞ **Repeat these steps until the whole scratch is gone**

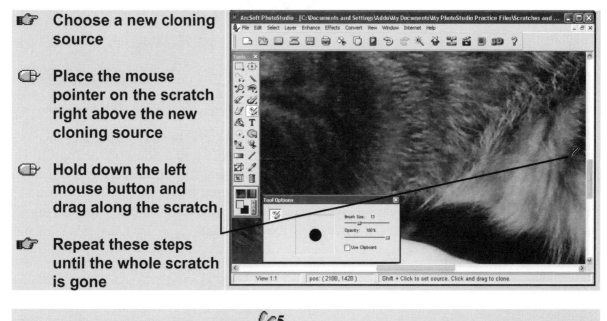

☞ Fit the photo to the window $\ell\ell^5$

☞ Hide the *Options Palette* $\ell\ell^1$

The photo has been repaired; not much is left of the scratch:

See the color supplement, plate 29

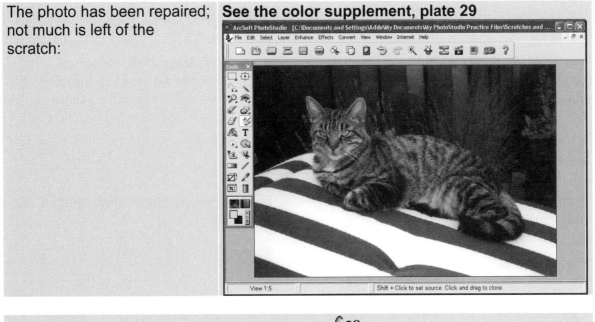

☞ **Close the photo and save the changes** 8

You've seen how you can improve and retouch your photos using *PhotoStudio*. In the next chapter, you'll learn how to work with selections.

Exercises

The following exercise will help you master what you've just learned. Have you forgotten how to perform a particular action? Use the number beside the footsteps to look it up in the appendix *How Do I Do That Again?*

Exercise: Removing Irregularities

In this exercise, you'll practice removing irregularities such as spots, dust specks, and scratches.

✔ Open the photo *Mailbox* using the *Browser.* 🦶6

✔ Maximize the window containing the photo. 🦶4

✔ Try to remove the spots on the pole using the *Scratch Removal* function. 🦶37

✔ Undo the last action. 🦶7

✔ Zoom in on the bottom of the pole. 🦶38

✔ Remove the spots on the pole using the *Clone* tool. 🦶39

✔ Sharpen the names on the mailbox. 🦶40

✔ Undo this action. 🦶7

✔ Blur the names on the mailbox. 🦶40

✔ Close the photo and don't save the changes. 🦶9

Background Information

Scanners

The most useful way to import an existing paper photo into the computer is by scanning it. You can scan not only printed photos, but also slides and negatives. The term *resolution* is used in scanning. The standard unit for resolution is the number of dots per inch (or *DPI*). The higher the DPI, the sharper the scan. You can specify the resolution yourself in your scanner software window. Choose the desired DPI based on what you want to do with the photo. Be sure you always adjust your scanner's DPI setting to match the purpose of the scan. Setting the default resolution too high can lead to enormous file sizes that your computer can barely process.

In addition to the resolution, the *color depth* is important: the number of colors the scanner can distinguish. A scanner's quality depends on the resolution, the color depth, and the scanning speed.

You can read more about your scanner settings in the background information for Chapter 8, *Importing, Editing, and Saving*.

The flatbed scanner is the most widely sold type of scanner. You place the photo on a glass plate and it's scanned by a device that moves beneath it.

-Continue reading on the next page.-

Some types of flatbed scanners can scan slides and negatives in addition to photos. The scanner comes with special slide holders, into which you can place a series of slides or a negative strip. One advantage is that this way you can scan several images at once. The accompanying software can split these images into separate photo files. This lets you digitize your old family photos or vacation memories at a fast pace.
After scanning, you can use *PhotoStudio* to enhance or retouch your photos as necessary.

There are also special scanners that can only scan slides or negatives.

If you have a large number of slides, photos, and negatives you'd like to digitize, a scanner is definitely an investment worth making. The features of the accompanying software are also important. For example, a scanner which can read in multiple images at once can save you a lot of time. Be sure to inquire about this at your computer store before purchasing a scanner.
More information and new developments in scanning can be found in articles in computermagazines or by browsing the Internet.

The Monitor

A *screen* or *monitor* also has a *resolution*. Here, the term refers to the number of horizontal and vertical *picture elements* (pixels) the monitor can display.

A resolution of 800 by 600, for example, means the monitor displays 800 pixels horizontally and 600 pixels vertically. The table here shows the most common resolutions.

640	**by**	**480**
800	**by**	**600**
1024	**by**	**768**
1152	**by**	**864**
1280	**by**	**1024**

The most common resolutions.

Because a larger screen surface has more room for pixels, larger monitors can handle higher resolutions. The term *image diagonal* expresses the size of the usable surface of the screen glass. For *Windows*, you really need a *17-inch* or *19-inch* monitor. Anything smaller will require additional handling to make the photos fit the screen.

A 15-inch and a 19-inch monitor

In *PhotoStudio* you can quickly display a photo shrunk to fit the screen using the option View , Fit In Window :

Tips

 Tip

The *Clone* Tool
You can also use the *Clone* tool on faces. For example, you can easily rub out a dark shadow under an eye and a blemish:

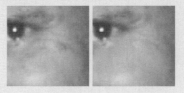

Tip

Old Photos
Try scanning an old, wrinkled, or damaged black-and-white photos some time. You'll be surprised at the improvements you can make to these photos using the *Clone* tool!

💡 Tip

Navigation Palette

You're already familiar with the tools *Zoom In* and *Zoom Out*. *PhotoStudio* has another way to navigate around a photo: the *Navigation Palette.* You can display this palette as follows:

👆 **Click on** `View` , `Show Navigation Palette`

You see the *Navigation Palette* at the bottom right of the window.

You can zoom in by dragging the slider:

The large window displays the sharply zoomed-in photo. In the *Navigation Palette*, the blue rectangle shows you which part of the photo is being displayed:

You can move the blue rectangle around using the little hand:

You can quickly display any desired part of the photo this way!

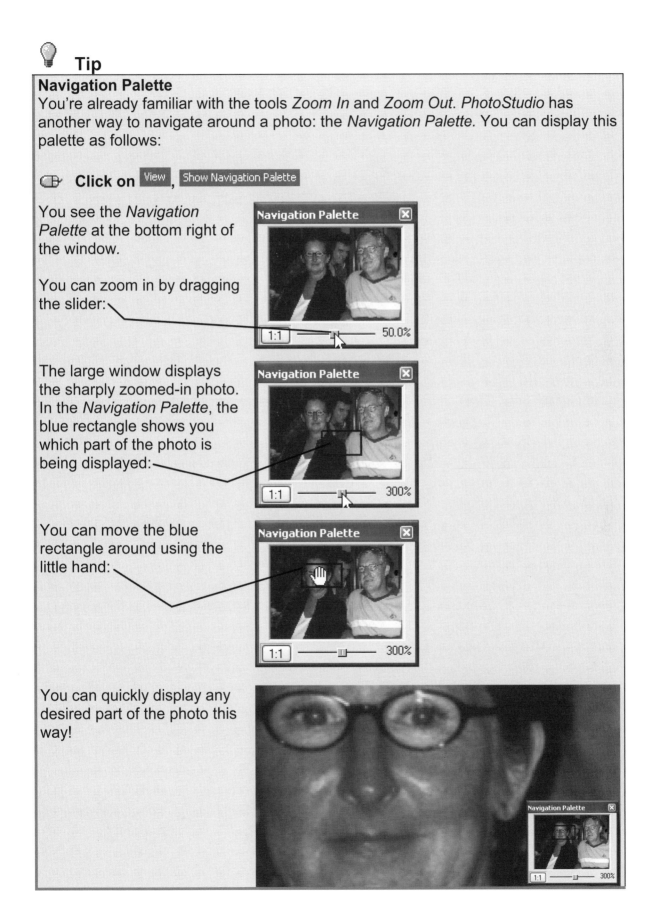

5. Working with Selections

The most important action to take before editing part of a photo is *selecting*. *PhotoStudio* has several selection options, such as selecting a rectangle or an oval. You can manually draw the shape you want to select with another tool, the *Lasso*. The *Magnetic Lasso* helps you select angular or irregular shapes very precisely. Yet another tool lets you make a selection based on color, so that you can easily select the blue sky in a photo, for example.
Once you've selected part of a photo, you can improve that part, or copy it and use it in a photomontage.

In this chapter, you'll learn how to:

- select using a shape
- move or copy a selection
- remove the selection boundary
- select freehand using the *Lasso*
- select an irregularly shaped object using the *Magnetic Lasso*
- soften the edges of a selection
- add shadow to a selection
- select based on color using the *Magic Wand*
- fill a selection with a pattern
- fill a selection with a color

Selecting Shapes

One of the most common actions in digital photo editing is selecting part of a photo. You can then apply all kinds of effects to that selection in order to improve the photo or to make a photomontage.

☞ **Start** *PhotoStudio* ℓℓ²

☞ **Open the photo** *Diver* **in the folder** *My PhotoStudio Practice Files* ℓℓ⁶

☞ **Maximize the window containing the photo** ℓℓ⁴

You see this photo of a diver:

There are many different ways to select part of a photo. The simplest way is using a shape.

Click on ⬚

The *Options Palette* appears.

You've already used the *Rectangle Select* tool before. In the *Options Palette* you can also choose a selection tool in the shape of a square, oval (ellipse), or circle. Go ahead and choose the square.

Click on ˅

Click on ⬚

☞ **Hide the *Options Palette*** 1

Now you can select part of the photo.

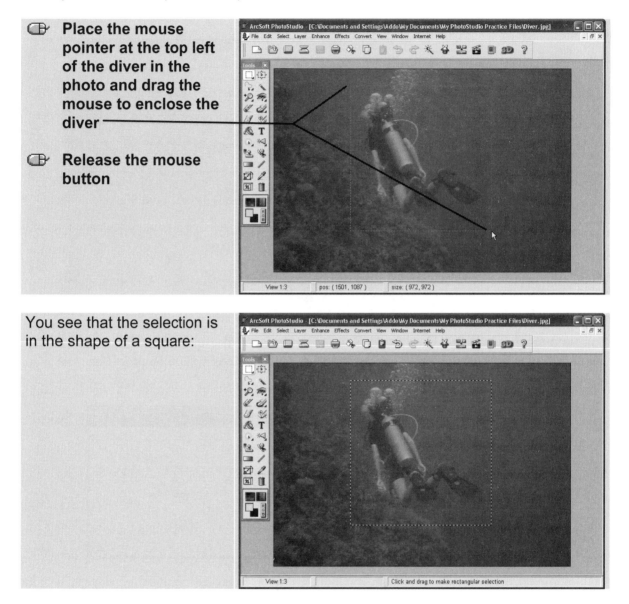

Place the mouse pointer at the top left of the diver in the photo and drag the mouse to enclose the diver

Release the mouse button

You see that the selection is in the shape of a square:

You can adjust the selection by sliding the selection boundary around.

> 🖱 **Place the mouse pointer inside the selection**
>
> The mouse pointer changes into ⌖.
>
> 🖱 **Drag the selection frame upward**

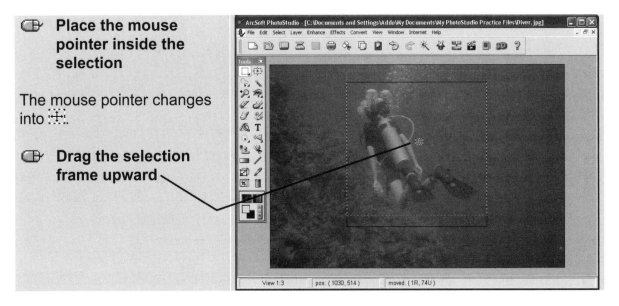

You can move or copy the selected part of the photo. You'll read how to do that in the next section.

Moving or Copying a Selection

You can easily move the selected area to another part of the photo by dragging it with the mouse. To do so, you'll use the *Move* tool.

> 🖱 **Click on** ⊕
>
> The mouse pointer changes into ⊞.

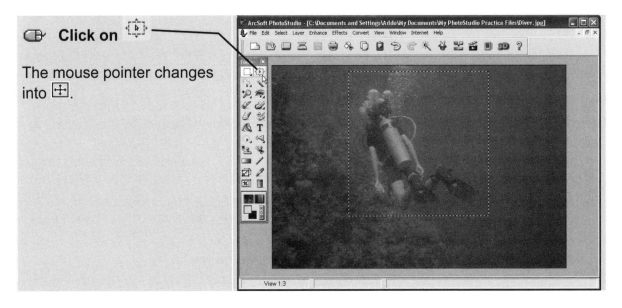

Place the mouse pointer ⊞ inside the selection and drag with the mouse

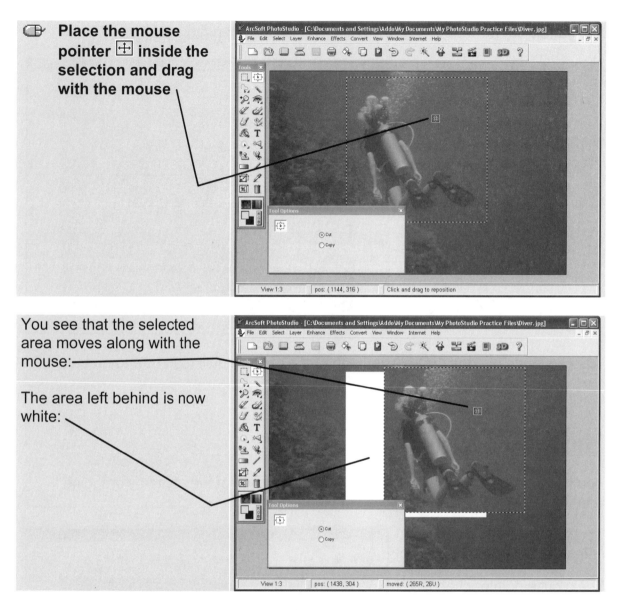

You see that the selected area moves along with the mouse:

The area left behind is now white:

The result looks pretty artistic, but you don't usually want to use it this way. It's more attractive to move the selection without disturbing the original photo. In that case it is better to copy the selection.

☞ **Undo the last action** 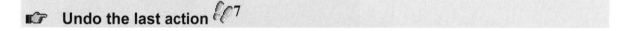7

Click on the radio button ○ beside Copy

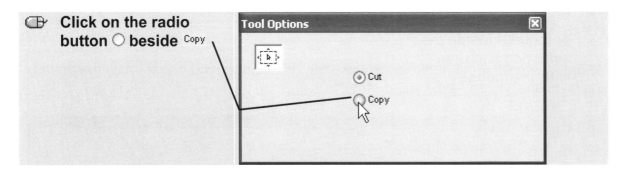

Now you can drag the selection away again.

Place the mouse pointer ⊞ inside the selection and drag with the mouse

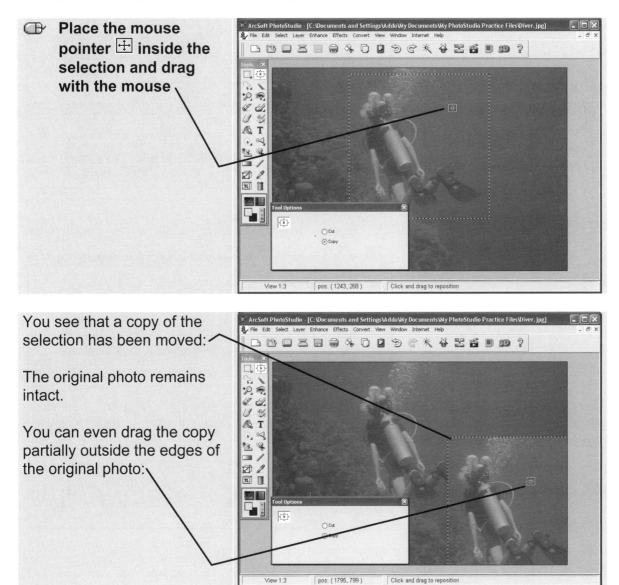

You see that a copy of the selection has been moved:

The original photo remains intact.

You can even drag the copy partially outside the edges of the original photo:

Removing the Selection Boundary

To better see what the photo looks like after this change, you can remove the dotted selection lines. Here's how you do that:

☞ **Click on** Select

☞ **Click on** None

☞ **Hide the *Options Palette*** 🖐️1

Now the result of your selection and copying is clearly visible:

☞ **Close the photo and <u>don't</u> save the changes** 🖐️9

Selecting with the Lasso

You've seen from the above that selecting with simple shapes like a square doesn't always achieve the most attractive results. Some items are selected along with the subject that you'd rather not have. Fortunately, *PhotoStudio* has a way to select more precisely: the *Lasso.*

☞ **Open the photo *Fish* in the folder *My PhotoStudio Practice Files* ℓℓ⁶**

☞ **Maximize the window containing the photo ℓℓ⁴**

You see this photo of a pretty tropical fish:

☞ **Click on**

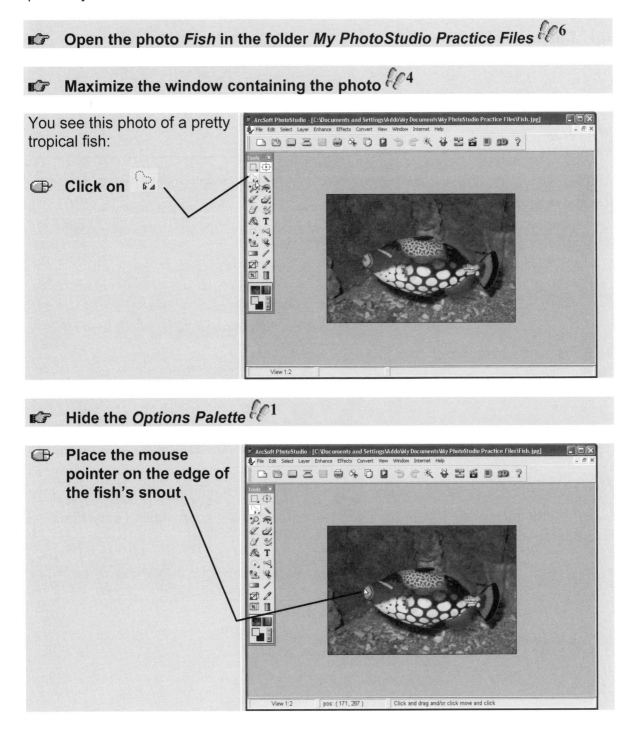

☞ **Hide the *Options Palette* ℓℓ¹**

☞ **Place the mouse pointer on the edge of the fish's snout**

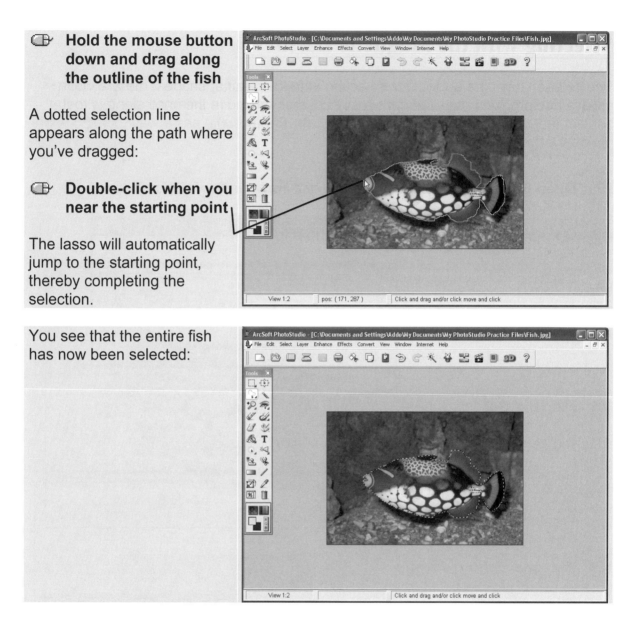

Hold the mouse button down and drag along the outline of the fish

A dotted selection line appears along the path where you've dragged:

Double-click when you near the starting point

The lasso will automatically jump to the starting point, thereby completing the selection.

You see that the entire fish has now been selected:

While the lasso allows you to select much more precisely than a shape does, it isn't always easy to make a really good selection. You need a very steady hand to work with this tool accurately. If your hand isn't so steady, you'll keep making selections with too much or too little of the object you want.

☞ **Undo the last action** ⁷

Selecting with the Magnetic Lasso

PhotoStudio has a better tool for selecting curved, irregular shapes: the *Magnetic Lasso.* The program uses the contrast in color or lighting in the photo for this tool.

☞ **Display the *Options Palette***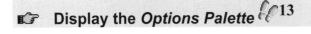

First, select the *Magnetic Lasso* in the *Options Palette.*

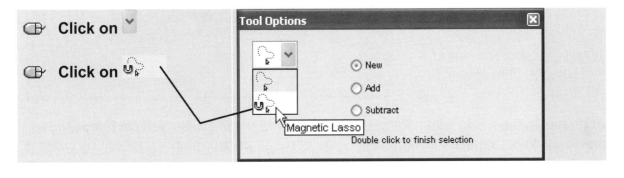

☞ **Hide the *Options Palette***

Now you can try selecting the fish with the *Magnetic Lasso.*

☞ Move the mouse pointer along the outline of the fish ——

A selection line appears. The *Magnetic Lasso* automatically adds anchor points to the selection:

At places in the photo with a lot of contrast, the *Magnetic Lasso* selects fairly precisely. Where there's less contrast, you can add anchor points yourself by clicking as you go.

Near the backfin, for example, you'll have to give the *Magnetic Lasso* a little help by clicking on points the selection line should contain:

✖ HELP! I didn't select the right thing.

If you click on the wrong spot while selecting with the *Magnetic Lasso*, you can undo

the bad selection by pressing ⌨Delete. The last anchor point you placed will be removed. Then you can select a new point.

When you get back to the starting point, you can complete the selection.

☞ **Double-click near the starting point**

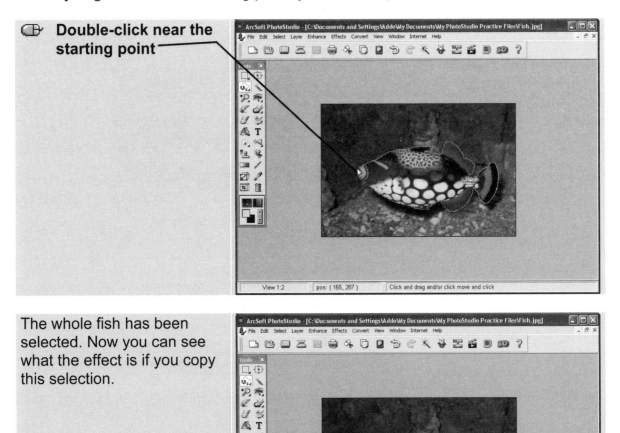

The whole fish has been selected. Now you can see what the effect is if you copy this selection.

☞ **Select the *Move* tool** ✍16

The option Copy should still be selected. If it isn't, then:

☞ **Click on the radio button ○ beside** Copy

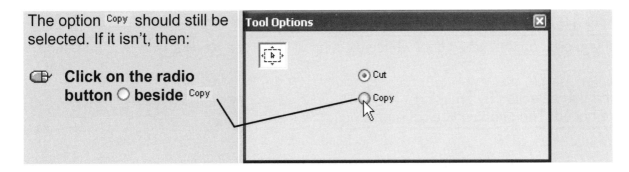

☞ Hide the *Options Palette* ✐¹

⬭ **Place the mouse pointer ⊞ inside the selection**

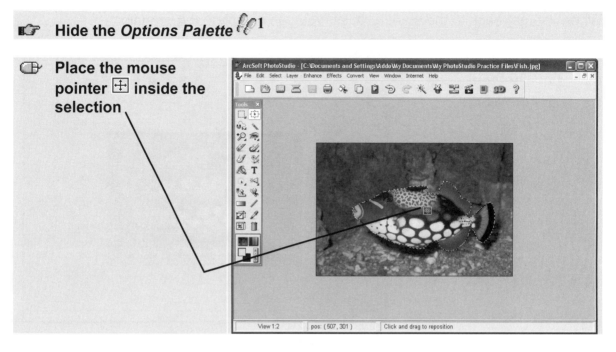

The fish is copied when you move the selection.

⬭ **Drag the selection upward**

Now there are two fish in your photo:

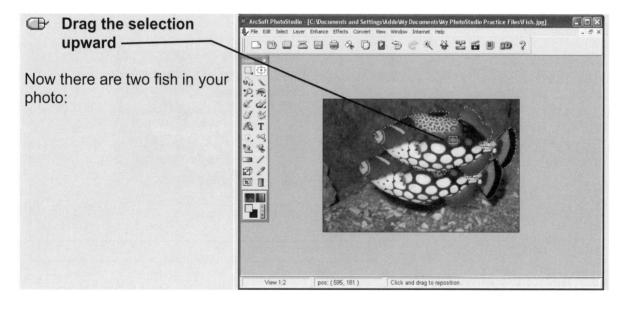

You can really see the effect well if you remove the selection boundary.

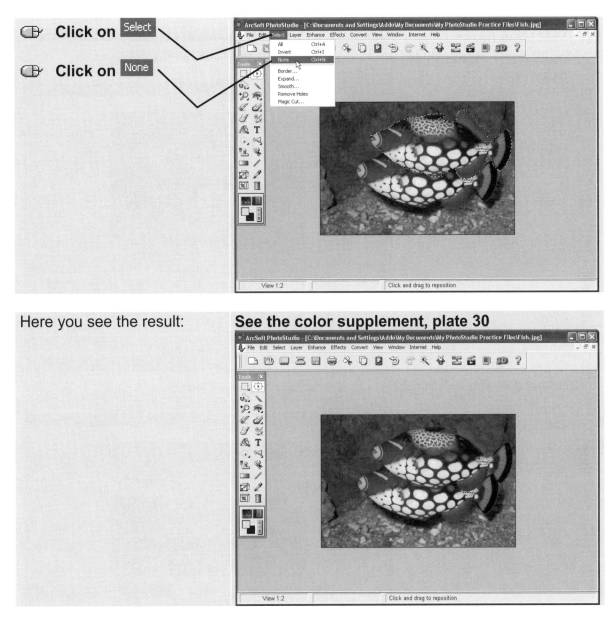

☞ **Click on** Select

☞ **Click on** None

Here you see the result: **See the color supplement, plate 30**

One disadvantage of all these selection methods is that the edges of the selection are sharp. This produces a less attractive result when you copy the selection. It's usually easy to see that the object has been "pasted into" the photo. You can do something about this by using the *Soft Edge* tool. You'll read more about that in the next section.

☞ **Undo the last two actions** 🐾7

Now you see the selected fish again.

Adding a Soft Edge

You can make the edges of a selection less sharp by using the *Soft Edge* tool. This makes the selection gradually blend into the background at the edges.

You see the original photo again, with the selection:

Here's how you use the *Soft Edge* on the selection you've made:

Click on Layer

Click on Soft Edge...

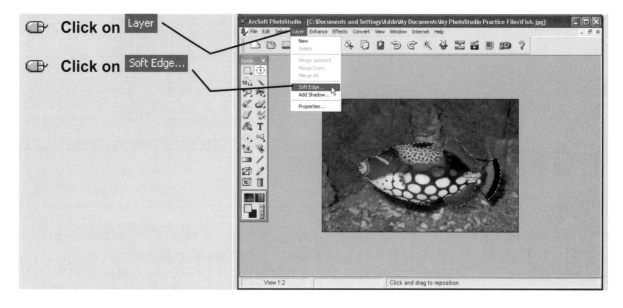

The *range* specifies how wide the transition between the edge pixels and the surrounding pixels should be. Let's choose a width of 10 pixels so you can see the effect of the *Soft Edge* clearly.

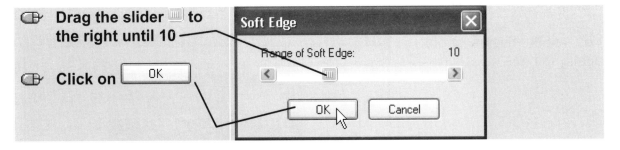

Now when you copy the selection, you'll see the effect of the *Soft Edge*.

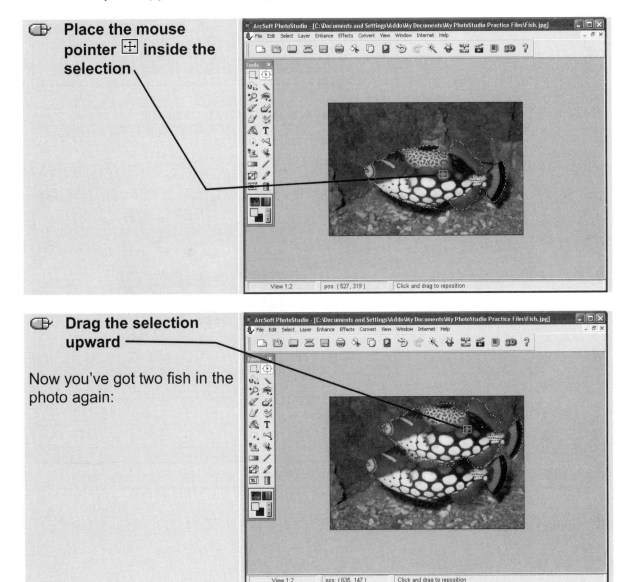

Place the mouse pointer ⊞ inside the selection

Drag the selection upward

Now you've got two fish in the photo again:

If you remove the selection border, you can see the effect of the *Soft Edge* more clearly.

☞ **Click on** Select

☞ **Click on** None

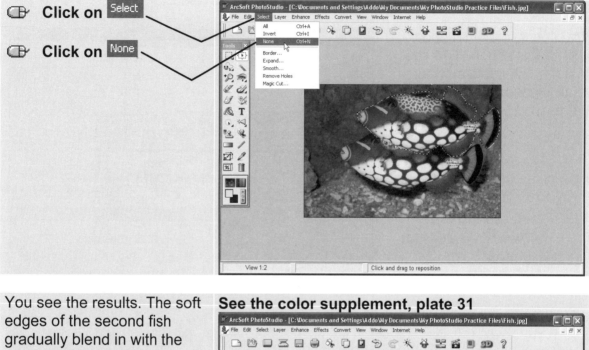

You see the results. The soft edges of the second fish gradually blend in with the environment:

See the color supplement, plate 31

⇨ **Please note:**

Using the *Soft Edge* tool with a large range does adversely affect the details at the edges of the selected object. This, too, can make the copied selection look artificial.

☞ **Undo the last two actions** 7

Now you see the selected fish with the soft edges again.

Adding Shadow

In addition to soft edges, you can add shadows to your selection.

You see the original photo
with the selection. You see
that the fish casts a shadow
on the stones as a result of
the flash:

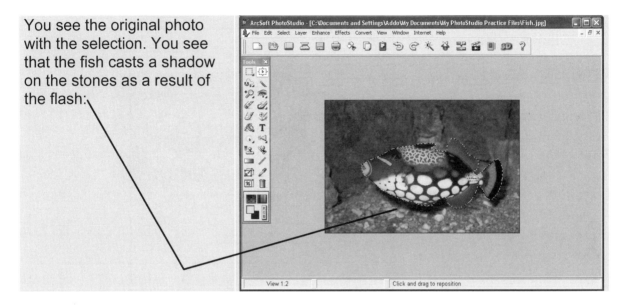

When you copy in a second fish, it'll look more realistic if this fish also casts a
shadow. You can add in the shadow as follows:

👉 **Click on** Layer

👉 **Click on** Add Shadow...

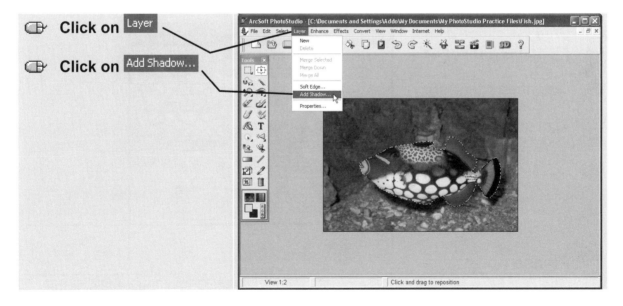

The *Add Shadow* window appears. You can adjust various settings for the shadow here. Let's begin by setting the *Pixel Offset.* This determines where the shadow should fall.

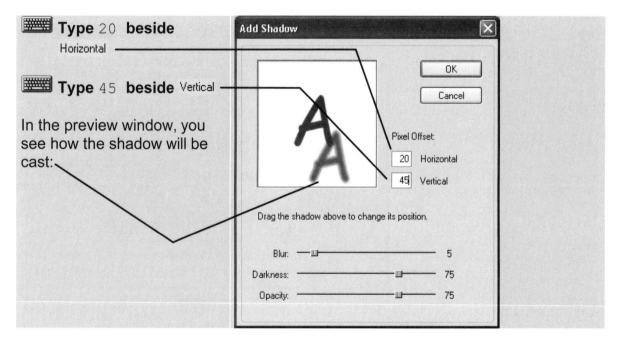

Next, you can darken the shadow and make it less transparent.

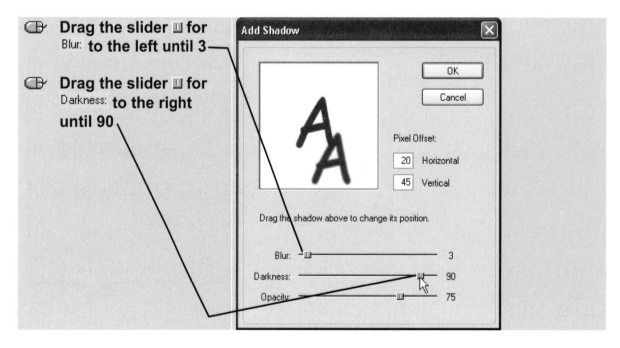

Now you can take a look at the effect on the selection.

👆 **Click on** ⟨ OK ⟩

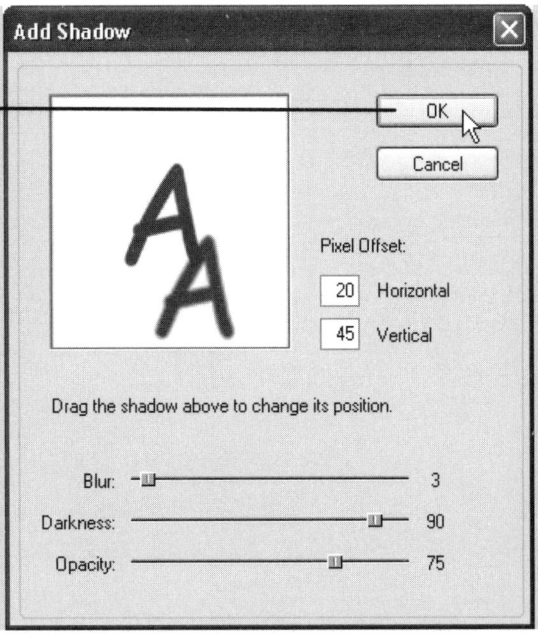

Add Shadow

OK

Cancel

Pixel Offset:

20 Horizontal

45 Vertical

Drag the shadow above to change its position.

Blur: 3

Darkness: 90

Opacity: 75

You see the selected fish and the shadow. It's hard to tell which shadow is new, and which was already in the photo:

After you copy the fish, you'll be able to see the new shadow better.

Place the mouse pointer ⊞ inside the selection

Drag the selection upward

Now you see that the top fish casts a shadow on the bottom one:

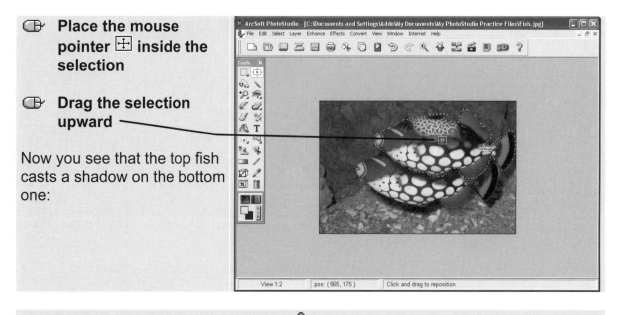

☞ **Remove the selection boundary** 🐾17

Without the selection boundary, the results are easier to see:

See the color supplement, plate 32

☞ **Close the photo and <u>don't</u> save the changes** 🐾9

Selecting with the Magic Wand

Up to this point, you've made selections based only on shapes and on the outline of an object. There's also another way. *PhotoStudio* provides a tool with which you can select parts of a photo with similar colors: the *Magic Wand*. Let's try out this tool on the photo you cropped earlier.

☞ **Open the photo *Cropped Picture Big Ben* in the folder *My PhotoStudio Practice Files* ℓℓ⁶**

☞ **Maximize the window containing the photo ℓℓ⁴**

You select the *Magic Wand* as follows:

Click on ✎

The mouse pointer changes into ✎.

You can adjust the settings for this tool in the *Options Palette*.

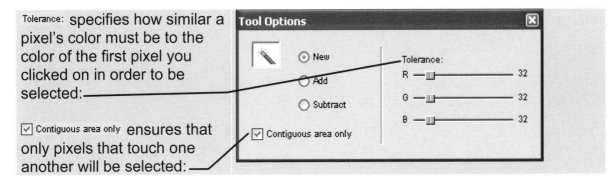

Tolerance: specifies how similar a pixel's color must be to the color of the first pixel you clicked on in order to be selected:

☑ Contiguous area only ensures that only pixels that touch one another will be selected:

The *tolerance* value you specify for the three color channels R (red), G (green), and B (blue) depends entirely on the photo in which you want to make the selection. Sometimes you'll have to experiment a bit before you get good results.

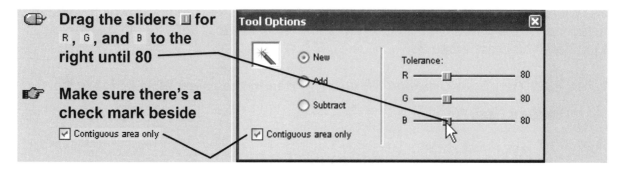

Drag the sliders ▯ for R , G , and ʙ to the right until 80

Make sure there's a check mark beside

You can also specify what kind of selection you want to make. The option New means a new selection will be made every time you click. The option Add adds the new selection to the previous selection, so that the selected area becomes larger. The option Subtract removes the new selection from the previous selection, so that the selected area becomes smaller.

Let's select the cloudy sky in the photo. The Add option works best for that.

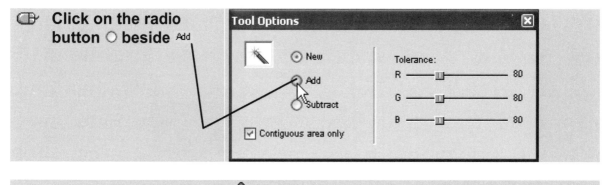

Click on the radio button ○ beside Add

Hide the *Options Palette* [1]

Now select the cloudy sky in the photo using the *Magic Wand*:

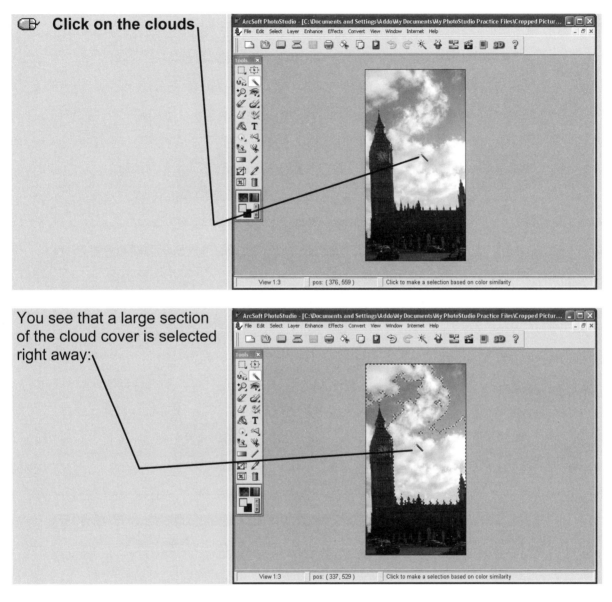

Click on the clouds

You see that a large section of the cloud cover is selected right away:

You can add in the rest of the sky by expanding the selection.

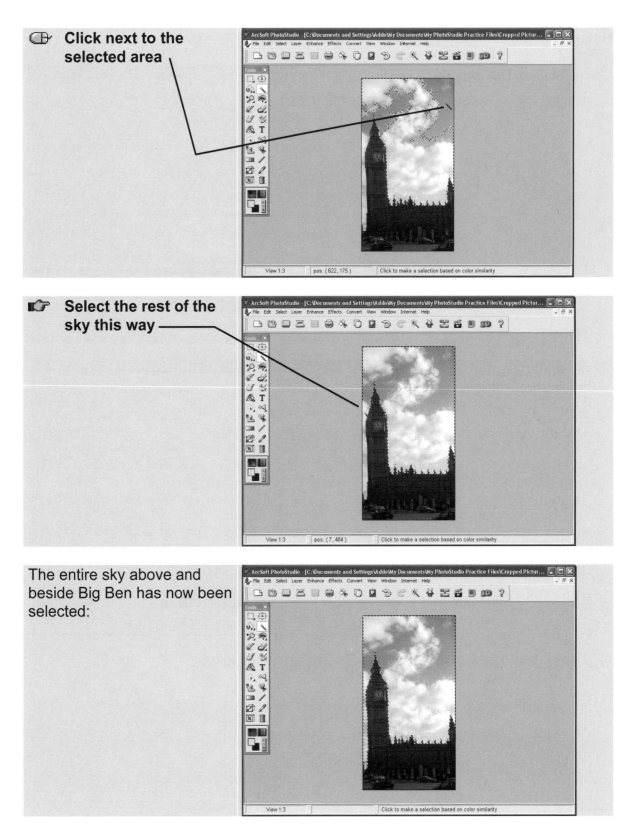

Click next to the selected area

Select the rest of the sky this way ——

The entire sky above and beside Big Ben has now been selected:

You can apply various fill effects to the selection you've just made. You'll work on that in the next section.

Fill Effects

You can achieve an interesting effect by replacing the selected pixels with a pattern or a color. You do this in *PhotoStudio* with the *Bucket Fill* tool. Here's how you select the bucket:

Click on

The mouse pointer changes into:

In the *Options Palette*, specify that you want to fill the selection with a pattern.

Click on

Click on

The mouse pointer changes into:

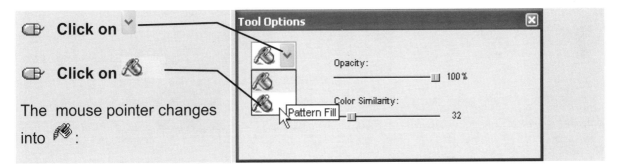

In this window, you can choose the pattern with which you want to fill the selection, for example the purple hand.

Click on

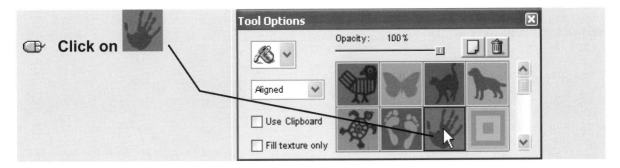

Now you can fill the selection with the pattern.

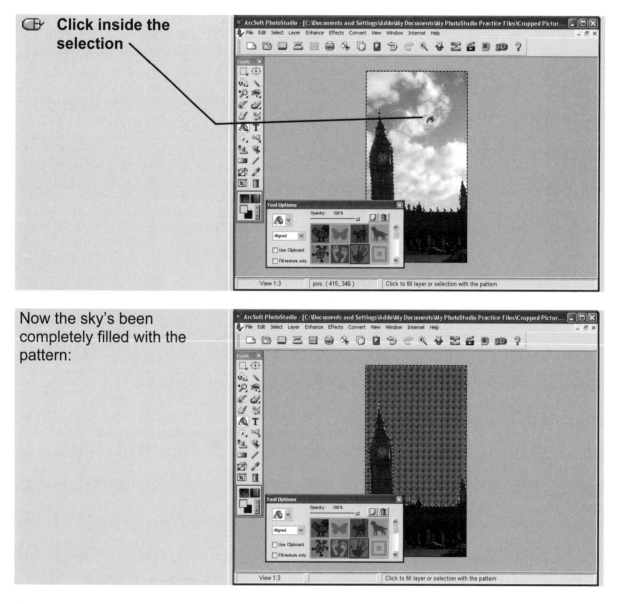

Click inside the selection

Now the sky's been completely filled with the pattern:

The pattern doesn't have to be completely opaque. By lowering the value for Opacity: , you can make sure the clouds remain visible.

☞ **Undo the last action** ℓℓ7

☞ **Drag the slider ▥ for** Opacity: **to the left until 30%**

☞ **Click inside the selection**

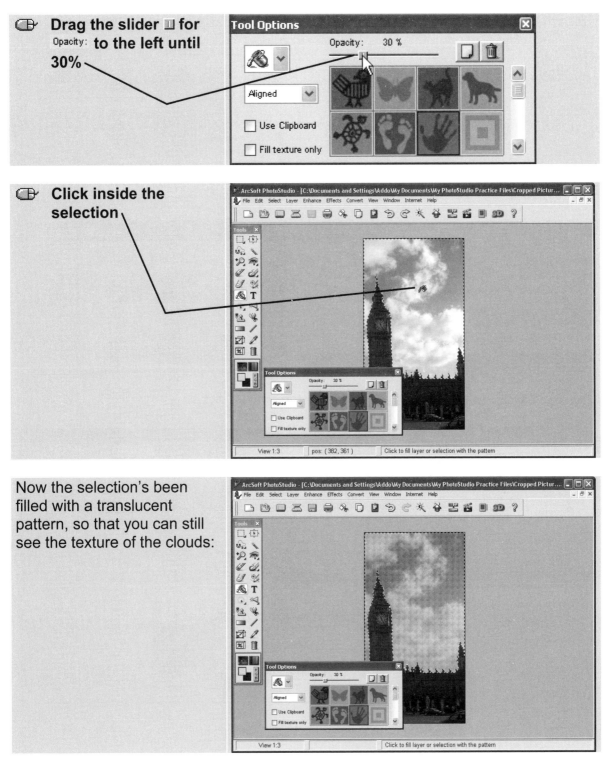

Now the selection's been filled with a translucent pattern, so that you can still see the texture of the clouds:

You can also choose to use the pattern, but not its color. You do that as follows:

☞ **Undo the last action** ℓℓ7

Click on the check box ☐ beside Fill texture only

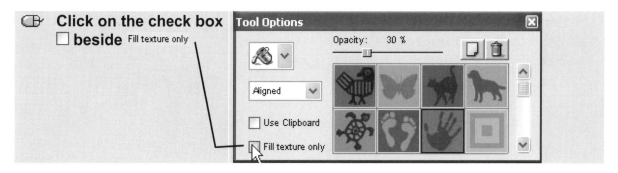

To really see the effect, you'd better increase the opacity.

Drag the slider ☐ for Opacity: **to the right until 80%**

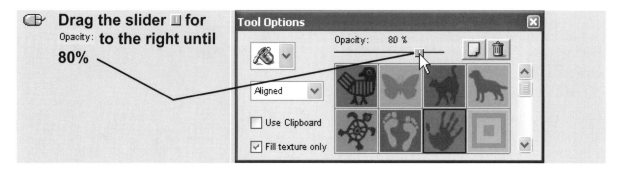

Now you can try out the effect with these settings.

Click inside the selection

The selection has now been filled with a translucent pattern in shades of gray:

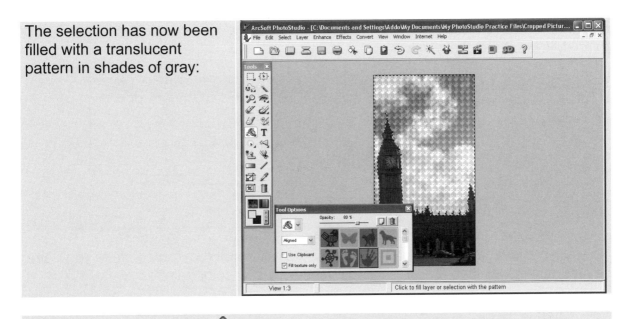

☞ **Undo the last action** 7

If you don't want to use a pattern, you can use a fill color instead. First, you'll need to choose a different bucket.

🖱 **Click on** ⌄

🖱 **Click on** 🪣

The mouse pointer changes into 🪣:

The *Bucket Fill* doesn't automatically fill the entire selection. It works with a tolerance value, just like the *Magic Wand* does. This value is called *Color Similarity* in the *Options Palette*. The lower the value for *Color Similarity*, the more a pixel must resemble the pixel you first clicked on with the bucket in order to be filled. If you raise the value, the clouds will be filled in one go.

🖱 **Drag the slider ⊡ for** Color Similarity: **to the right until 132**

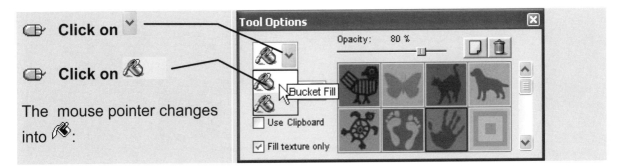

If you make the fill color translucent, the texture of the clouds will still be visible. To do that, lower the *Opacity* value.

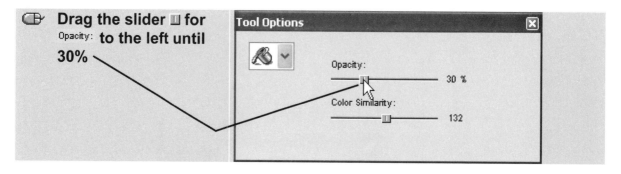

Now all you have to do is choose a color. At the bottom of the *Tools Palette* you'll see several options for that. Go ahead and choose the 256-color palette.

If you move over the color palette with the mouse pointer, the pointer changes into a pipette 🖋 with which you can select the desired color.

On the *Tools Palette*, you see the color you've chosen here in the top *Color Swatch*:

☞ **Click inside the selection**

The clouds will be filled with the chosen pinkish color.

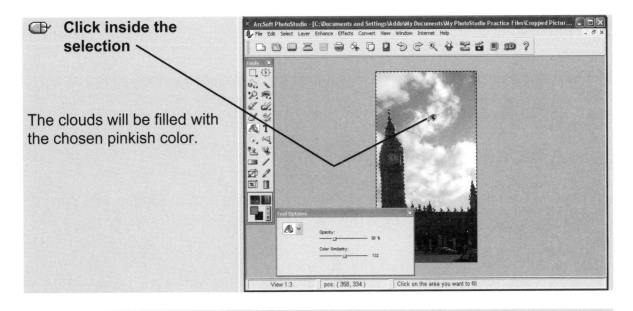

☞ Hide the *Options Palette* ✆1

☞ Remove the selection boundary ✆17

The photo looks very different now:

See the color supplement, plate 33

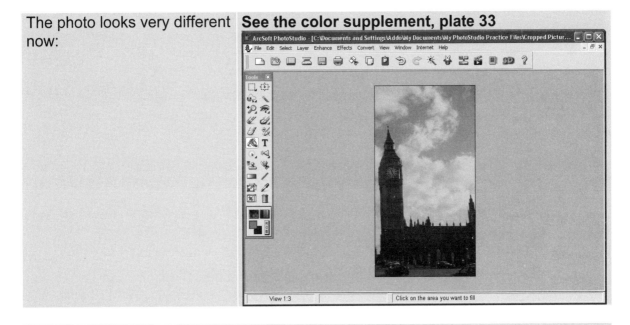

☞ **Close the photo and <u>don't</u> save the changes** ✆9

Exercises

The following exercises will help you master what you've just learned. Have you forgotten how to perform a particular action? Use the number beside the footsteps to look it up in the appendix *How Do I Do That Again?*

Exercise: Making Selections

In this exercise, you'll practice making selections with the help of various selection tools.

✔ Open the photo *Mailbox* using the *Browser*. 🦶⁶

✔ Maximize the window containing the photo. 🦶⁴

✔ Select the top part of the mailbox. 🦶⁴¹

✔ Move the selection. 🦶⁴²

✔ Undo the last action. 🦶⁷

✔ Copy and move the selection. 🦶⁴³

✔ Remove the selection boundary. 🦶¹⁷

✔ Close the photo and don't save the changes. 🦶⁹

Exercise: Extending a Selection

In this exercise, you'll practice selecting and extending a selection.

✔ Open the photo *Cropped Picture Big Ben* using the *Browser*. 🦶⁶

✔ Select the sky using the *Magic Wand* tool. 🦶⁴⁴

✔ Extend the selection until the entire sky has been selected. 🦶⁴⁵

✔ Close the photo and don't save the changes. 🦶⁹

Tips

Tip

Removing Part of a Selection

If you don't want to use part of a selected area, you can remove that part from the selection you've made.

Click on the radio button ○ beside Subtract

Select the part you want to delete from the selection

Be sure the starting point for the new selection is outside the current selection.
Inside the existing selection, the mouse pointer only allows you to move the current selection frame.

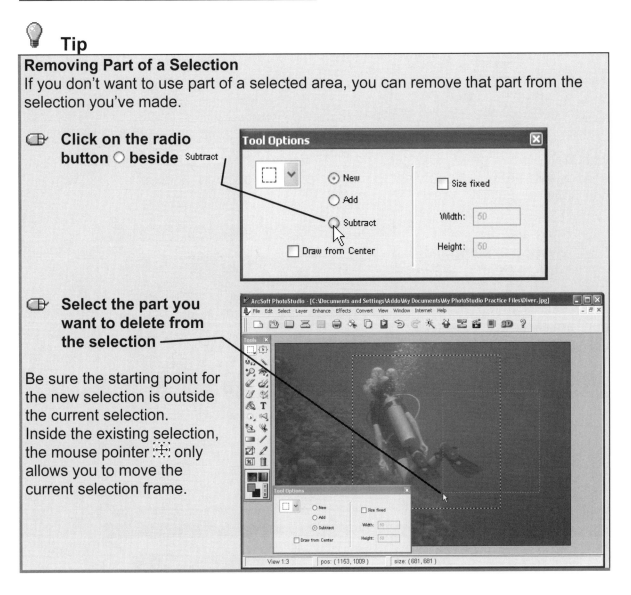

💡 **Tip**

Magic Cut
In *PhotoStudio* you can use the *Magic Cut* tool to select and cut an object out of a photo. Here's how you start the *Magic Cut*:

👆 **Click on** `Select`
👆 **Click on** `Magic Cut...`

In the *Magic Cut* window, you can draw a line around the area you want to select with the help of a pencil. Using 🖊 ●∨, you can choose among pencils of various thicknesses. If you want to make a precise selection, choose a pencil with a fine point.

👆 **Click and drag with the mouse along the edge of the fish** ——

A red selection border appears at the places you've dragged the mouse over:

👆 **Double-click when you're almost back at the starting point**

Up to this point, *Magic Cut* looks a lot like selecting with the *Lasso*.
The difference is that you can refine your *Magic Cut* selection:

👆 **Click on** `Next >>`

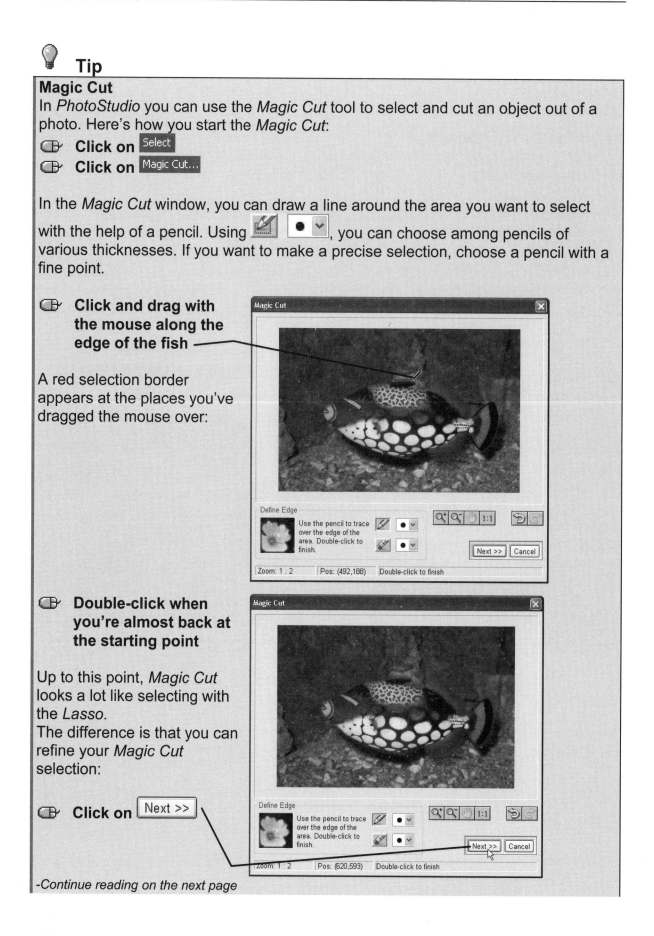

-*Continue reading on the next page*

In the window you see now, you can adjust your selection. You can do that not only by enlarging the selection with the pencil, but also by reducing the selection with the eraser. Here's how you select the *Eraser.*

☞ **Click on** 🖉

☞ **Drag the eraser over the parts of the selection you want to remove**

If you accidentally remove too much, you can use the buttons ↺ ↻ to undo or redo your last action:

When you're satisfied with the selection you've made, you can complete the *Magic Cut.*

☞ **Click on** Finish

Now you see an enlarged view of the selection you've made. *PhotoStudio* has saved it in a new photo file named *Untitled-TrueColor-01:*

6. Working with Layers

In *PhotoStudio* you can make use of *layers* when editing your photos. When you open a photo for the first time, the photo itself becomes the first layer called Layer-0. If you make changes to this layer, the original photo will be altered. This won't happen if you make changes in a layer covering the first layer. This new layer may contain text or a figure. You can also copy (part of) Layer-0 and improve or retouch it. The big advantage of this method is that you can edit each layer independently without affecting the background layer or other layers.

You can compare layers to sheets of glass stacked on top of one another. If part of one layer is empty, you'll see the underlying layers through it. Beneath all the layers is Layer-0, the background layer.

Until you merge the layers, each layer is independent from the others in the image. This means you can experiment with different compositions without making permanent changes to the whole image. With a little practice, you can attain excellent results with layers.

In this chapter, you'll learn how to:

- create a new layer by copying
- view the layers in a photo
- crop a layer with the *Shape* tool
- edit a layer
- add a text layer using the *Text* tool
- save an image with layers
- invert a selection
- merge layers
- create a photomontage
- add text using the *3D Text Factory*
- choose a different text color
- enlarge the canvas
- create a panoramic photo by combining two layers
- improve a panoramic photo

Creating a New Layer by Copying

With the help of the selection methods you learned in the previous chapter, it's a snap to create layers in an image.

☞ **Open the photo *Red Eyes* in the folder *My PhotoStudio Practice Files*** 🐾⁶

☞ **Maximize the window containing the photo** 🐾⁴

You see the photo you edited earlier:

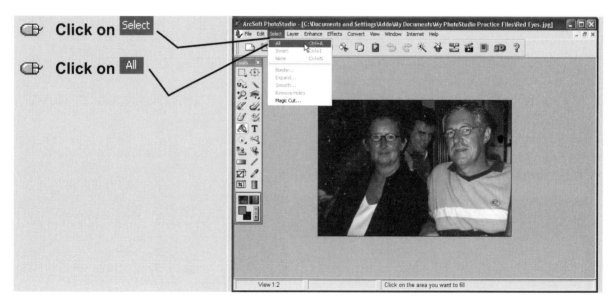

Go ahead and select the entire photo.

👆 **Click on** `Select`

👆 **Click on** `All`

A selection boundary appears
around the photo:

Let's create a new layer from this selection by copying it.

Click on Edit

Click on Copy

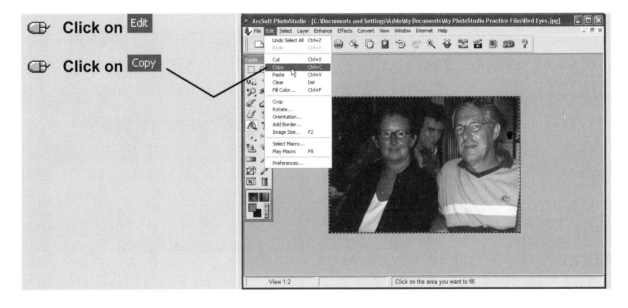

The copy of the photo has now been placed on the clipboard. Go ahead and paste it over the existing photo.

☞ **Click on** Edit

☞ **Click on** Paste

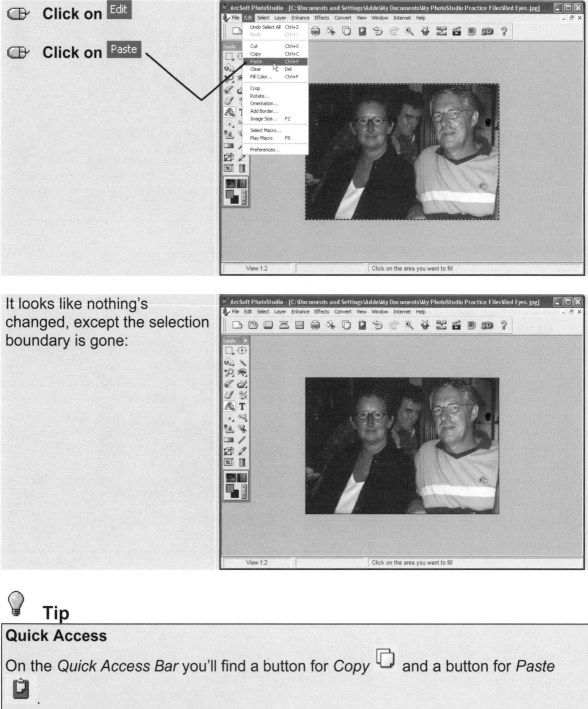

It looks like nothing's changed, except the selection boundary is gone:

💡 **Tip**

Quick Access

On the *Quick Access Bar* you'll find a button for *Copy* 🗗 and a button for *Paste*
📋 .

If you don't see this toolbar, then:

☞ **Click on** View
☞ **Click on** Show Quick Access Bar

Viewing the Layers in a Photo

The copy of the photo has become a separate layer in the image. You can view this layer in the *Layers Palette*. Here's how you display the *Layers Palette*:

Click on View

Click on Show Layers Palette

The *Layers Palette* appears:

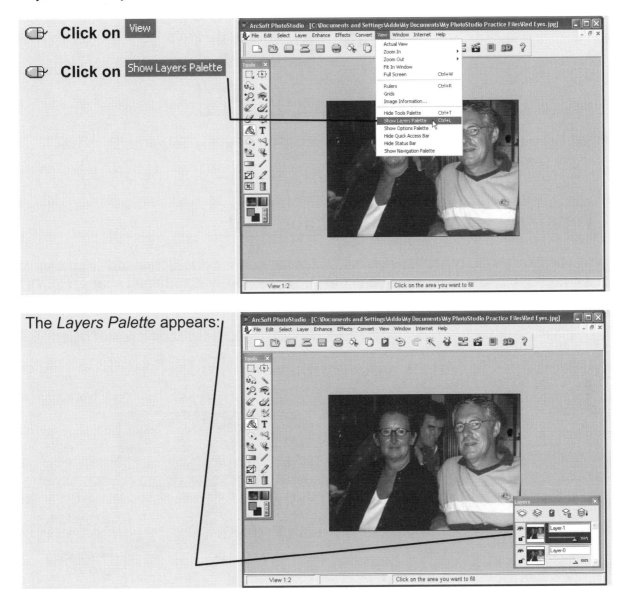

In the *Layers Palette*, you see the layers that make up the photo.

The new layer with the copy
of the photo:

The original photo:

In the *Layers Palette*, the blue layer is the active layer. In the next section you're
going to crop this layer.

Cropping a Layer with the Shape Tool

In this section you're going to use a new selection method: the *Shape* tool. You can
use it to crop a photo or a layer in a photo into a previously determined shape. Here's
how you select the *Shape* tool:

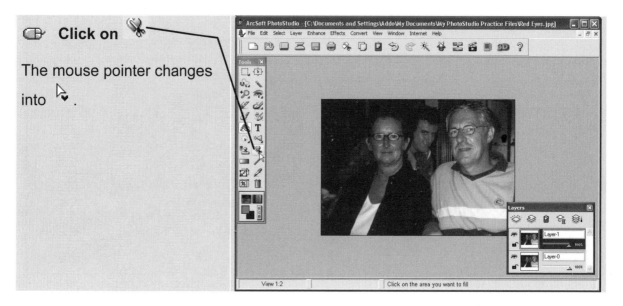

You can choose from a large number of shapes in the *Options Palette*. Let's try the square with ragged edges.

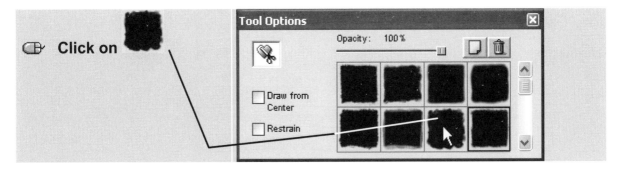

☞ **Click on**

Now you can make a selection in Layer-1. Let's select the three heads, leaving a good bit of space around them.

☞ **Place the mouse pointer at the top left near the woman and drag, holding the mouse button down, to the man's right shoulder**

☞ **Release the mouse button**

Once again, it doesn't look like anything's happened. You've just changed Layer-1. After this change, Layer-0 has suddenly become the active layer:

Layer-0 is the unchanged original photo, the same one you now see on the screen.

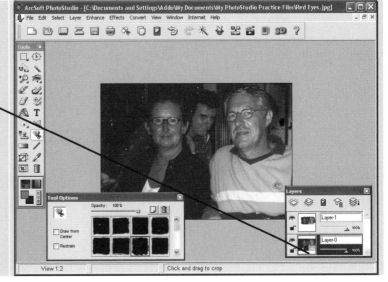

If you now hide Layer-0, you can see what's happened to Layer-1. Here's how you do that:

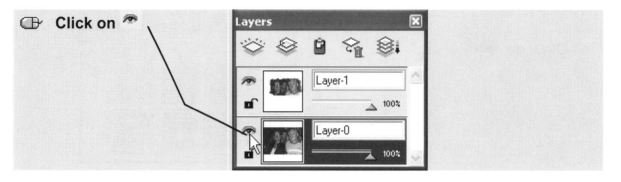

The original photo has now disappeared. You see only the section you cropped in Layer-1. Here's how you bring Layer-0 back into view:

Editing a Layer

With the help of the various effects *PhotoStudio* provides, you can add an artistic twist to your photo with just two layers. For example, you can turn Layer-0 into a charcoal drawing.

☞ **Hide the *Options Palette*** ✎ 1

    ⊡ **Click on** Effects

    ⊡ **Click on** Fine Art

    ⊡ **Click on** Charcoal...

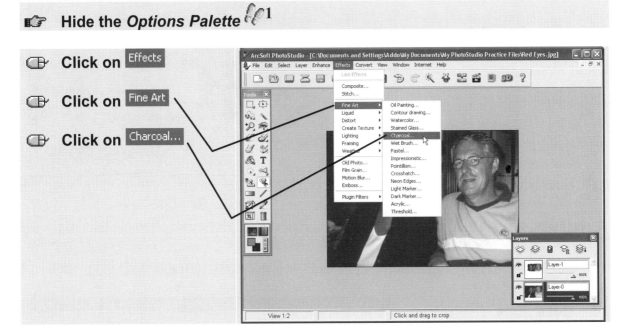

In the *Charcoal* window you can change the settings for this effect. You don't need to change any of the settings this time.

    ⊡ **Click on** OK

You see that Layer-0 has now been turned into a charcoal drawing. Because the cropped Layer-1 lies on top of it, you still see the faces in color:

See the color supplement, plate 34

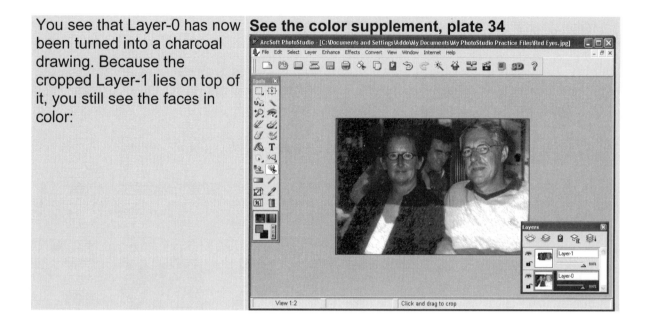

Adding a Text Layer

You can add a text layer to these two layers. You do that using the *Text* tool.

👉 **Click on** **T**

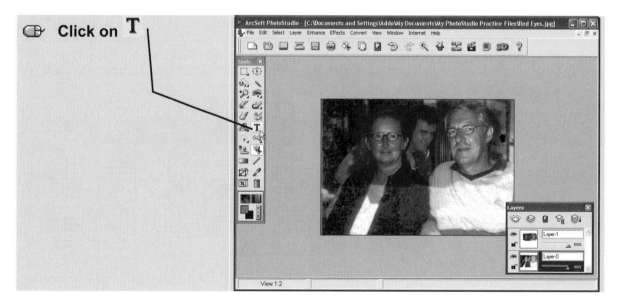

Now you can enter the text in the *Options Palette.*

Click in the white box

Type:
`In the picture together!`

Let's make the letters a little larger.

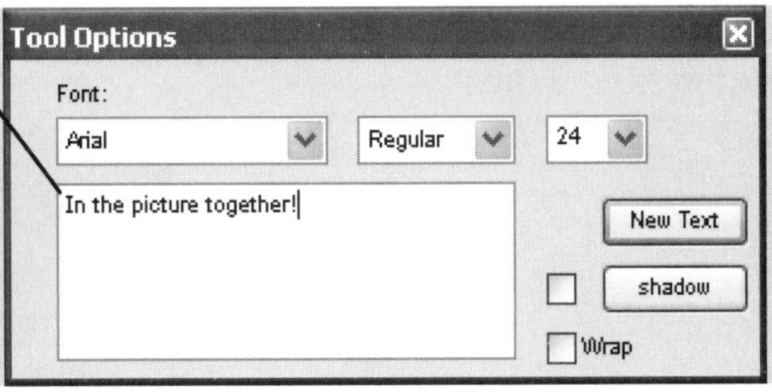

Double-click on 24

Type:
`72`

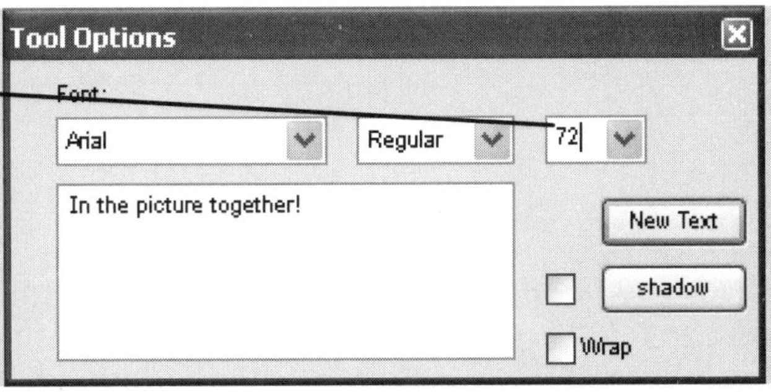

You immediately see the result in the photo:

A new layer with the name Layer-2 has automatically been added to the *Layers Palette*:

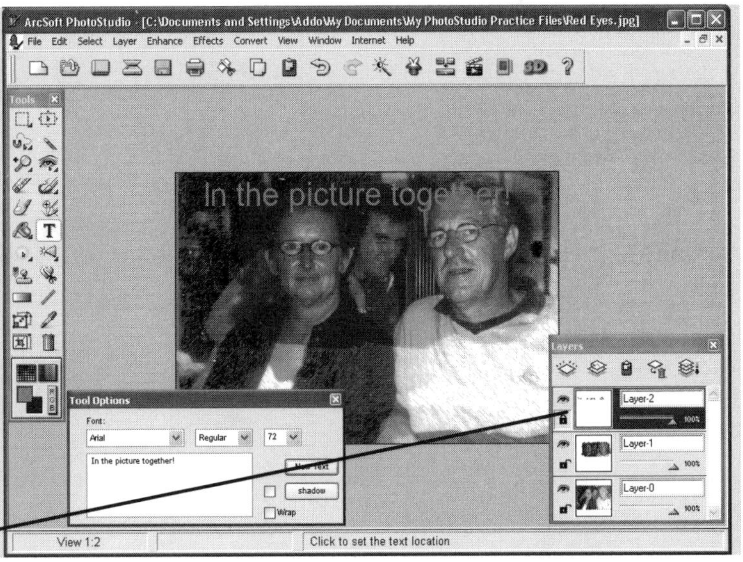

The text has been placed at the top left. Of course, you can move it.

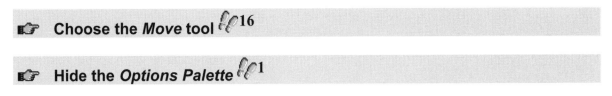

Choose the *Move* tool 16

Hide the *Options Palette* 1

☞ **Place the mouse**
   pointer on the text

☞ **Drag the text to the**
   bottom of the photo

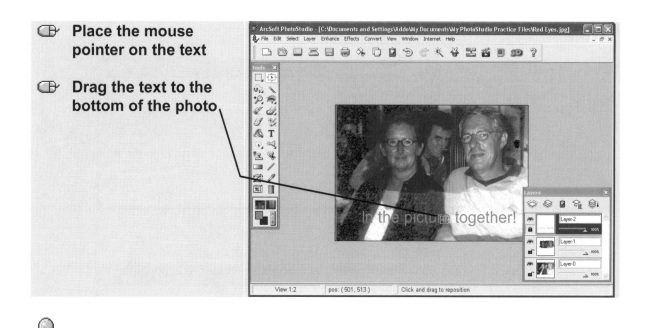

Tip

Restricted Layer

The text layer you created with the *Text* tool is automatically a *restricted layer*. That means you can't draw over the transparent parts of the layer. That can be useful if you want to paint the text a different color, for example, without affecting the surrounding area.

You can recognize a restricted layer by the closed padlock 🔒 :

If you want to remove the restriction, click on the 🔒 . The closed padlock then becomes an open padlock 🔓 .

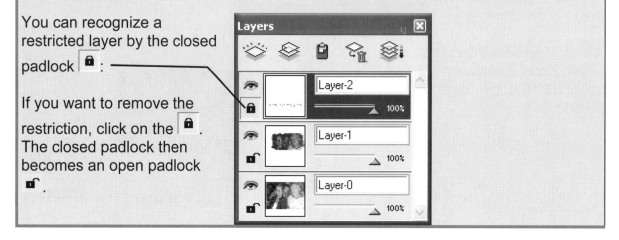

Saving an Image with Layers

PhotoStudio gives you the option of saving the photo in a file format that preserves the layers. That way you can edit them more later.

Click on File

Click on Save As...

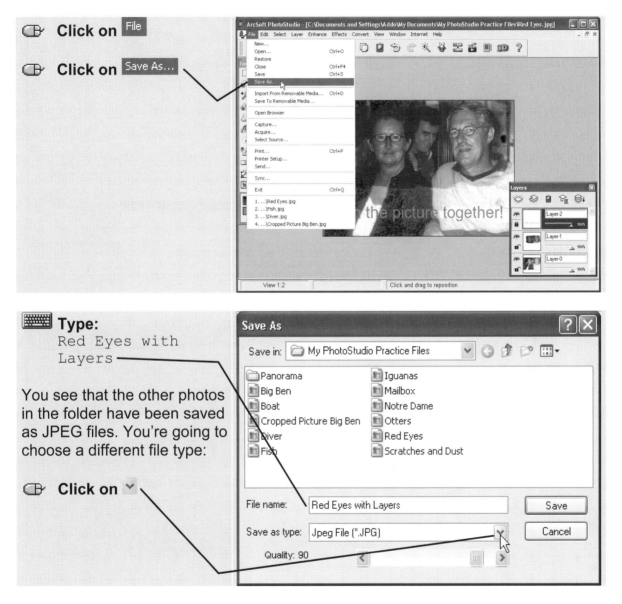

Type:
Red Eyes with Layers

You see that the other photos in the folder have been saved as JPEG files. You're going to choose a different file type:

Click on ⌄

Save the file in PSF format. This is the format in which the independent layers are preserved.

🖰 **Click on**

PhotoStudio File (*.PSF)

Save As

Save in: My PhotoStudio Practice Files

Panorama   Iguanas
Big Ben   Mailbox
Boat   Notre Dame
Cropped Picture Big Ben   Otters
Diver   Red Eyes
Fish   Scratches and Dust

File name: Red Eyes with Layers   Save

Save as type: Jpeg File (*.JPG)   Cancel

Quality: 90   PhotoStudio File (*.PSF)
              Jpeg File (*.JPG)
              Windows Bitmap (*.BMP)
              Tagged Image File (*.TIF)
              Portable Network Graphics (*.PNG)
              PC Paintbrush (*.PCX)
              Targa (*.TGA)
              FlashPix (*.FPX)
              EPS (*.EPS)

🖰 **Click on** [Save]

Save As

Save in: My PhotoStudio Practice Files

Panorama

File name: Red Eyes with Layers   Save

Save as type: PhotoStudio File (*.PSF)   Cancel

Quality: 90

The photo has now been saved as *Red Eyes with Layers.psf.*

You can close the photo now.

👆 **Click on** ✖

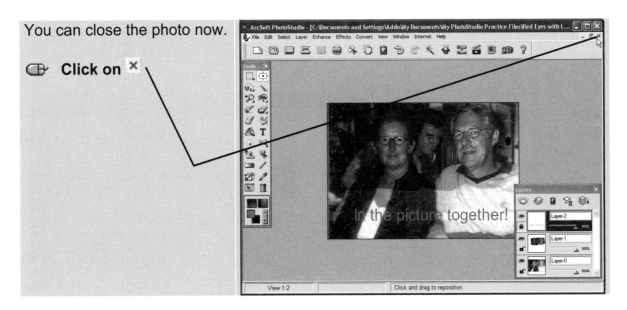

You've put together a composition consisting of three layers: the background layer, the cropped layer, and the text layer. That may sound like a lot, but in this program you can stack over 300 layers on top of each other! To edit so many layers, you might need to expand your computer's memory.

Inverting a Selection

In the previous chapter, you selected the cloud cover in the photo of Big Ben using the *Magic Wand*. Let's do that again:

☞ **Open the photo *Cropped Picture Big Ben* in the folder *My PhotoStudio Practice Files*** 𝓁𝓁6

☞ **Maximize the window containing the photo** 𝓁𝓁4

☞ **Select the *Magic Wand* tool** 𝓁𝓁18

You can adjust the settings for this tool in the *Options Palette*.

☞ **Adjust the settings as you see them here**

> **Tool Options**
>
> ⭘ New
> ◉ Add
> ⭘ Subtract
> ☑ Contiguous area only
>
> Tolerance:
> R ——🔲—— 80
> G ——🔲—— 80
> B ——🔲—— 80

☞ Hide the *Options Palette* 🖱¹

Select the cloudy sky in the photo using the *Magic Wand*:

🖱 **Click on the clouds** ⎯

☞ **Repeat this step until the entire cloud cover has been selected**

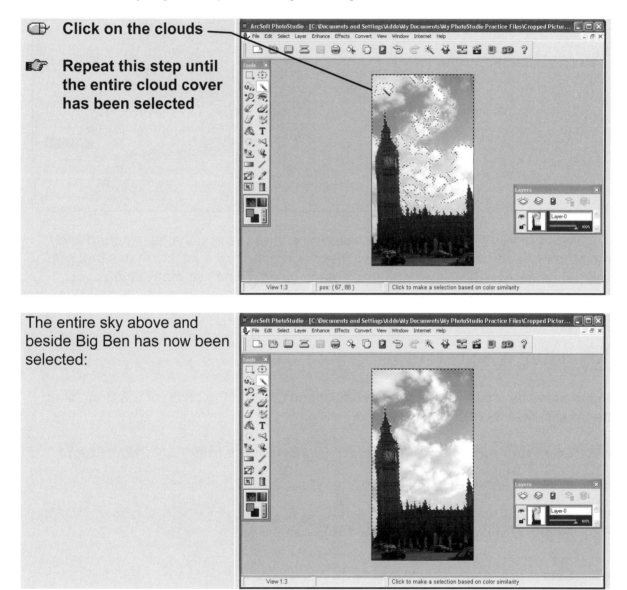

The entire sky above and beside Big Ben has now been selected:

One handy function in *PhotoStudio* is the option to invert a selection. In the case of Big Ben, you've used the *Magic Wand* to select the sky. If you invert this selection, you'll select everything in the photo except the sky in the blink of an eye.

Click on Select

Click on Invert

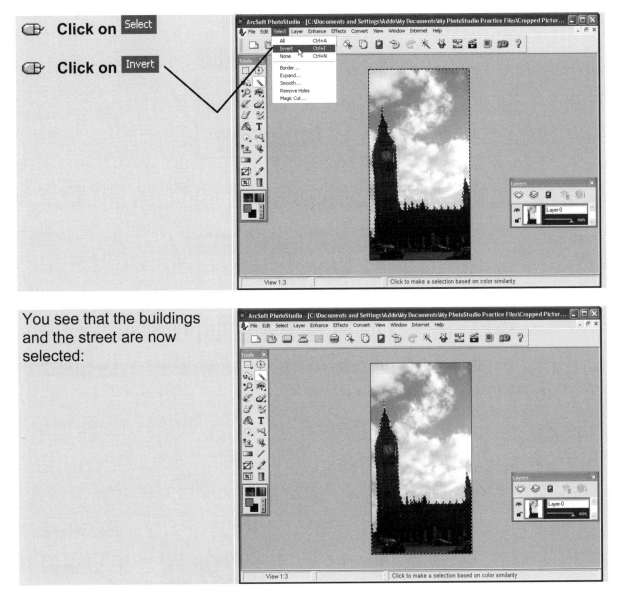

You see that the buildings and the street are now selected:

The sky in the photo looks fine. Big Ben, on the other hand, is very dark as a result of backlighting. In the next section, you're going to do something about that with the help of a new layer.

Creating a New Layer Using the Layers Palette

You can create a new layer from the selection you've just made by copying and pasting. The *Layers Palette* contains buttons for doing this.

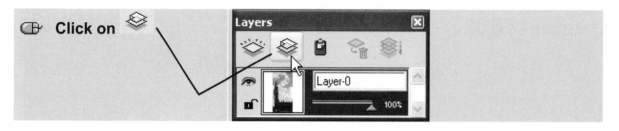

The selection has now been copied and is on the *Windows* clipboard, which you can't see. Go ahead and paste the contents of the clipboard into the image as a new layer.

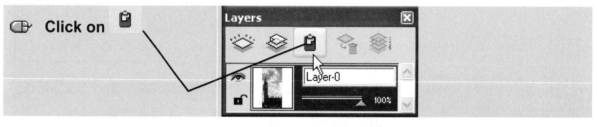

Again, it doesn't look like anything's changed, except the selection boundary has disappeared:

In the *Layers Palette*, you see that the copy of the selection has become Layer-1:

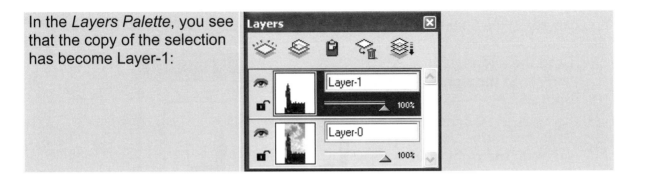

Lightening a Layer

The photo will look much better if you lighten the layer containing the buildings.

👆 **Click on** Enhance

👆 **Click on**
Brightness and Contrast...

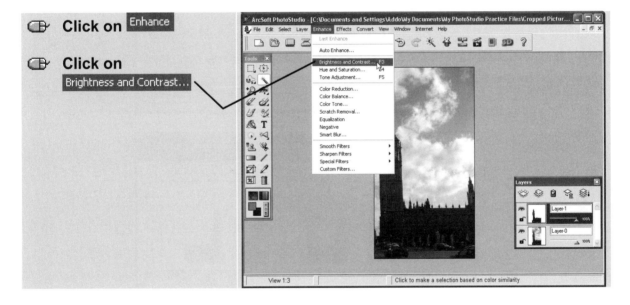

You can adjust the amount of correction in the *Brightness and Contrast* window.

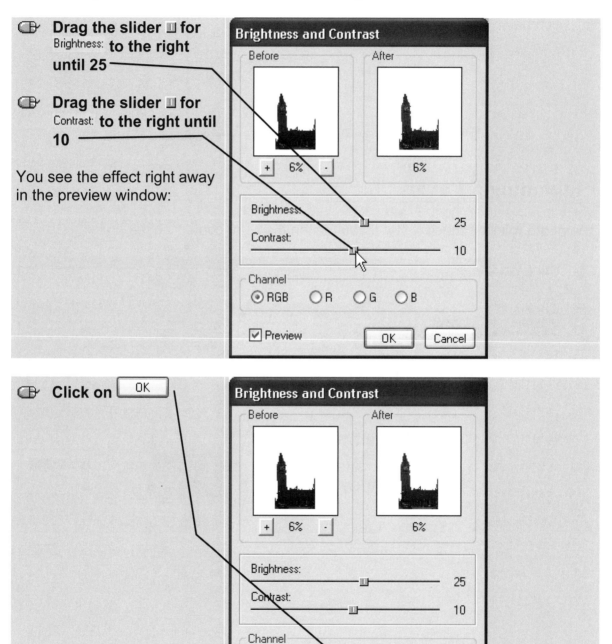

Drag the slider ⊞ for
Brightness: **to the right
until 25**

Drag the slider ⊞ for
Contrast: **to the right until
10**

You see the effect right away
in the preview window:

Click on [OK]

The photo is much brighter and clearer now. To really see the difference, you can hide Layer-1 temporarily.

☞ **Click on** 👁

See the color supplement, plate 35

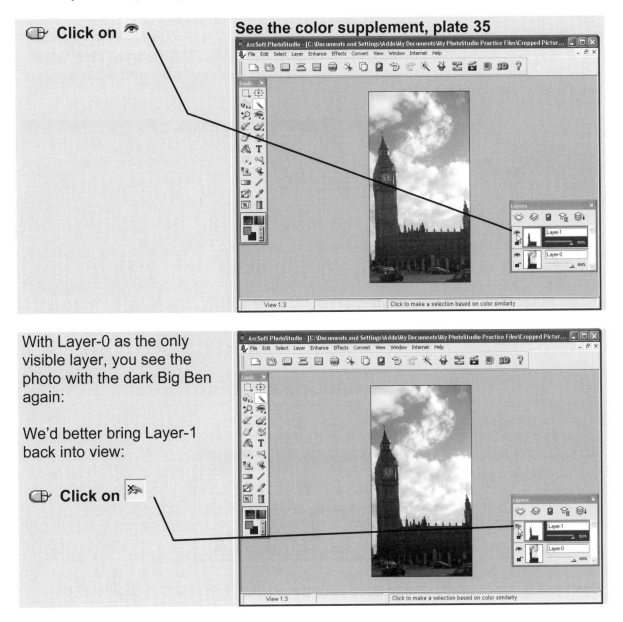

With Layer-0 as the only visible layer, you see the photo with the dark Big Ben again:

We'd better bring Layer-1 back into view:

☞ **Click on** ▨

Merging Layers

Earlier you saved a photo as a PSF file. That's the file format in which the layers are preserved so that you can continue editing them later. When you're finished editing the layers in a photo, you can also merge them. The separate layers are then added together, so to speak, so you can save the photo as it appears on your screen. Here's how you merge the layers:

Click on `Layer`

Click on `Merge All`

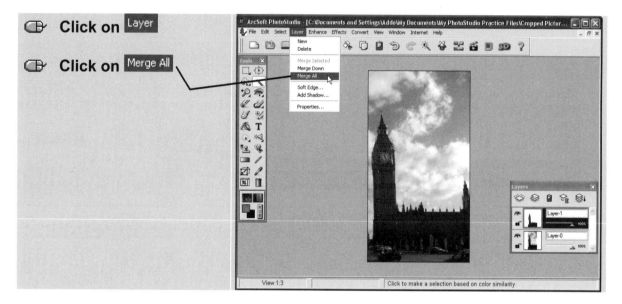

Now something's changed in the *Layers Palette*.

The photo now consists of only one layer, with the name *Merged*:

This means you can't make any more changes to the layer with the original photo and the layer with just the buildings. You can save and close the photo now, just as you're used to doing.

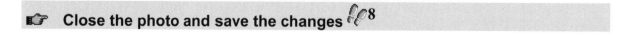

☞ **Close the photo and save the changes** ✍ 8

Shrinking a Photo for a Photomontage

With your knowledge of selections and layers, you can already create a nice photomontage.

☞ **Open the photo *Fish* in the folder *My PhotoStudio Practice Files*** ℓℓ⁶

☞ **Maximize the window containing the photo** ℓℓ⁴

You see the photo of the fish you've worked on before:

You're going to shrink the fish, select it, then paste it into another photo. Here's how you shrink the photo:

☞ **Click on** Edit

☞ **Click on** Image Size...

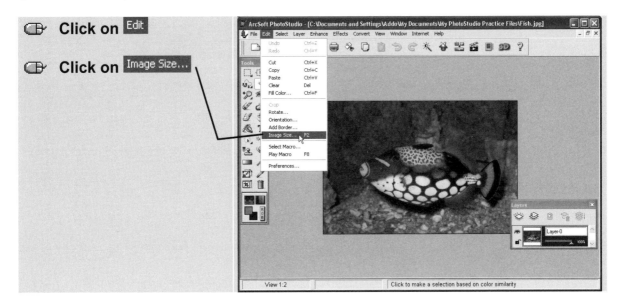

In the *Image Size* window, adjust the size to 50% of the current size.

⌨ **Type:** 50 **beside** WScale:

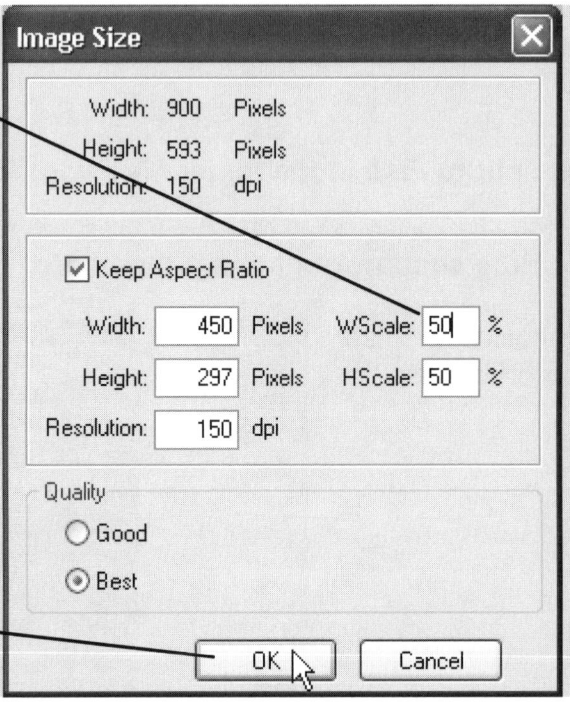

You see that the values for Width:, Height: and HScale: automatically change.

👆 **Click on** ⟮ OK ⟯

Image Size ✕

Width: 900 Pixels
Height: 593 Pixels
Resolution: 150 dpi

☑ Keep Aspect Ratio

Width: 450 Pixels WScale: 50 %

Height: 297 Pixels HScale: 50 %

Resolution: 150 dpi

Quality
○ Good
◉ Best

⟮ OK ⟯ ⟮ Cancel ⟯

The photo's gotten quite a bit smaller:

☞ **Fit the photo to the window** 📖⁵

Making a Selection for a Photomontage

You can use the *Magnetic Lasso* to select the fish.

👉 **Click on** 〄

🩹 HELP! I don't see the *Magnetic Lasso*.

Like several other tools, the *Magnetic Lasso* and the regular *Lasso* share a button on the *Tools Palette*.

You can recognize a shared location by the tiny triangle at the bottom right of the button: 〄

Here's how you can quickly access the tool you want to use:

👉 **Click with the <u>right</u> mouse button on** 〄

👉 **Click on** 〄 Magnetic Lasso

👉 Hide the *Options Palette* 〄 1

Now you can select the fish.

Click on the edge of the fish's snout with the mouse pointer

Move the mouse pointer along the outline of the fish

A selection boundary appears:

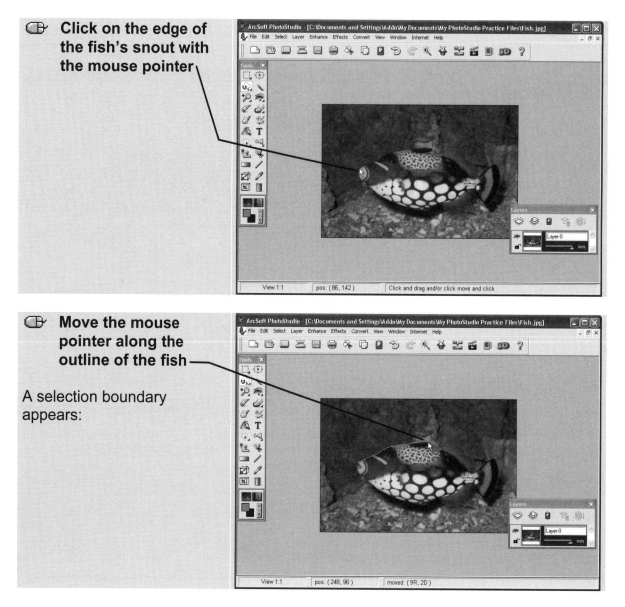

You'll have to give the *Magnetic Lasso* a little help along the backfin by clicking on the points through which the selection boundary should run:

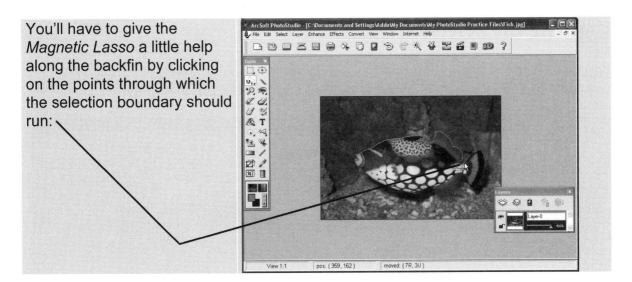

When you reach the starting point again, you can complete the selection.

Double-click near the starting point

The entire fish has been selected:

Copying the Selection

You only need the fish for the photomontage you're about to make. If you copy the selection containing the fish, you can paste it into another photo shortly.

☞ **Click on** Edit

☞ **Click on** Copy

The copy of the fish is now on the *Windows* clipboard. You can close the photo of the fish now; that won't change the contents of the clipboard.

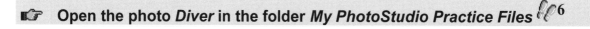

☞ **Close the photo *Fish* and <u>don't</u> save the changes** [9]

Now you're going to paste the fish into the photo of the diver.

☞ **Open the photo *Diver* in the folder *My PhotoStudio Practice Files*** [6]

You see the photo of the diver:

You can paste in the fish using the *Layers Palette*.

☞ **Click on** 📋

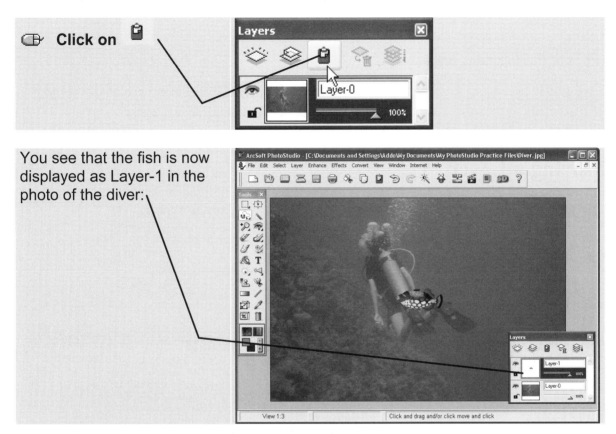

You see that the fish is now displayed as Layer-1 in the photo of the diver:

Go ahead and add a thin soft edge to the layer with the fish, so the fish blends nicely into the environment.

☞ **Click on** Layer

☞ **Click on** Soft Edge...

☞ **Drag the slider ▦ to the left until 2**

☞ **Click on [OK]**

<table>
<tr><td colspan="2">**Soft Edge**   ☒</td></tr>
<tr><td>Range of Soft Edge:</td><td>2</td></tr>
<tr><td colspan="2">◁ ▦ ────────────── ▷</td></tr>
<tr><td colspan="2">[OK]   [Cancel]</td></tr>
</table>

Moving a Layer

The fish is covering the diver right now. You can easily move it away.

☞ **Select the *Move* tool** *∬*16

☞ **Hide the *Options Palette*** *∬*1

☞ **Drag the fish up and to the right**

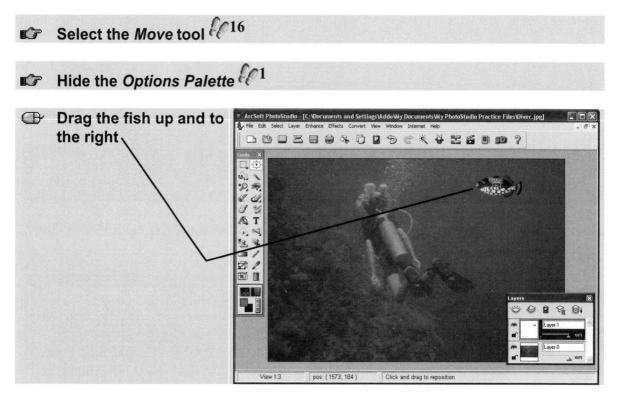

Now the fish no longer covers the diver, but you can still clearly see that it doesn't belong in the original photo. You're going to do something about that in the next section.

Making a Layer Translucent

To make the fish fit better into the background, you can make it translucent. You do this in the *Layers Palette*.

Drag the slider △ for Layer-1 to the left until 50%

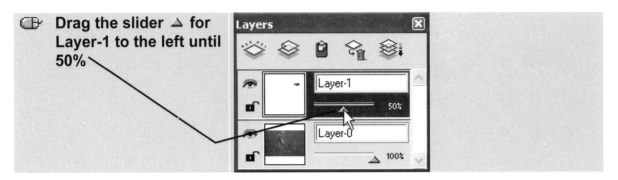

Now the fish will be 50% transparent:

You see that the fish has become more translucent:

See the color supplement, plate 36

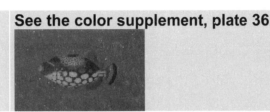

The photomontage looks much more realistic now:

See the color supplement, plate 37

Adding a Layer with 3-D Text

You can make the photomontage look like a postcard by adding a text layer. You can use a copy of Layer-0 for this.

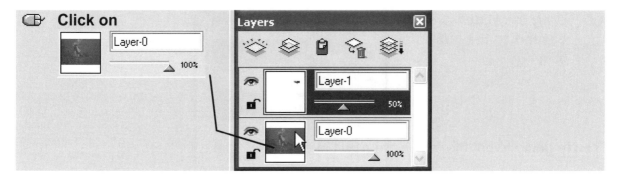

Layer-0 is now the active layer. Go ahead and use the *Layers Palette* to copy and paste this layer.

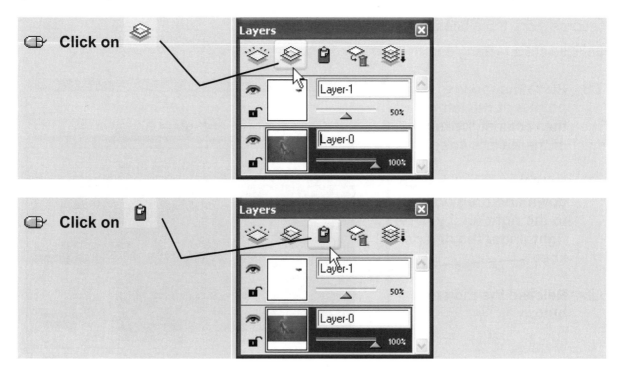

You see that a new layer named Layer-2 has been added:

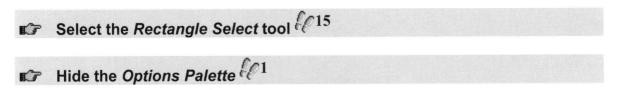

You're going to put the text in the new Layer-2. First, make a selection.

☞ **Select the** *Rectangle Select* **tool** 👣15

☞ **Hide the** *Options Palette* 👣1

Let's select a rectangle from the bottom left of the photo up to the diver's knee.

👆 **Place the mouse pointer at the left on the rocks at the height of the diver's knee**

👆 **Hold the mouse button down and drag down to the right until you're right under the diver's knee**

👆 **Release the mouse button**

The text will go in this rectangle.

The 3D Text Factory

The *3D Text Factory* is a small program within *PhotoStudio* with which you can add three-dimensional text to your photo. Here's how you start the *3D Text Factory*:

Click on

HELP! I get an error message.

Do you see this error message?

> **3D Text Factory**
>
> ⚠ Please select an area under 1024x1024 pixels.
>
> OK

Then you've made a selection greater than 1024 by 1024 pixels. The *3D Text Factory* can only work with selections smaller than 1024 by 1024 pixels.

☞ **Click on** OK

☞ **Remove the selection boundary** ✌[17]

☞ **Make a new, somewhat smaller selection**

☞ **Restart the *3D Text Factory***

You see the *3D Text Factory* window:

You can choose among various types of three-dimensional letters in this part of the window:

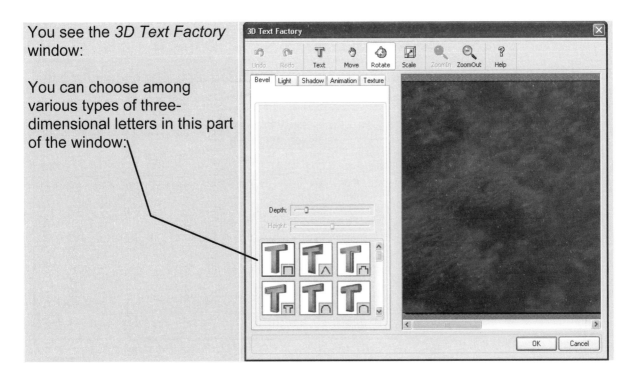

Keep the default type for the time being. Now you can open the window where you're going to type in the text.

☞ **Click on** Text

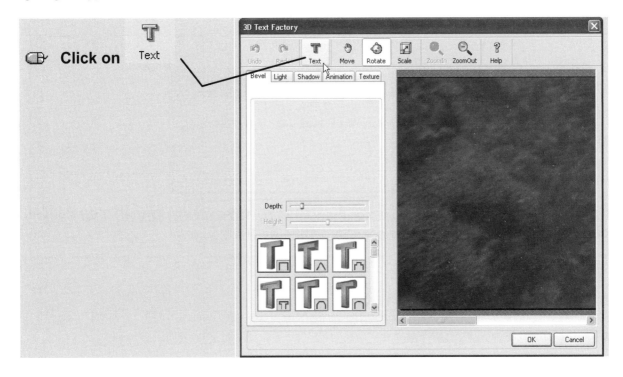

The *Edit Text* window opens. You can choose a font and font size here.

Click on ☐ —

You can use the slider ☐ to view the rest of the fonts in the list.

Click on a font, for example Arial Black

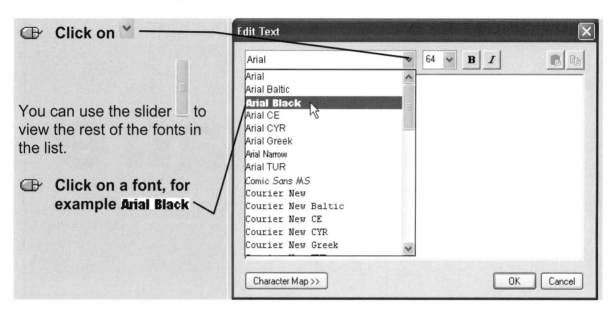

Let's select a font size of 80 points.

Click on ☐

Click on 80

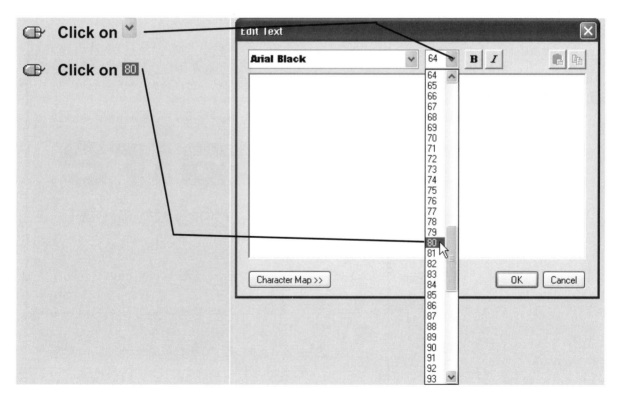

Now you can type in your text.

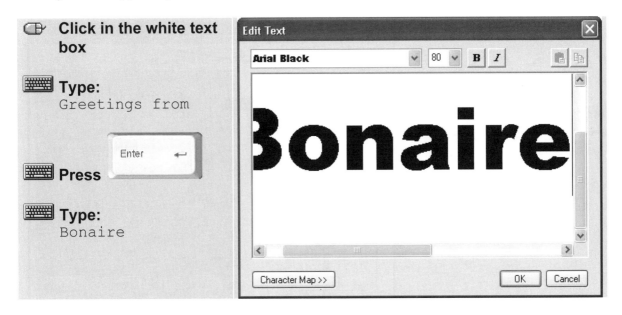

When you're satisfied with the text, you can see what it will look like in three dimensions.

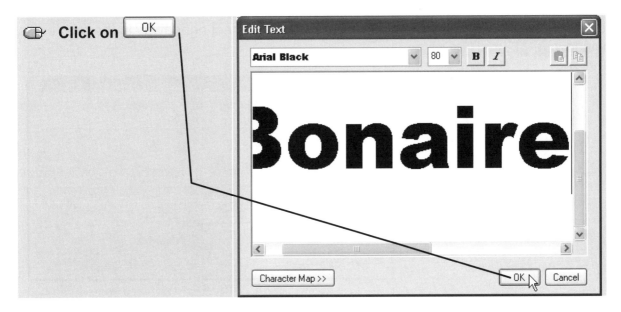

You see part of the text. If you zoom out, the text will be easier to see.

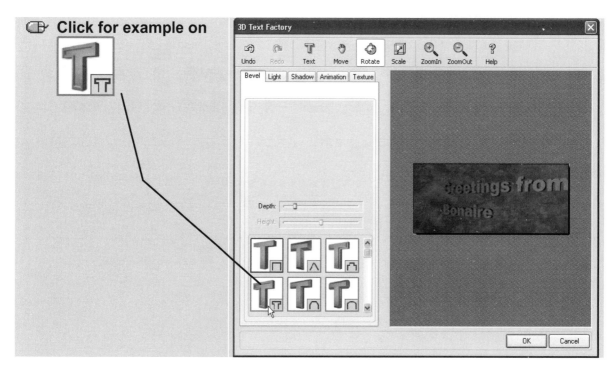

☞ **Click seven times on**

ZoomOut

Now you see the entire text.

If you choose a different type of edge, you'll see the effect right away in the preview window.

☞ **Click for example on**

Changing the Text Color

PhotoStudio has selected blue text. Of course, you can change that.

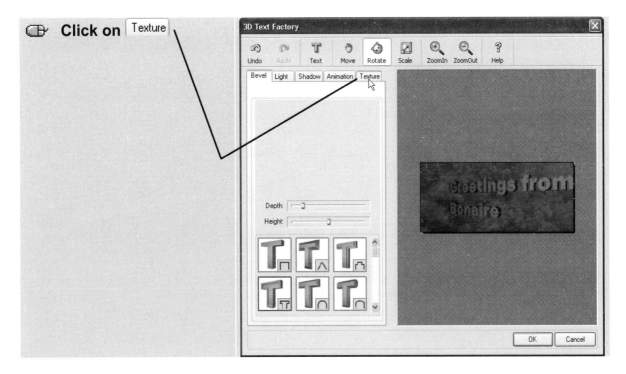

On the *Texture* tab, choose sea-green.

Click on ⬛ ▾

Click on ◻

You'll see the change right away in the preview window.

Rotating the 3-D Text

PhotoStudio also provides the option of rotating the three-dimensional text. You do that as follows:

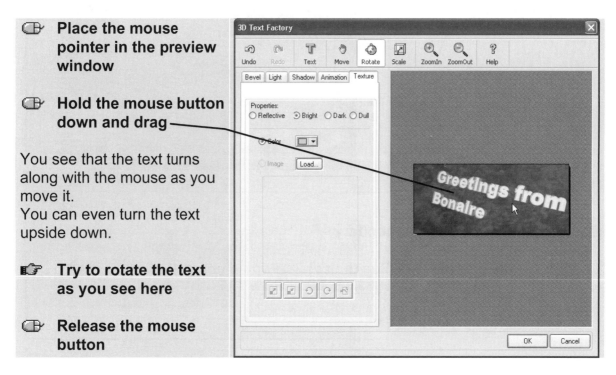

☞ **Place the mouse pointer in the preview window**

☞ **Hold the mouse button down and drag**

You see that the text turns along with the mouse as you move it.
You can even turn the text upside down.

☞ **Try to rotate the text as you see here**

☞ **Release the mouse button**

You've made enough adjustments to the text now.

☞ **Click on** OK

The text has been added to the photomontage, but the selection boundary is still blinking:

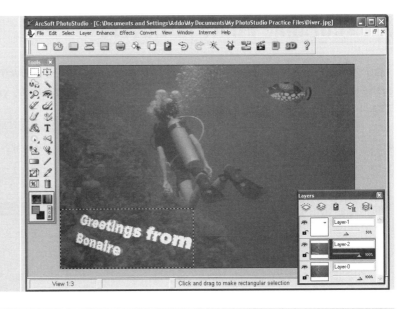

☞ **Remove the selection boundary** 📖¹⁷

Now you see the final result: **See the color supplement, plate 38**

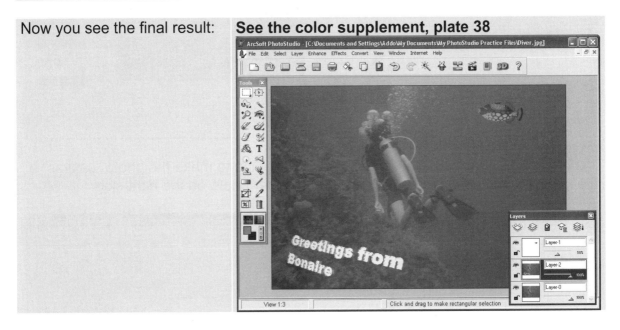

You're finished making this photomontage.

☞ **Merge the layers in the photo** 📖¹⁹

☞ **Save the photo with the name** *Greetings* 📖²⁰

☞ **Close the photo** 📖²¹

A Panoramic Photo in Layers

You may have tried before to capture the gorgeous view from a scenic lookout in a series of photos. With the help of layers in *PhotoStudio*, you can join these photos together to create a single panoramic photo.

☞ **Open the photo *Panorama 1* in the folder *Panorama* in the folder**

My PhotoStudio Practice Files 📎⁶

You see this photo of a bay on the island of St. Maarten:

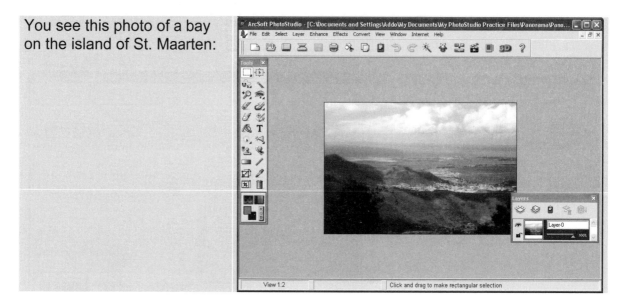

This photo is the basis for the panorama. You're going to make the photo "canvas" a little larger so you can place the layer with the other photo on the right side.

👉 **Click on** `Edit`

👉 **Click on** `Add Border...`

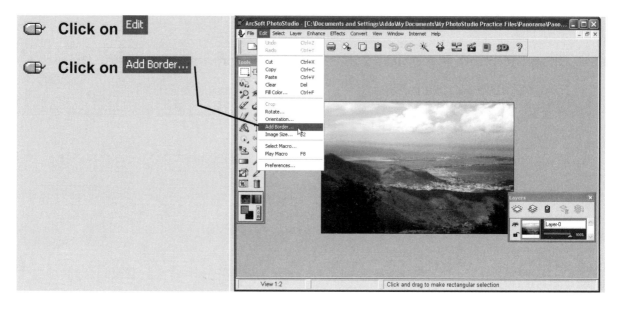

Let's add a border of 800 pixels.

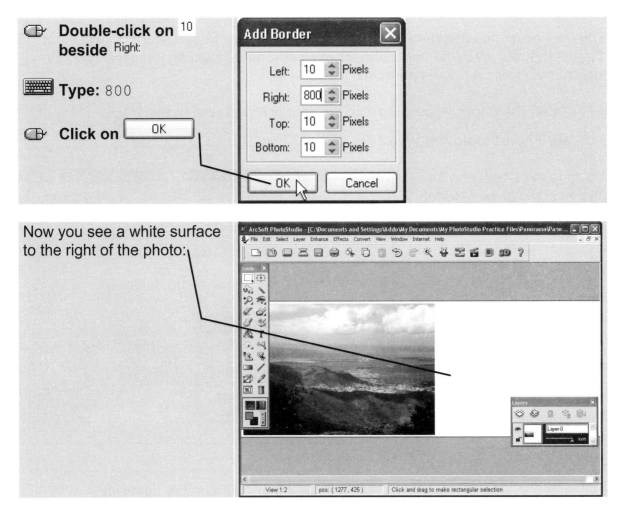

⊂⊅ **Double-click on** 10 **beside** Right:

⌨ **Type:** 800

⊂⊅ **Click on** OK

Now you see a white surface to the right of the photo:

You can open the other half of the panorama now.

☞ **Open the photo *Panorama 2* in the folder *Panorama* in the folder *My PhotoStudio Practice Files* 6**

You see the other half of the panorama:

In the *Layers Palette*, make a copy of the only layer in this photo, Layer-0.

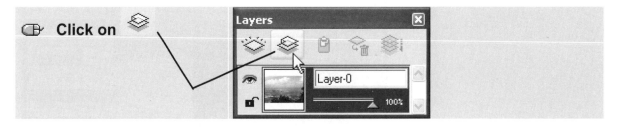

The copy of the layer is now on the clipboard.

☞ **Close the photo *Panorama 2* and <u>don't</u> save the changes** *ℓℓ*⁹

You see the first photo again:

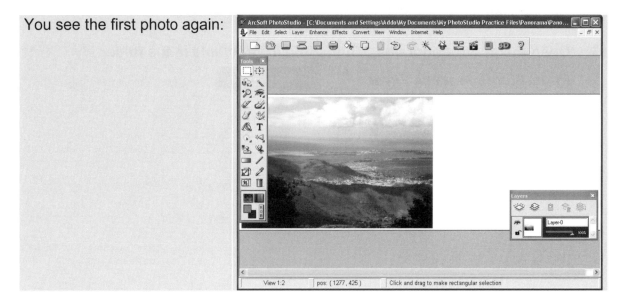

In the *Layers Palette*, paste the copied layer as a new layer in the photo *Panorama 1*.

☞ **Click on** 📋

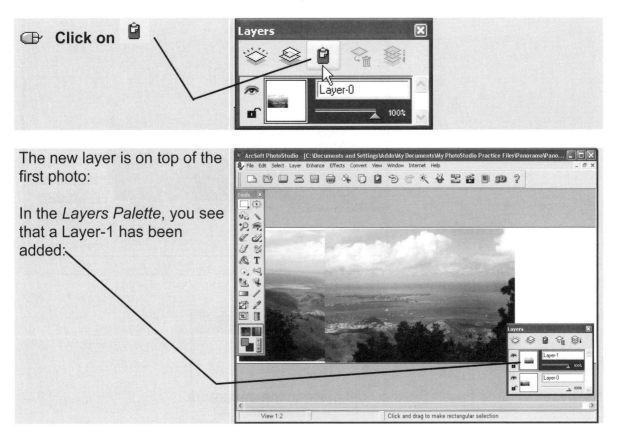

The new layer is on top of the first photo:

In the *Layers Palette*, you see that a Layer-1 has been added:

If you make Layer-1 translucent, you'll be able to move it into place in the panorama much more easily.

☞ **Drag the slider △ to the left until 60%**

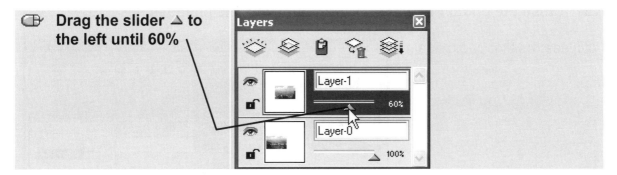

Now you see Layer-0 through Layer-1:

See the color supplement, plate 39

☞ Select the *Move* tool ✍16

☞ Hide the *Options Palette* ✍1

Now you can drag Layer-1 to the right place in the panorama.

🖱 **Drag Layer-1 along Layer-0 until the images match up**

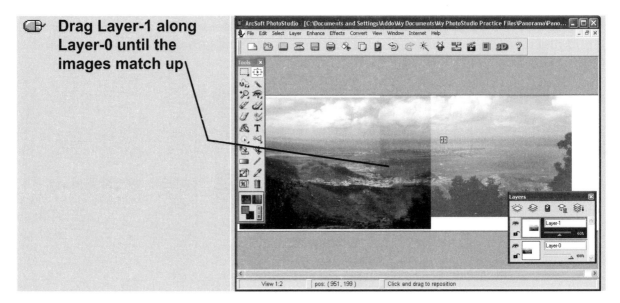

💡 Tip

Difference in Perspective

You may have noticed that it's very hard to place Layer-1 so that all elements of the photo fit perfectly onto Layer-0. This is because the photo was taken at a great distance. The slightest movement of the camera upward or downward between taking the two photos will create a difference in perspective. As a result, the overlapping parts aren't equally distant.

That makes it look like there's an extra island:

You also see the trees in the foreground double:

If you focus on lining up the green ridge, the panorama will look good after you remove the transparency in Layer-1:

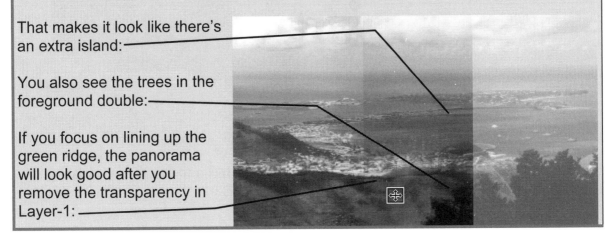

When you're satisfied with the panorama, you can make Layer-1 opaque again.

👆 **Drag the slider ◮ to the right until 100%**

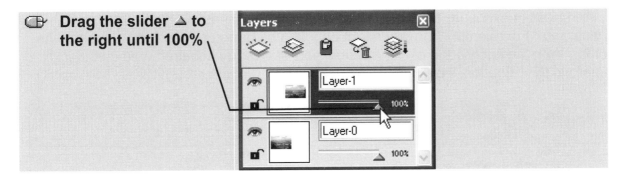

The composition is o.k. now, but the transition between the two photos is clearly visible:

See the color supplement, plate 40

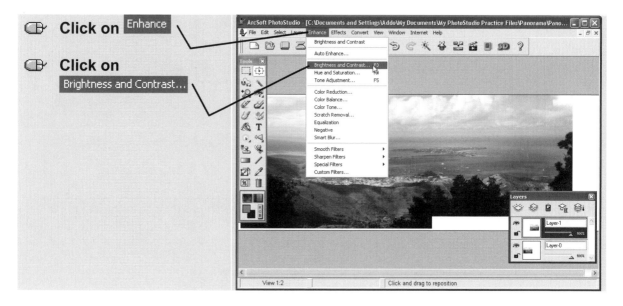

In the next section, you'll continue to work on the panorama to make the transition between the two layers less obvious.

Improving a Panoramic Photo

Differences in exposure can occur when you make a series of photos for a panorama. For example, the sun might be just a bit brighter in one photo than in the other. With the knowledge of *PhotoStudio* you've already acquired, you can quickly improve this situation. You can begin by lightening up Layer-1 a bit.

Click on Enhance

Click on Brightness and Contrast...

Let's make Layer-1 a little brighter, and lower the contrast.

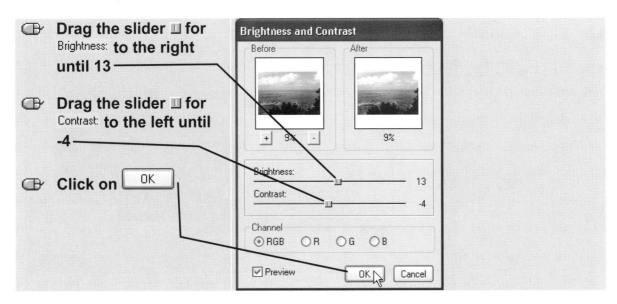

☞ **Drag the slider ⬚ for** Brightness: **to the right until 13**

☞ **Drag the slider ⬚ for** Contrast: **to the left until -4**

☞ **Click on** OK

The layers' brightness levels correspond pretty well now. If you look at the sky and the sea, however, you notice that Layer-0 is a little greener than Layer-1:

See the color supplement, plate 41

You can remove some yellow from Layer-0, so that this layer becomes a little bluer. First you'll need to activate Layer-0.

☞ **Click on**

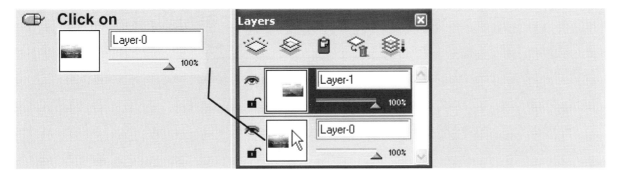

You can adjust the layer's color in the *Color Balance* window.

Click on Enhance

Click on Color Balance...

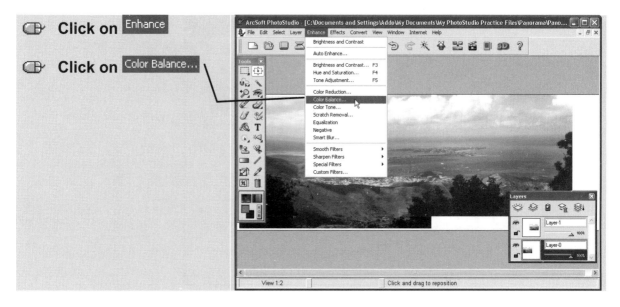

Let's remove some yellow from the midtones in Layer-0.

Drag the slider ▯ for Yellow **to the right until 20**

Click on the radio button ○ beside

Midtones

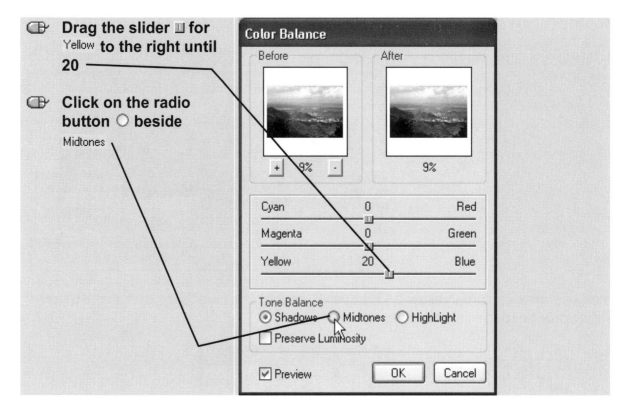

☞ **Click on the check box** ☐ **beside** Preserve Luminosity

☞ **Click on** OK

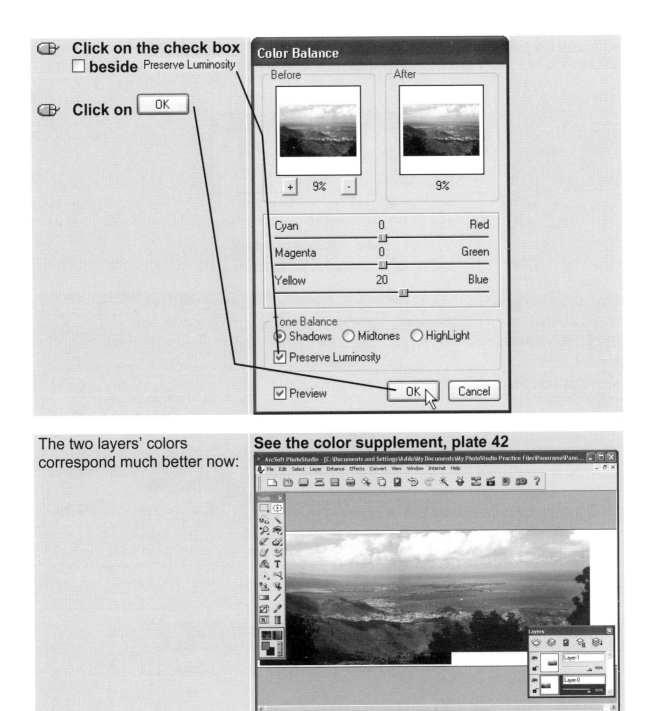

The two layers' colors correspond much better now:

See the color supplement, plate 42

Although the colors look better now, the sharp edge between Layer-0 and Layer-1 is still easy to see. You can fix this by giving Layer-1 a soft edge. First, make Layer-1 the active layer.

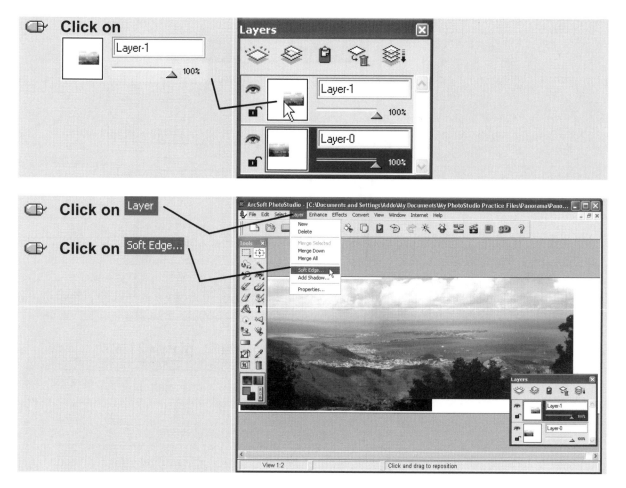

Go ahead and select a soft edge 20 pixels wide.

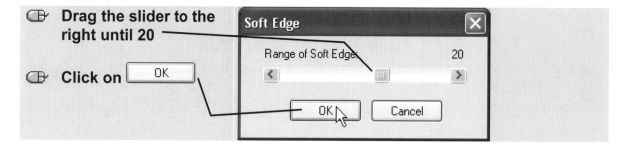

Layer-1 now has a soft edge. As a result, the two layers blend more nicely into one another:

☞ **Fit the photo to the window** ⁰⁵

Now you can see the whole panorama:

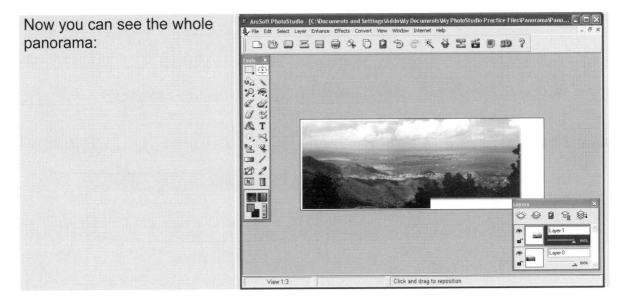

You don't need to change anything more in the individual layers, so you can merge them.

☞ **Merge the layers in the photo** ¹⁹

☞ **Close the *Layers Palette*** ²²

Cropping the Panorama

The panoramic photo isn't completely finished. Because you added a border that's a little too wide, you see a white edge on the right side. The bottom of the panorama isn't quite straight, either.

You see that the edges of the panorama aren't straight:

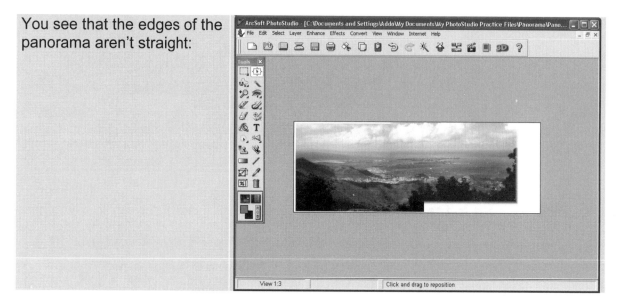

To really complete your panoramic photo, you can crop it into a rectangle.

☞ **Select the *Rectangle Select* tool** 𝓁𝓁¹⁵

☞ **Click on the radio button ○ beside** New

☞ **Hide the *Options Palette*** 𝓁𝓁¹

Now select a rectangle inside the panoramic photo, just inside the soft edges.

Place the mouse
pointer at the top left
next to the edge

Hold the mouse button
down and drag to the
bottom right next to
the soft edge

Release the mouse
button

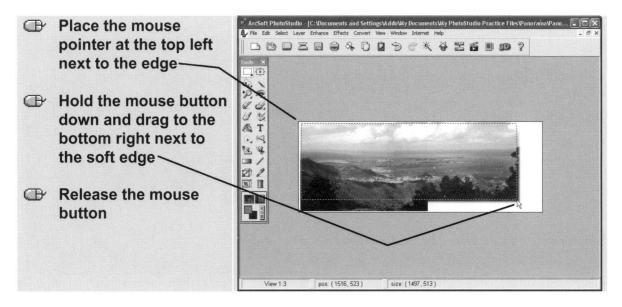

You can crop the photo now.

Click on Edit

Click on Crop

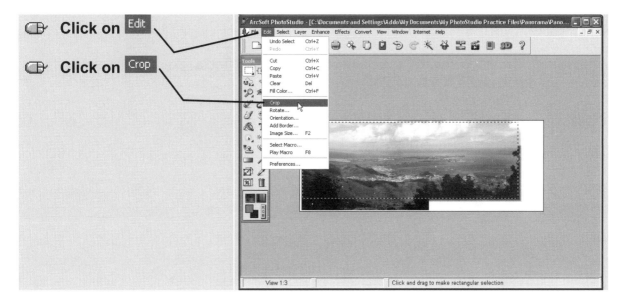

The panoramic photo is complete:

See the color supplement, plate 43

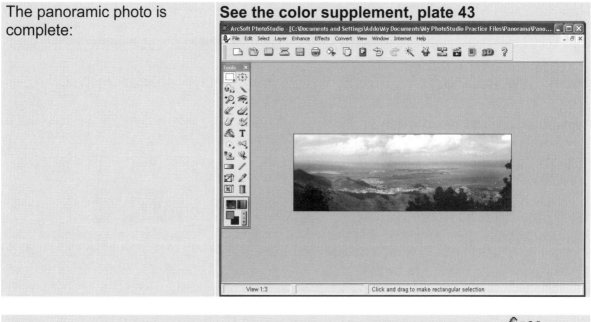

☞ **Save the photo *Panorama* with the name *Panorama St Maarten* ✐20**

☞ **Close the photo ✐21**

PhotoStudio provides several special techniques and effects. You'll learn about several of these in the next chapter.

Exercises

The following exercise will help you master what you've just learned. Have you forgotten how to perform a particular action? Use the number beside the footsteps to look it up in the appendix *How Do I Do That Again?*

Exercise: Layers

In this exercise, you'll practice working with layers.

☑ Open the photo *Fish* using the *Browser.* 6

☑ Maximize the window containing the photo. 4

☑ Select the photo. 46

☑ Copy the photo and paste it as a new layer. 47

☑ Cut out the fish using the *Shape* tool. 48

☑ Apply the *Charcoal* effect to the layer that's been cut. 49

☑ Add a text layer with the text: `Greetings.` 50

☑ Move the text layer to the top middle of the photo. 51

☑ Merge the layers. 52

☑ Close the photo and don't save the changes. 9

Tips

Tip

Buttons in the *Layers Palette*
At the top of the *Layers Palette*, there are several buttons you can use to quickly perform certain actions. The functions for these buttons are listed below.

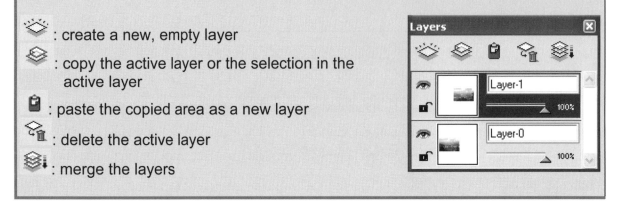

: create a new, empty layer

: copy the active layer or the selection in the active layer

: paste the copied area as a new layer

: delete the active layer

: merge the layers

Tip

More Layers In View
You can increase the size of the *Layers Palette* so you can see more layers. Then you won't have to keep scrolling to the layer you want to edit.

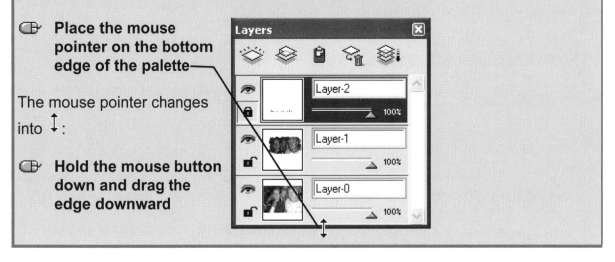

☞ **Place the mouse pointer on the bottom edge of the palette**

The mouse pointer changes into ↕ :

☞ **Hold the mouse button down and drag the edge downward**

Tip

Rulers and Grids

If you want to line up your composition precisely in *PhotoStudio*, you can use the rulers and grids. You display these as follows:

☞ **Click on** View

☞ **Click on** Rulers **or on** Grids

This is what the screen looks like with the rulers and the grids:

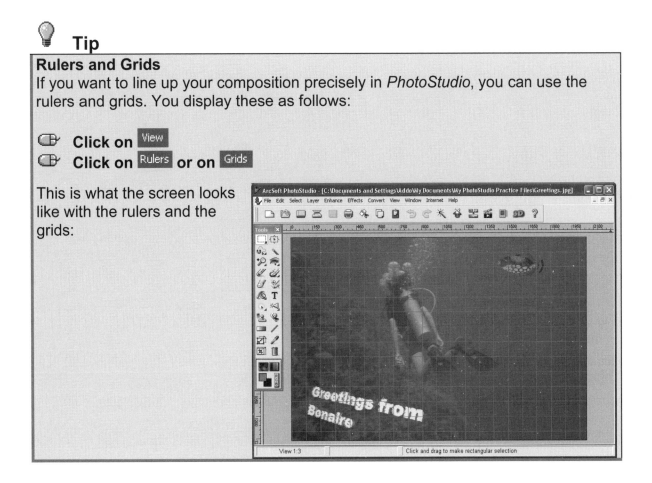

7. Special Effects

In this chapter, you'll become acquainted with a number of special effects and techniques in *PhotoStudio*. You'll learn to work with different effects that you can use to add an artistic twist to your photos. You can even frame your photos.
With the help of the *Stitch* function, you can put two photos together to make a panoramic photo. You'll also see how you can straighten a slanted building and adjust the perspective in a photo. If you want to change even more in a photo, you can apply interesting effects with the distortion filters.

In this chapter, you'll learn how to:

- use various effects
- frame a photo
- create a panoramic photo with the *Stitch* function
- make a photo look old
- straighten a slanted building
- adjust a photo's perspective
- use the distortion filters

Effects

In the chapter *Improving Photos*, you were introduced to some filters that can enhance a photo. Those filters sharpen or blur a photo, or remove dust and scratches. *PhotoStudio* provides many more filters. You'll find them in the group *Effects.* You can use a number of these effects to give your photo an artistic feel.

☞ **Open the photo *Notre Dame* in the folder *My PhotoStudio Practice Files*** 📖6

☞ **Maximize the window containing the photo** 📖4

You see this photo of two tourists in front of the Notre Dame in Paris:

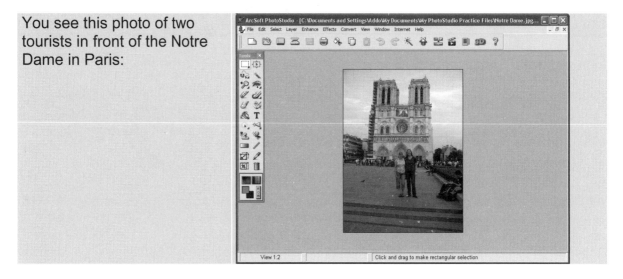

The Stained Glass Effect

You're going to try out an effect in the *Fine Art* group first.

👆 **Click on** Effects

👆 **Click on** Fine Art

👆 **Click on** Stained Glass...

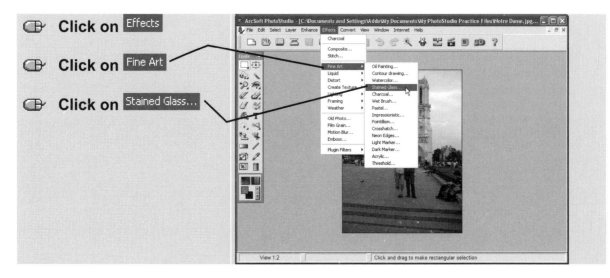

With this effect you can make your photo look like a stained-glass window. You don't need to change any settings in the *Stained Glass* window.

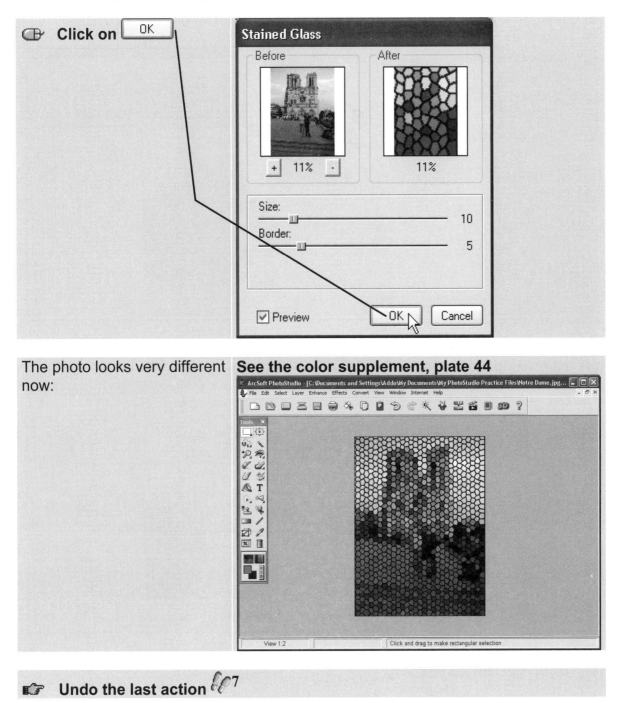

The photo looks very different now:

See the color supplement, plate 44

☞ Undo the last action 🖐7

The Moonlight Effect

Go ahead and try out another effect, this time in the *Lighting* group.

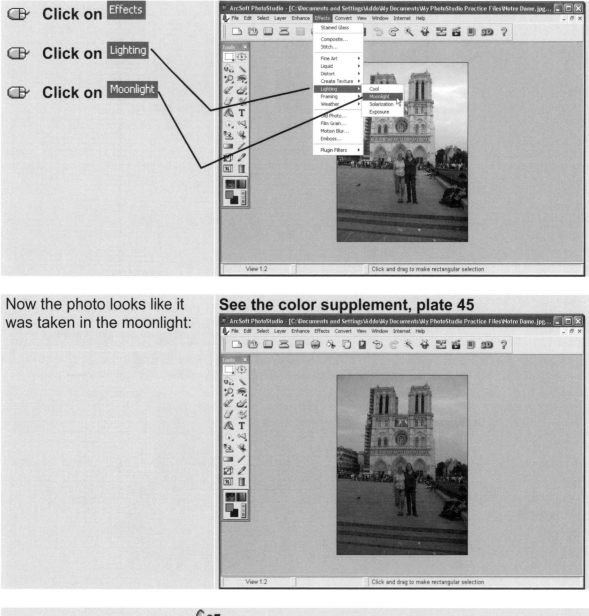

Click on Effects

Click on Lighting

Click on Moonlight

Now the photo looks like it was taken in the moonlight:

See the color supplement, plate 45

☞ **Undo the last action** 7

The Blinds Effect

You'll find several more interesting effects in the *Create Texture* group.

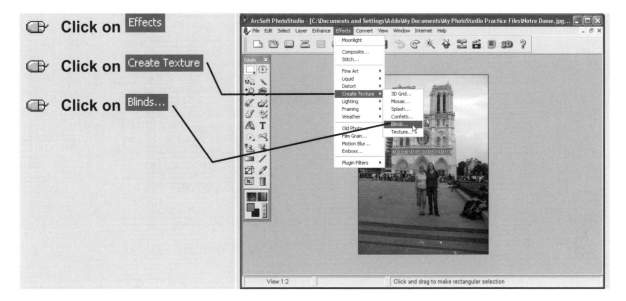

Click on Effects

Click on Create Texture

Click on Blinds...

This effect makes the photo look like it's been printed on venetian blinds. In the *Blinds* window you can adjust, for example, the width.

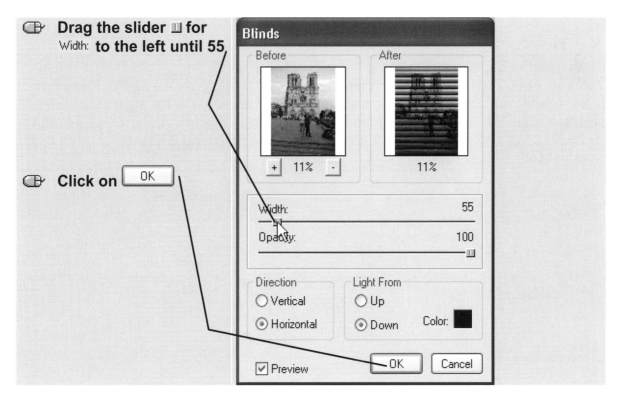

Drag the slider 🔲 for Width: **to the left until 55**

Click on OK

The photo looks very unusual now:

See the color supplement, plate 46

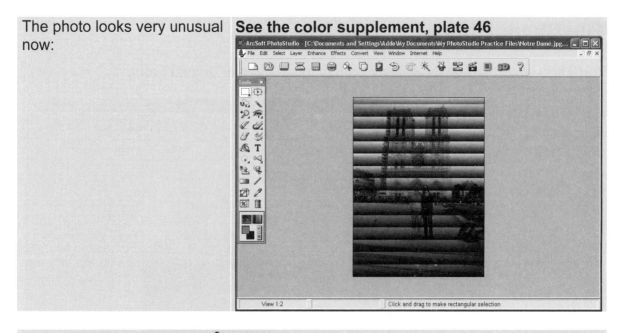

☞ **Undo the last action** $\ell\ell^7$

Of course, whether or not you like the results of these effects is a matter of taste. You can experiment with them to your heart's content: if you don't like the result, you can always undo the effect.

💡 **Tip**

Selections and Layers
You can, of course, also apply an effect to just a small section of a photo. If you first make a selection and then choose an effect, this effect will only be applied to the selected area. When you're working with layers, keep in mind that the effect will only be applied to the currently active layer. You can recognize the active layer by its blue color in the *Layers Palette*.

Framing a Photo

You can put a frame around your photo using a different group of effects. Let's give it a try.

Click on Effects

Click on Framing

Click on Clear Frame...

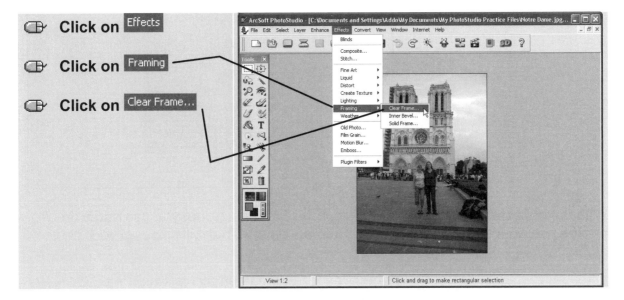

In the *Clear Frame* window, you can adjust the settings for the frame if you wish. Right now we'll just see what the result is using the default settings.

Click on OK

The photo's been given a
modern frame:

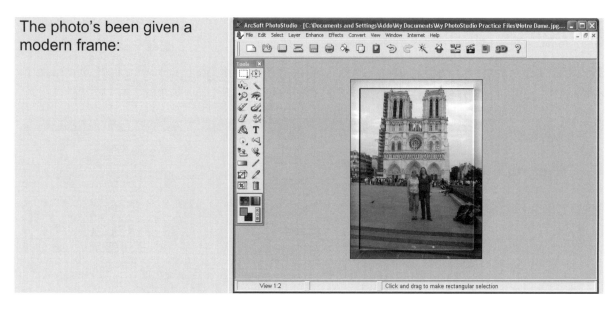

With the help of the various frame types in the *Framing* group, you can add extras to photos you want to print out and paste into an album. That will spice up your photo album in the blink of an eye.

☞ **Close the photo and <u>don't</u> save the changes** ℓℓ⁹

The Stitch Function

In the previous chapter, you created and improved a panoramic photo with the help of layers. There's another way to do that. *PhotoStudio* provides a special function with which you can almost automatically stitch together two photos, given certain conditions: There must be a recognizable point of agreement between the photos, called the *target*. The target must have enough contrast. In addition, the perspectives from which the photos were taken must not differ too greatly. You're going to try it out with two photos you saved earlier in the folder *Panorama*.

☞ **Open the photo *Panorama A* in the folder *Panorama* in the folder**

   My PhotoStudio Practice Files ℓℓ⁶

☞ **Maximize the window containing the photo** ℓℓ⁴

You see this photo of Dutch windmills in the historic village of Zaanse Schans:

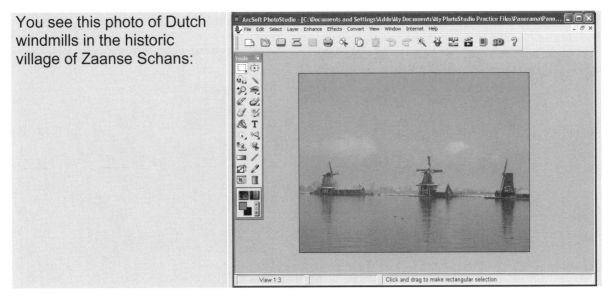

Now you can open the other photo that'll go into the panorama.

☞ **Open the photo *Panorama B* in the folder *Panorama* in the folder *My PhotoStudio Practice Files* ℓ℘6**

Here you see the other half of the panorama you're going to make:

The windmill on the left is also in the other photo. You're going to use this windmill as the target for stitching the photos together:

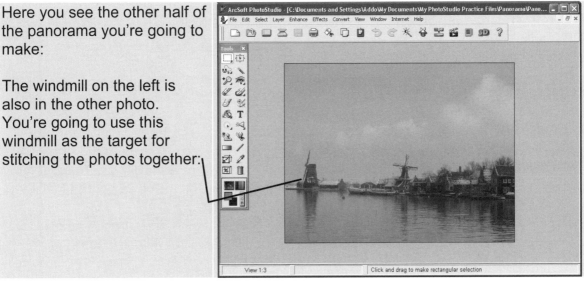

The *Stitch* function has a button on the *Quick Access Bar*.

Click on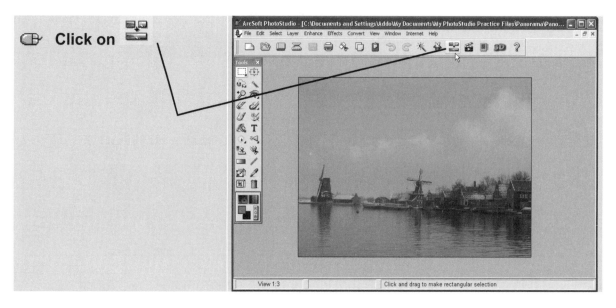

The *Stitch* window opens.

According to *PhotoStudio*, the photo *Panorama A* should be stitched onto the right side of the photo *Panorama B*:

In the preview windows, you can see what the panorama will look like. This setting isn't right for the panorama. The real target is this windmill:

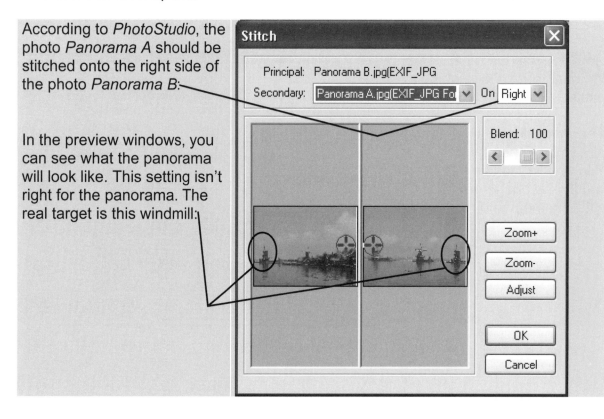

The photo *Panorama A* shouldn't go on the right, but rather on the left of *Panorama B*. Here's how you change this setting:

Click on ∨ beside `Right`

Click on `Left`

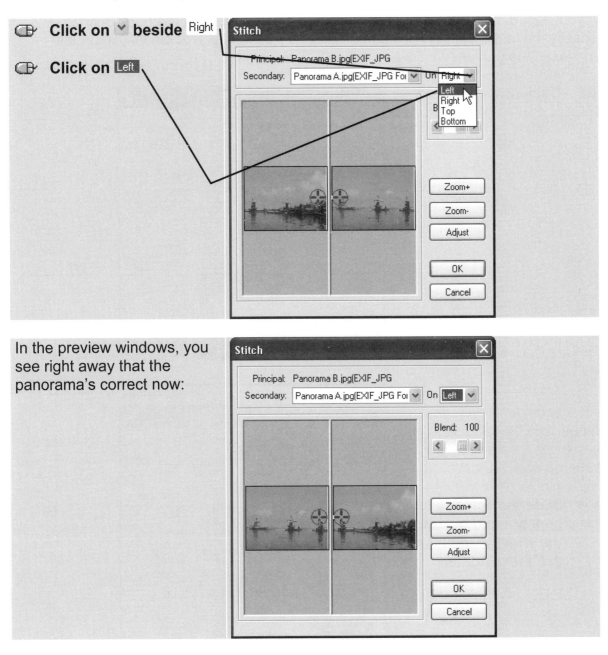

In the preview windows, you see right away that the panorama's correct now:

Placing the Target

If you want to be certain the photos will be properly stitched together, you'll need to specify the target exactly. You can do this very easily if you zoom way in on the photos in the preview windows.

Click three times on Zoom+

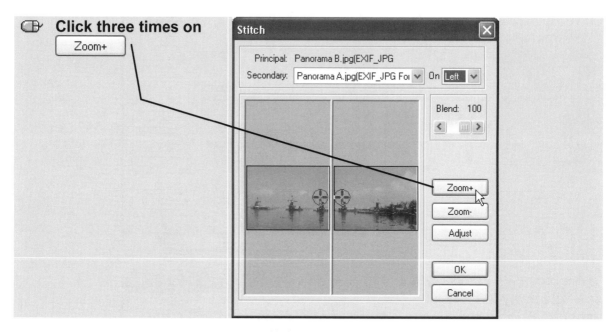

After zooming in, you no longer see the windmill. You can bring it back into view with the scrollbars:

Slide the scrollbars beneath and beside the window until you see the windmill

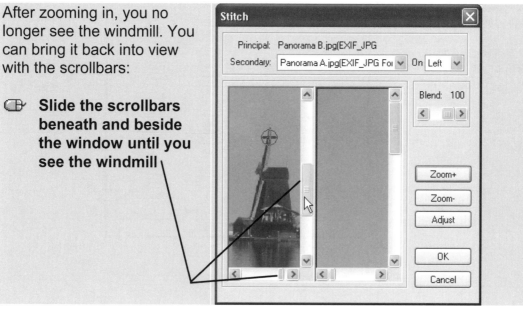

Go ahead and do the same thing in the preview window on the right.

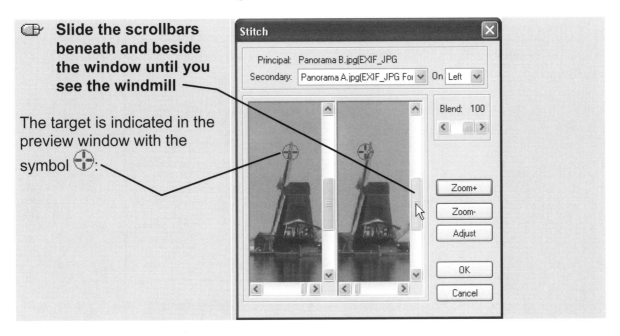

☞ **Slide the scrollbars beneath and beside the window until you see the windmill**

The target is indicated in the preview window with the symbol ⊕:

By dragging or clicking with the mouse, you can move the target. For this panorama, we'll use the tip of the white roof in the center of the windmill for the target.

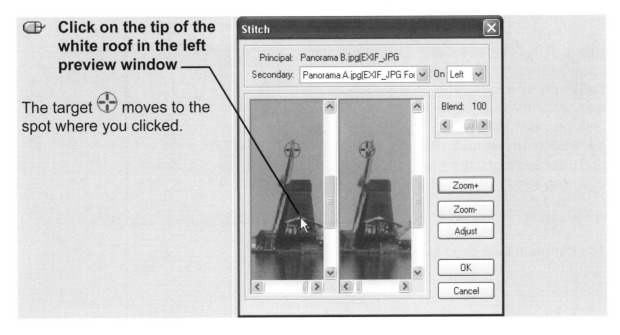

☞ **Click on the tip of the white roof in the left preview window**

The target ⊕ moves to the spot where you clicked.

👆 **Click on the tip of the white roof in the right preview window**

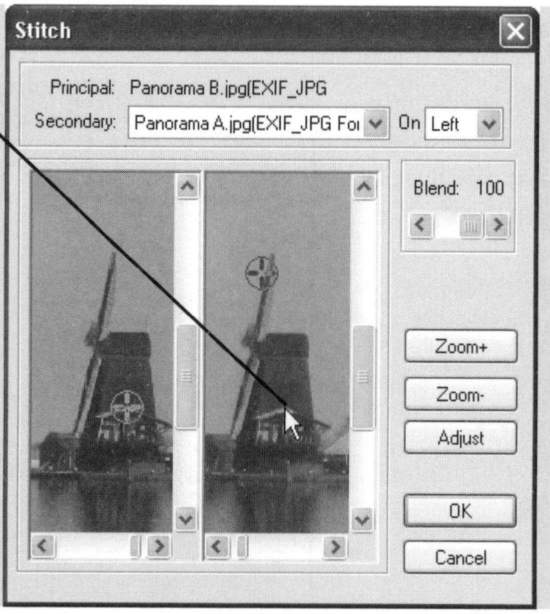

The target is now at the same point in both preview windows:

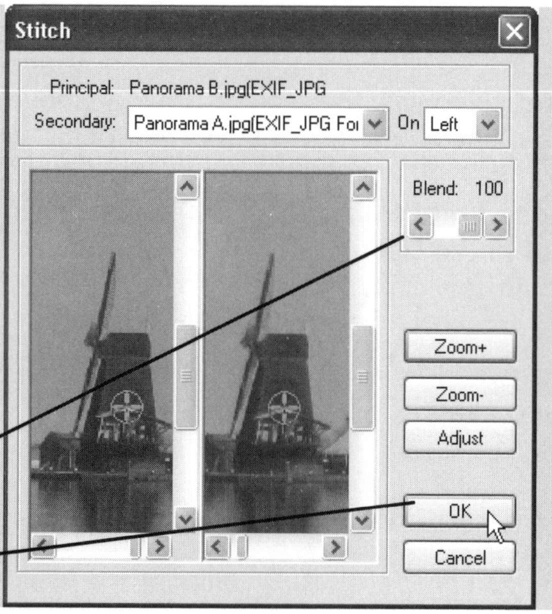

Blend: 100

Using  [< ▢ >] , you can specify how the two photos should blend into one another. The current setting, 100, provides the gentlest transition:

👆 **Click on** [OK]

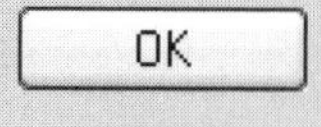

The panorama will be created now.

The panoramic photo appears.

Because a gentle blend was specified, you don't see any edge between the two photos.

The panoramic photo has been placed in a new file named [Untitled-Stitched-02]:

See the color supplement, plate 47

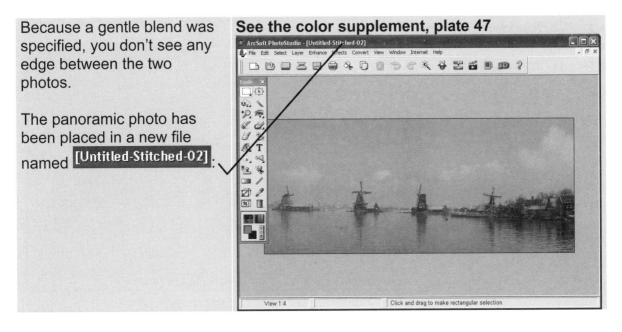

HELP! I'm seeing double.

Has the windmill you used as the target developed double blades?

Then you didn't put the target in exactly the same spot in the two preview windows. Go ahead and give it another try!

☞ **Close the photo *Untitled-Stitched* and <u>don't</u> save the changes** [9]

☞ **Repeat the steps for creating the panorama**

Now you can save the panoramic photo.

🖱️ **Click on** File

🖱️ **Click on** Save As...

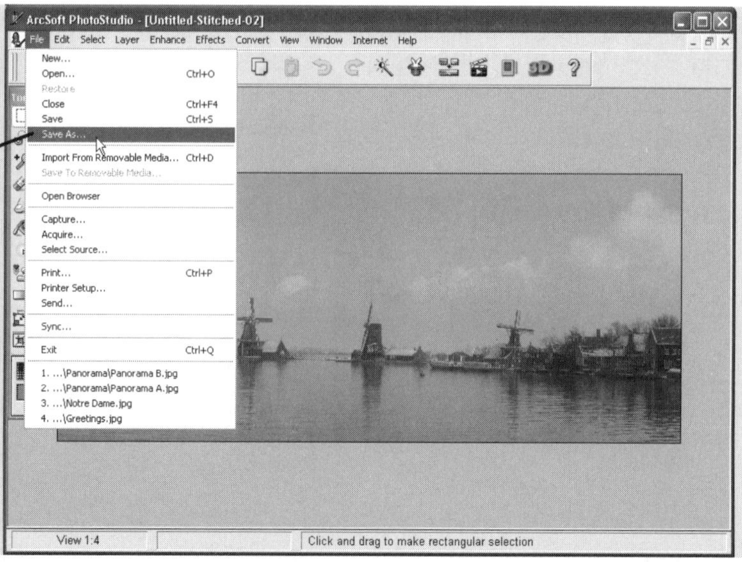

⌨️ **Type:**
Panorama Windmills

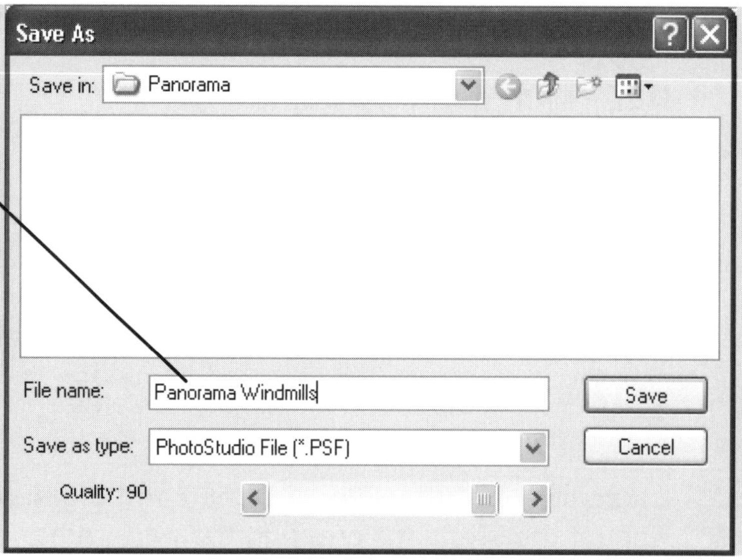

Because *PhotoStudio* created the new photo file for the panoramic photo, it assumes you want to save the photo as a PSF file. That isn't necessary, however, since the photo isn't composed of layers that you want to edit again later. You can choose the JPEG file format instead.

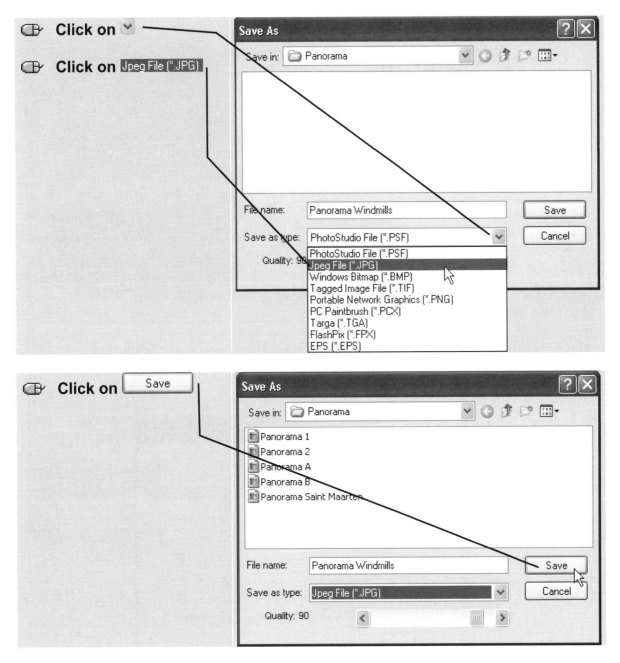

In the next section, you're going to turn this panoramic photo into an old photo.

The Old Photo Effect

You've no doubt seen them, those old-fashioned photos in sepia tints. In *PhotoStudio*, you can turn your modern digital photo into a photo that looks like it was taken a hundred years ago.

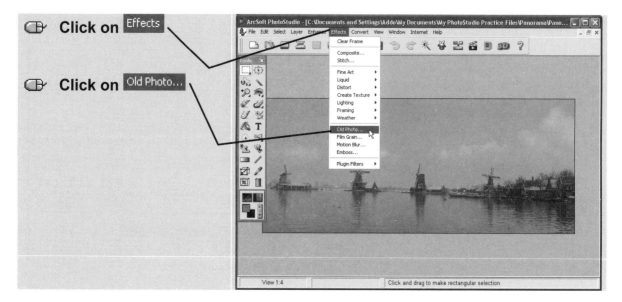

Click on Effects

Click on Old Photo...

In the preview window and in the underlying photo, you see that the photo has changed color and become blurry. You can also change the border of the photo and make it a little spotty.

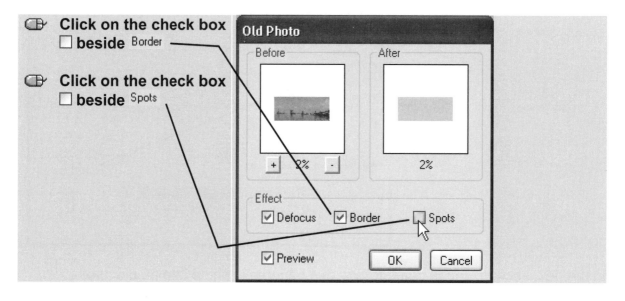

Click on the check box □ beside Border

Click on the check box □ beside Spots

HELP!
Clicking on the check box doesn't give immediate results.

It takes a little time to display these effects. You'll have to be patient before you see the check mark and the effect appear. You can follow the progress at the bottom of the *PhotoStudio* window: Processing: 92%

You see the result in the underlying photo:

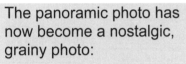

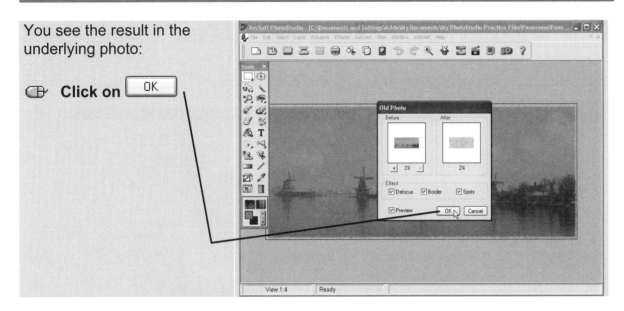

The panoramic photo has now become a nostalgic, grainy photo:

See the color supplement, plate 48

☞ **Close the photo *Panorama Windmills* and <u>don't</u> save the changes** *{9*

☞ **Close the photos *Panorama A* and *Panorama B*** *{21*

Straightening a Building

Buildings and towers often end up a little slanted in a photo. Perhaps you weren't holding your camera straight, or you were standing off to one side. In *PhotoStudio*, it takes very little effort to straighten a building.

☞ **Open the photo *Cropped Picture Big Ben* in the folder *My PhotoStudio Practice Files* ✐⁶**

☞ **Maximize the window containing the photo ✐⁴**

You see the photo of Big Ben in which you previously adjusted the exposure.

As you can see, the tower is leaning a little to the left:

You're going to try to straighten Big Ben back up. You can do that with the *Transform* tool.

☞ **Click on** ⬚

The mouse pointer changes into ↕.

Eight small square handles appear in the corners and along the edges of the photo:

You also see the *Options Palette*:

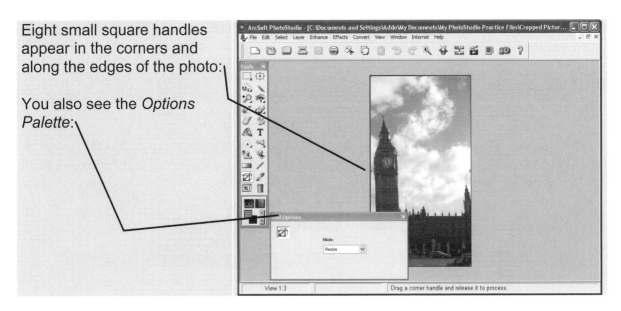

In the *Options Palette*, choose the *Skew* function.

👆 **Click on** ⌄

👆 **Click on** Skew

The mouse pointer changes into ↗.

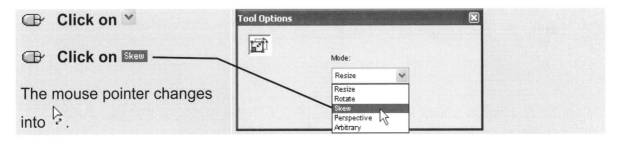

☞ **Hide the *Options Palette*** 𝓲𝓮¹

With the help of the corner handles, you're going to slant the photo, which will make Big Ben stand straight.

👆 **Place the mouse pointer ↗ on the top right corner handle**

👆 **Hold the mouse button down and drag the corner handle a little to the right**

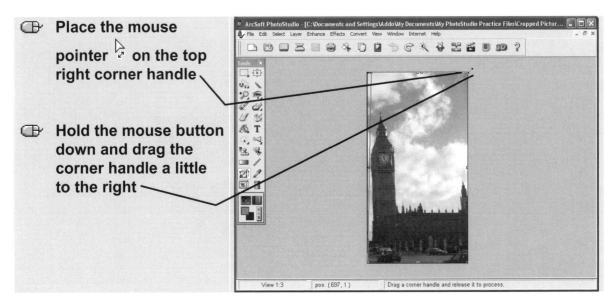

You see the effect right away in the photo. Big Ben is straight, but now there's a small white border on the left side:

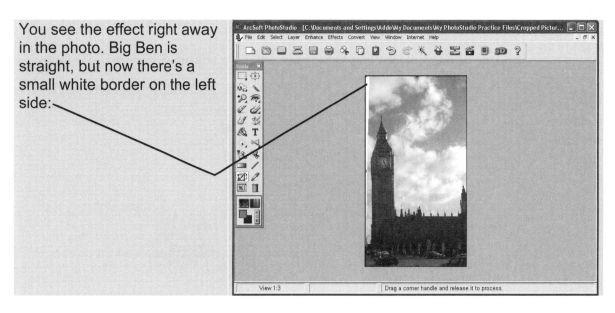

Here is how to get rid of this border:

☞ **Select the *Rectangle Select* tool** 🔏15

☞ **Hide the *Options Palette*** 🔏1

Using the *Rectangle Select* tool, make a selection in the photo so that the white border falls just outside it.

👆 **Place the mouse pointer at the top left next to the white border**

👆 **Hold the mouse button down and drag to the bottom right**

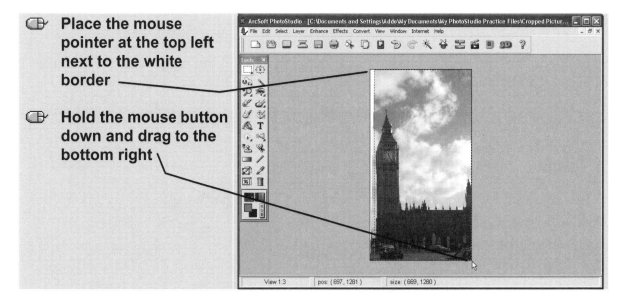

You can quickly cut out this selection with the *Crop* tool.

Click on

💡 **Tip**

The Same Function
The *Crop* tool does exactly the same thing as the commands Edit, Crop which you've used up to this point. Using the *Tools Palette*, you can carry out the command with a single mouse click.

Big Ben is straight and the white border is gone:

The disadvantage of straightening and cropping the photo is that it's become a little smaller. It's a good idea to straighten the photo before you make the very first crop next time.

☞ **Close the photo and <u>don't</u> save the changes** 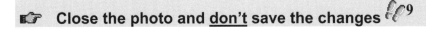⁹

Adjusting the Perspective

Another problem you might have with buildings in photos is that they seem to tilt backward. *PhotoStudio* has a solution for this, too: you can adjust the perspective.

☞ **Open the photo *Notre Dame* in the folder *My PhotoStudio Practice Files*** *ℓℓ*6

☞ **Maximize the window containing the photo** *ℓℓ*4

You see the photo of the Notre Dame. The bottom of the building looks larger than the top. As a result, it appears to tilt backward:

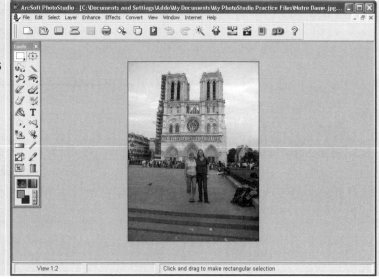

You're going to try to change this with the *Transform* tool.

🖰 **Click on**

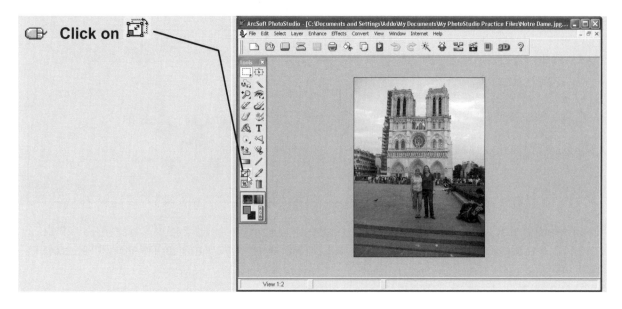

In the *Options Palette*, choose the *Perspective* function.

👆 **Click on** ⌄

👆 **Click on** Perspective

The mouse pointer changes into ▷.

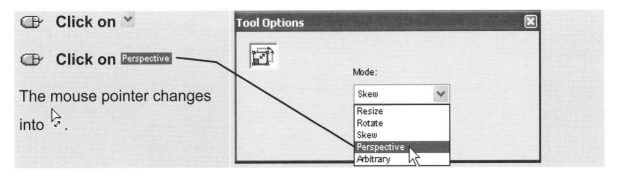

👉 **Hide the *Options Palette*** 📖¹

The corner and edge handles have appeared around the photo again.

👆 **Place the mouse pointer on the left bottom corner handle**

👆 **Hold the mouse button down and drag the corner handle a little to the right**

The same adjustment is automatically applied on the right side:

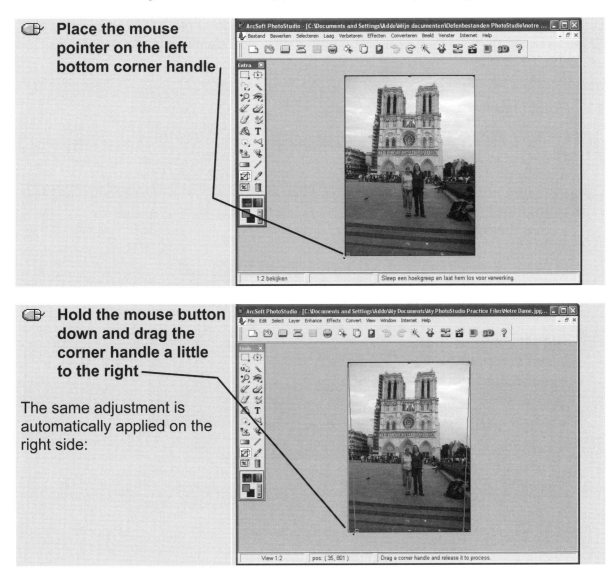

When you release the mouse button, you see that the photo has gotten narrower at the bottom. The Notre Dame looks much better now:

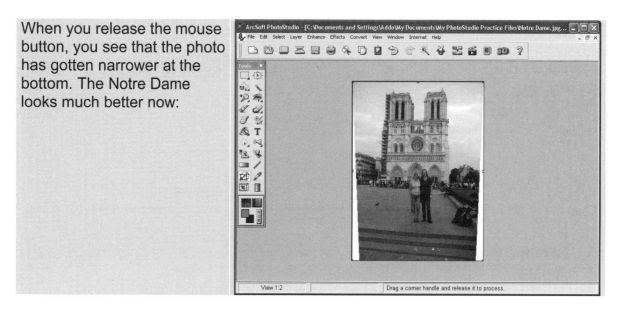

Because you've altered the perspective, the shape of the photo has changed. As a result white borders have appeared on both sides. You can fix this problem by cropping the photo.

☞ **Select the *Rectangle Select* tool** *15*

☞ **Hide the *Options Palette*** *1*

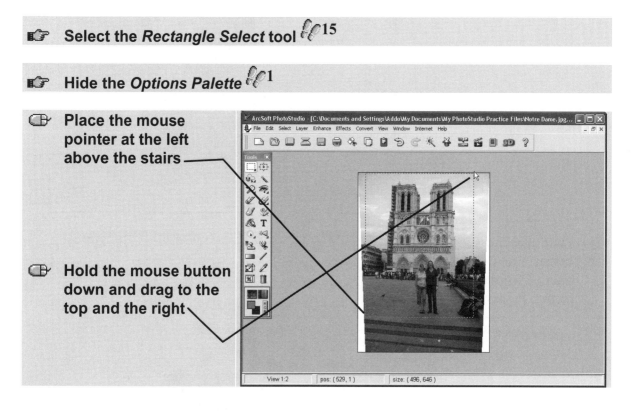

Place the mouse pointer at the left above the stairs

Hold the mouse button down and drag to the top and the right

Now you can crop this
selection:

☞ **Click on** 🖽

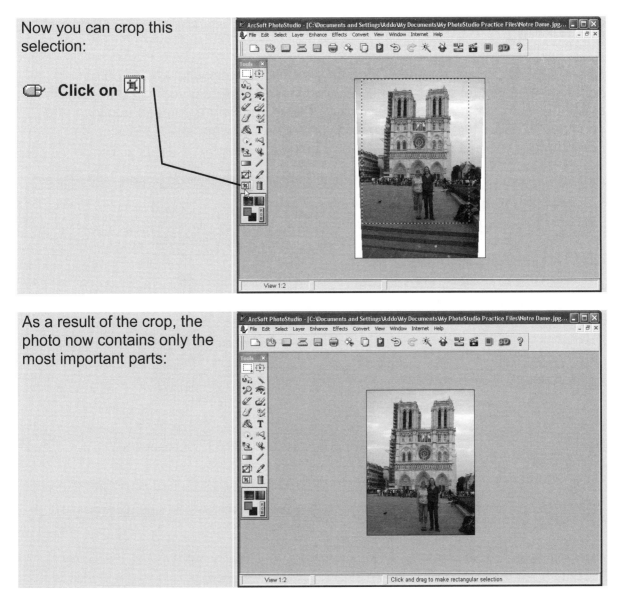

As a result of the crop, the
photo now contains only the
most important parts:

Countless tourists have photographed the Notre Dame in Paris. No one's impressed
to see you've been there anymore. In the next section, you'll read how you can make
this monument look a little different in your photo, so that it makes an impression
after all.

Distorting a Photo

PhotoStudio provides several features in the *Distort* group with which you can achieve interesting effects in a photo. Using these feautures, you can transform a building into a structure no architect could dream up. Before you can apply an effect, you have to select the part of the photo you want to be effected.
For example, you can select the windows in the left tower:

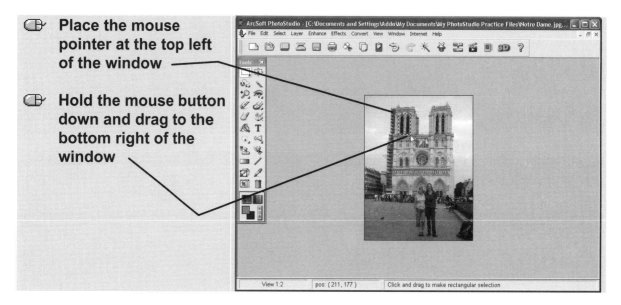

☞ **Place the mouse pointer at the top left of the window**

☞ **Hold the mouse button down and drag to the bottom right of the window**

Go ahead and select the *Twist* effect.

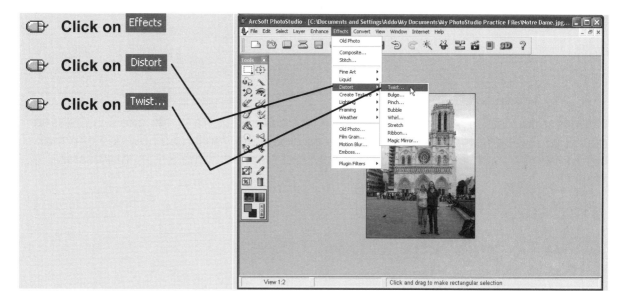

☞ **Click on** Effects

☞ **Click on** Distort

☞ **Click on** Twist...

In the *Twist* window, you can adjust the settings for this effect.

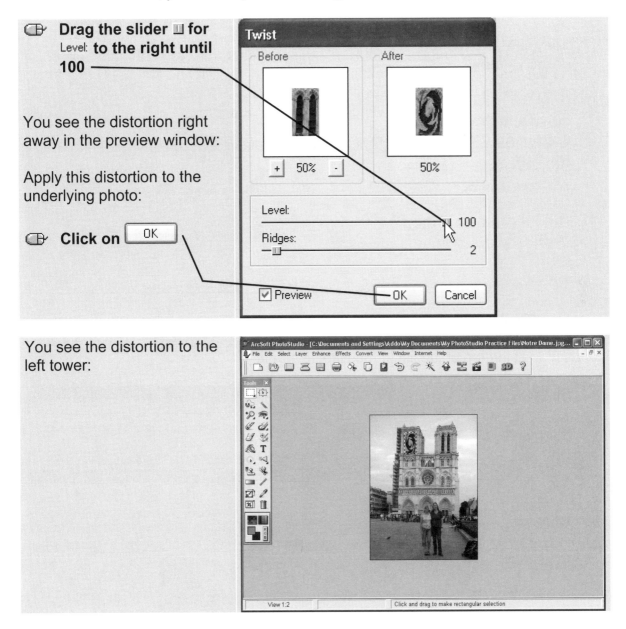

☞ **Drag the slider ▥ for** Level: **to the right until 100**

You see the distortion right away in the preview window:

Apply this distortion to the underlying photo:

☞ **Click on** OK

You see the distortion to the left tower:

Now do the same thing to the right tower.

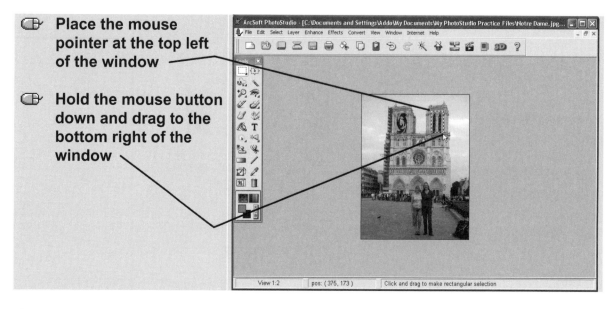

Select the *Twist* effect again. In *PhotoStudio*, you can quickly apply the last effect you used to a new selection. You don't have to specify the settings again. The effect you last used is at the top of the list in the *Effects* menu.

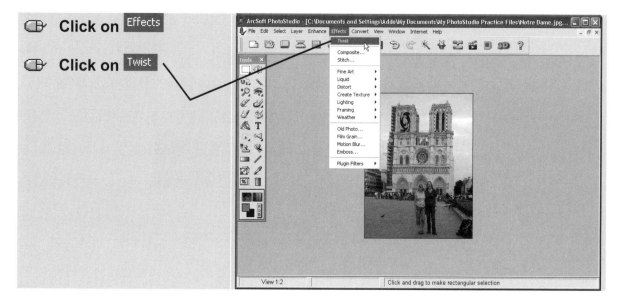

Both towers are twisted now:

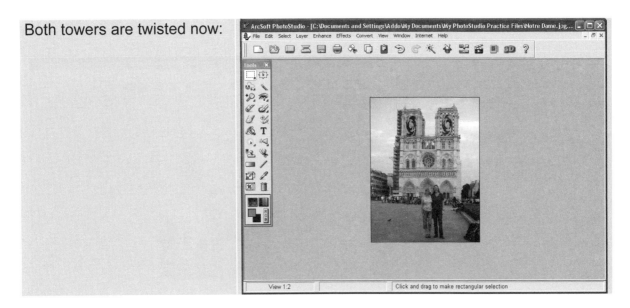

As a last effect, you're going to tackle the three windows in the center of the Notre Dame.

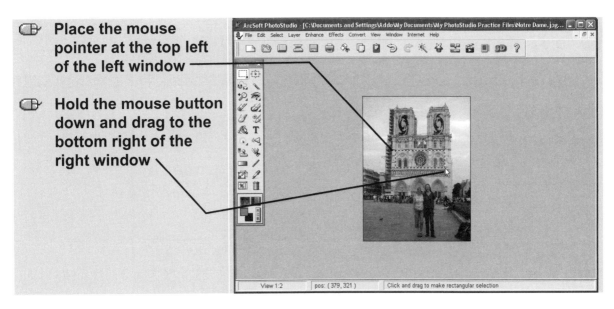

☞ **Place the mouse pointer at the top left of the left window**

☞ **Hold the mouse button down and drag to the bottom right of the right window**

Try the *Pinch* effect on these windows.

Click on Effects

Click on Distort

Click on Pinch...

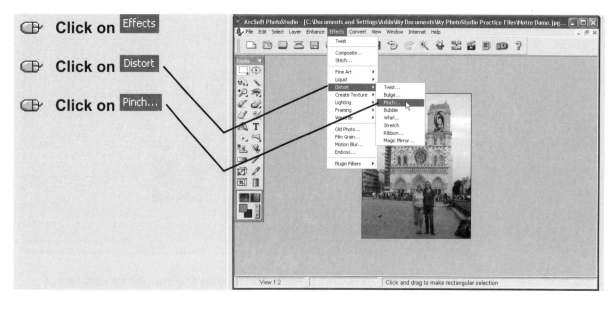

You can increase the intensity of the effect in the *Pinch* window.

Drag the slider for Intensity: **to the right until 75**

Now apply this distortion.

Click on OK

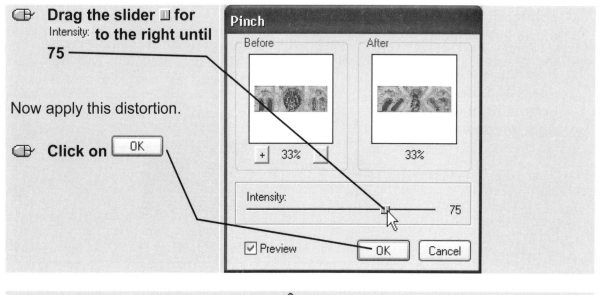

☞ **Remove the selection boundary** 17

Now you can really see the
final result of the distortions.
The Notre Dame has
undergone a transformation:

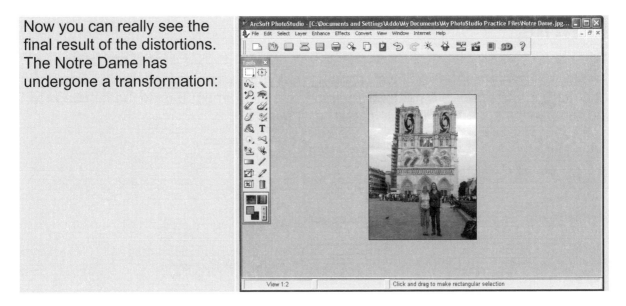

With a little practice, you can achieve good results with the effects in the *Distort*
group.

☞ **Close the photo and <u>don't</u> save the changes** *9*

In this chapter, you've applied special effects to photos. In the next chapter, you'll
read about importing photos into *PhotoStudio*.

Exercises

The following exercise will help you master what you've just learned. Have you forgotten how to perform a particular action? Use the number beside the footsteps to look it up in the appendix *How Do I Do That Again?*

Exercise: Special Effects

In this exercise, you'll practice applying special effects.

✔ Open the photo *Cropped Picture Big Ben* using the *Browser*. %%6

✔ Maximize the window containing the photo. %%4

✔ Apply the *Moonlight* effect. %%53

✔ Undo the last action. %%7

✔ Straighten the building using the *Transform* function. %%54

✔ Crop the photo so that the white border disappears. %%30

✔ Select Big Ben's clock. %%41

✔ Distort the clock with the *Twist* effect in the *Distort* group. %%55

✔ Select the whole photo. %%46

✔ Apply the *Old Photo* effect. %%56

✔ Add a frame to the photo. %%57

✔ Close the photo and don't save the changes. %%9

Tips

💡 Tip

Effect Browser

With the help of the *Effect Browser*, you can preview the results of various effects. You can start the *Effect Browser* from the *Quick Access Bar*.

🖱️ **Click on** 🐰

At the top, you see a list where you can select the desired effect:

In the preview window at the right, you see how the effect will look:

Various settings are available for each effect.

When the ☑Preview option is selected, you also see the chosen effect in the underlying photo:

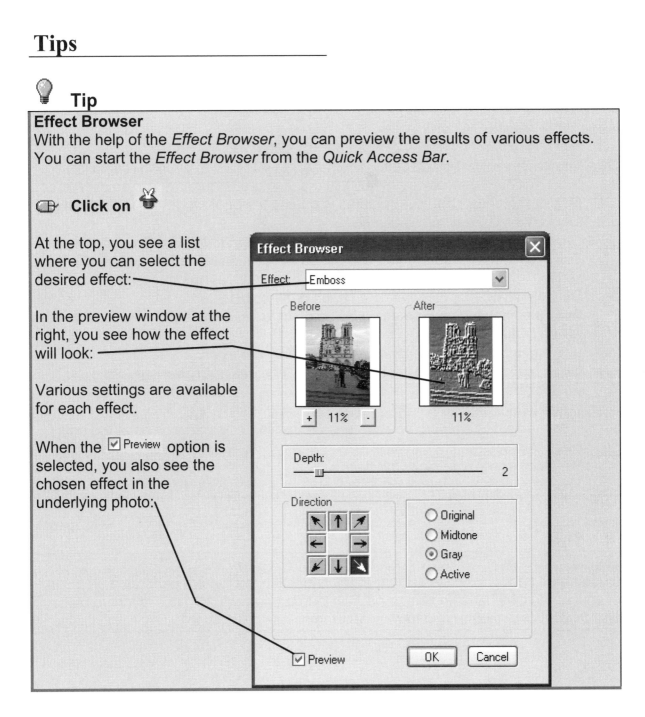

Tip

Taking Photos for a Panorama
When taking a series of photos to combine into a panorama using the *Stitch* function, you should pay special attention to the following points.

   Make sure there's enough overlap between images.
The photos should overlap one another 15 to 40%. If the overlap is smaller, *Stitch* will have difficulty automatically creating the panorama. But an overlap of 50% or more also creates problems in putting the photo together. The blending function won't work very well, either.

Choose beforehand whether or not to use the zoom function on your camera.
You'll get the best result if you use the same focal distance for all photos in the series.

Don't move when you're taking a series of photos.
Take the photos from the same viewpoint; otherwise, the continuity of the series will be broken.

Use the optical viewfinder instead of the LCD screen.
If you hold the camera close to your eye, it'll be easier to keep the same viewpoint.

Use a tripod.
With the help of a tripod, you can ensure that the camera remains at the right place and height.

Be judicious in your use of the flash.
The flash increases the likelihood of differences in exposure.

Tip

Layers
If you aren't having success using the *Stitch* function to create a panorama, you can, of course, do it by hand. In Chapter 6, you learned how you can use layers to place photos over one another and form a panorama.

8. Importing, Editing, and Saving

The fastest way to get digital photos onto your computer is to import them directly from your digital camera. *PhotoStudio* provides you with a handy interface for quickly importing and saving photos.

In addition, scanning is still one of the most widely used methods for digitizing photos. In itself, scanning a photo is a simple process. Nonetheless, it's good to know how a scanner works, because you can choose different scanning qualities. You make your choice depending on what you want to use the digital photo for. In this chapter, you'll get the information you need to make that decision.

A scanned photo usually needs some editing, such as cropping. If you're going to save the scanned photo onto your computer's hard disk, you can choose among various file formats. Some file formats produce much larger files than others. This can be important if you want to send your photos through e-mail, for example, or use them on a website.

In this chapter, you'll learn how to:

- import photos from your digital camera
- import a photo using your scanner
- adjust the scanner settings
- edit a scanned photo
- save a photo in a different file format

Importing Photos from Your Digital Camera

The program *PhotoStudio* contains software for digital cameras, so that you can import photos directly from a digital camera. To be able to do so, you should make sure that the drivers for your digital camera have been properly installed.

⇨ **Please note:**

The process of importing photos from a digital camera or a scanner uses either *WIA support* or a *TWAIN interface*. When you install the software that comes with the device, the appropriate drivers are copied to your computer.
TWAIN is a platform-independent API (application program interface) which allows you to operate the scanner or camera directly from *PhotoStudio* using the device's software.
For scanners and cameras that use *WIA support*, *PhotoStudio* works together with *Windows Me* or *Windows XP* and the device's software to import the images. *WIA* stands for *Windows Image Acquisition*.

In the following examples, we assume you'll be using *WIA support* in *Windows XP*. If you don't have *Windows XP* or *Me* on your computer, your camera or scanner will use the *TWAIN interface* only. In that case, the screen shots in the examples may be different from what you see on your screen.

⇨ **Please note:**

Digital cameras can connect to computers in various ways. Consult your camera's manual to find out how this works for your camera.

If you don't have a digital camera, just read through this section.

☞ **Make sure the software delivered with your camera is installed on your computer**

☞ **Connect your digital camera to your computer (see your camera's manual) and turn the camera on**

☞ Start *PhotoStudio* $\mathcal{U}^2$

You can quickly check whether your camera can be accessed directly from *PhotoStudio*.

Click on File

Click on Select Source...

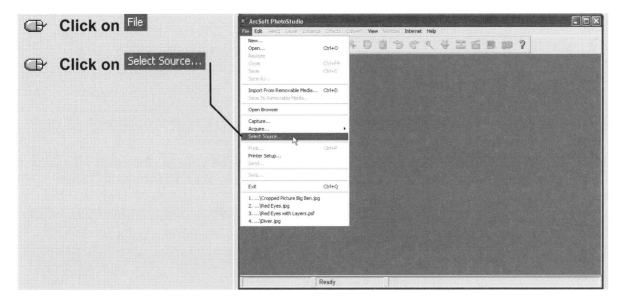

A list of all the devices you can access directly from *PhotoStudio* appears. These might be photo cameras, but they can also be webcams, scanners, or video cameras. Select the name of your digital camera. That might be a different camera than shown in this example.

Click on
WIA-hp photosmart 735 1.0 (32-32)

Click on Select

HELP! My camera isn't in the list.

If you connected your camera after you opened *PhotoStudio*, it's possible that the program hasn't noticed the camera yet.

☞ **Close** *PhotoStudio*
☞ **Check your camera's connection**
☞ **Turn your camera on**
☞ **Start** *PhotoStudio*
☞ **Try to access your camera again**

After you've selected your camera, nothing will change on your screen. *PhotoStudio* now knows you want to import photos from your camera. You do that as follows:

☞ **Click on** `File`

☞ **Click on** `Acquire...`

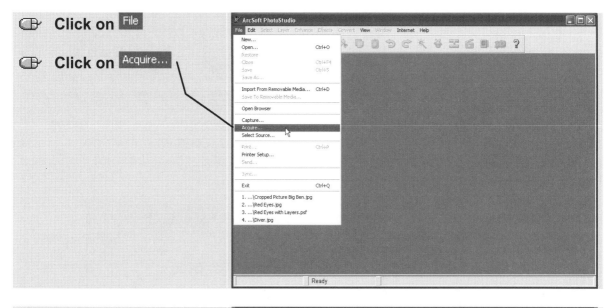

In the *Get Pictures from hp photosmart 735* window, you see thumbnails of the photos that are on this camera:

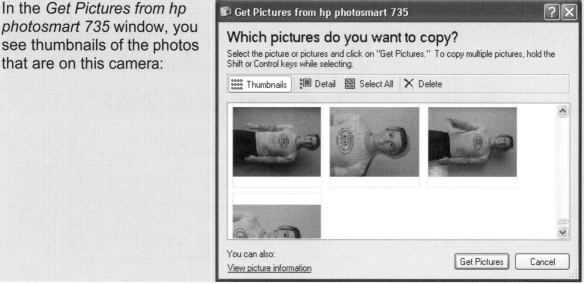

💡 Tip

Delete the Photo?

If you click on ✕ Delete in the *Get Pictures from hp photosmart 735* window, the selected photo will be deleted from the camera. If you hadn't yet saved this photo, you won't be able to recover it. *PhotoStudio* will ask if you really want to delete the photo. If you clicked on the Delete button by accident and want to keep the picture, then:

👉 **Click on** No

You can quickly select all the photos on the camera.

👉 **Click on** ⊞ Select All

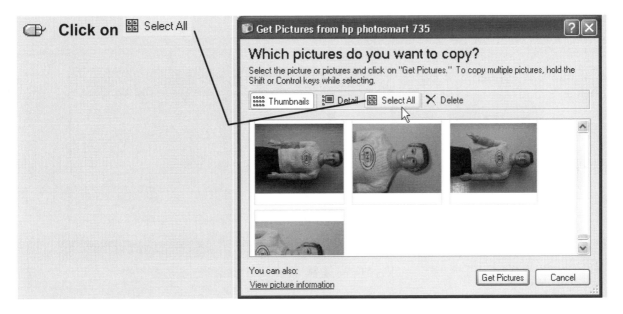

Then you can copy these photos from your camera to *PhotoStudio*.

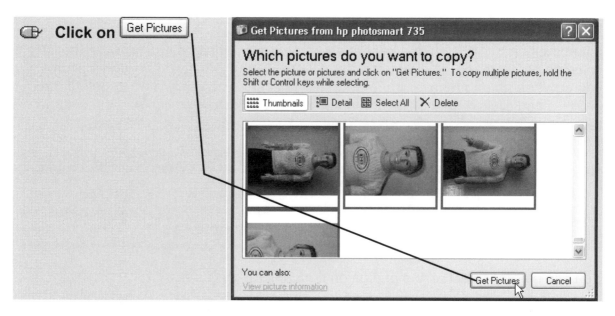

Click on Get Pictures

The photos will now be opened one by one.

A status bar appears for each photo:

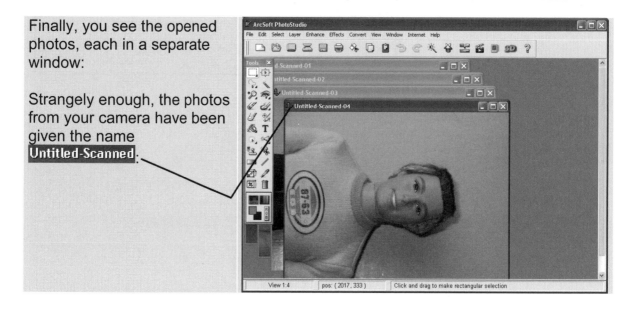

Finally, you see the opened photos, each in a separate window:

Strangely enough, the photos from your camera have been given the name Untitled-Scanned.

Saving

You can save these photos now, so that they'll be stored on your computer's hard disk. For simplicity's sake, go ahead and save the photos with their current names: *Untitled-Scanned-01, Untitled-Scanned-02, Untitled-Scanned-03*, and *Untitled-Scanned-04*.

Click on File

Click on Save As...

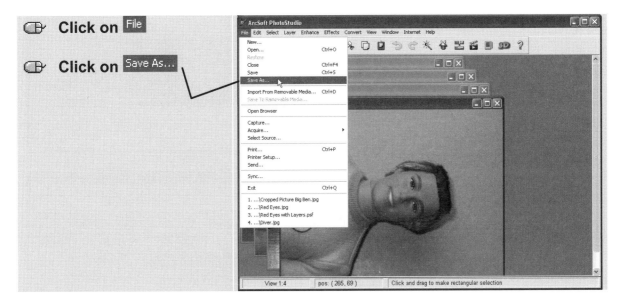

Because you've imported the photos into *PhotoStudio*, the program assumes you want to save the files in PSF format. Since the photos don't consist of separate layers you want to edit later, choose the JPEG file format instead.

Click on ˅

Click on Jpeg File (*.JPG)

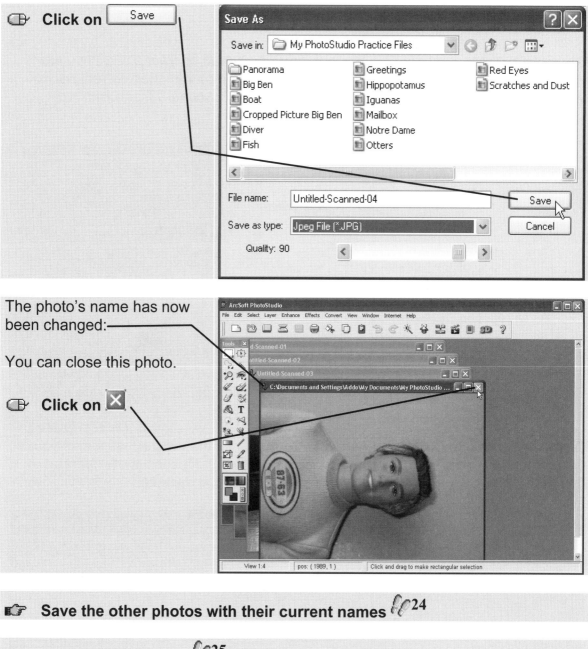

Click on | Save |

The photo's name has now been changed:

You can close this photo.

Click on ⊠

☞ **Save the other photos with their current names** 🦶24

☞ **Close all the photos** 🦶25

Importing Photos from Your Scanner

In the following example, you'll learn how to scan a photo in *PhotoStudio*. Different software is delivered with each brand of scanner. In this example, we assume the scanner has WIA support.

 Please note:

You may see different windows for your scanner if you aren't using *Windows XP* or *Windows Me*. This is also the case if your scanner doesn't have WIA support. If you don't have a scanner connected to your computer, just read through this section.

☞ **Make sure the software delivered with your scanner is installed on your computer**

☞ **Make sure the scanner is on**

☞ **Place a photo in the scanner**

Before you can scan, you need to select your scanner as the import source.

👆 **Click on** File

👆 **Click on** Select Source...

You see a list of devices. This list will look different on your computer than in this example. You'll select your own scanner.

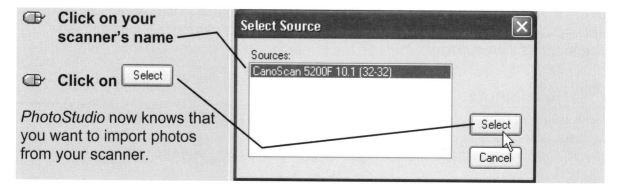

☞ **Click on your scanner's name**

☞ **Click on** Select

PhotoStudio now knows that you want to import photos from your scanner.

Here's how you start the scanning program:

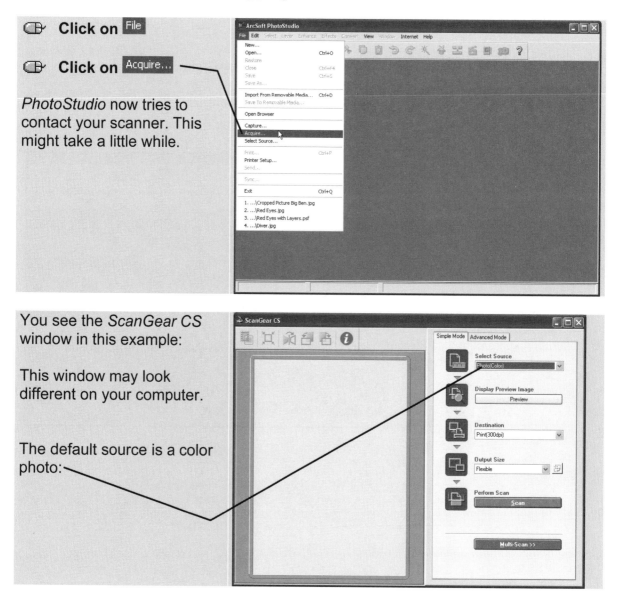

☞ **Click on** File

☞ **Click on** Acquire...

PhotoStudio now tries to contact your scanner. This might take a little while.

You see the *ScanGear CS* window in this example:

This window may look different on your computer.

The default source is a color photo:

Adjusting Your Scanner Settings

You begin by adjusting the scan quality. This quality is also called *resolution*. Resolution is expressed in *DPI: dots per inch.*

Depending on what you want to use the photo for, choose a setting from 75 to a maximum of 2400 DPI. A photo you want to put on a website, for example, doesn't need a very high quality. In that case, 75 DPI is sufficient. If you want to print a photo after scanning it, you can choose a resolution that matches the maximum resolution of your printer. If you want to extensively edit a photo, scan it at the highest resolution.

Bear in mind that resolutions of 1200 DPI and higher create enormous files, many megabytes in size.

In the background information at the end of this chapter, you'll find more information on the connection between resolution and a photo's print size.

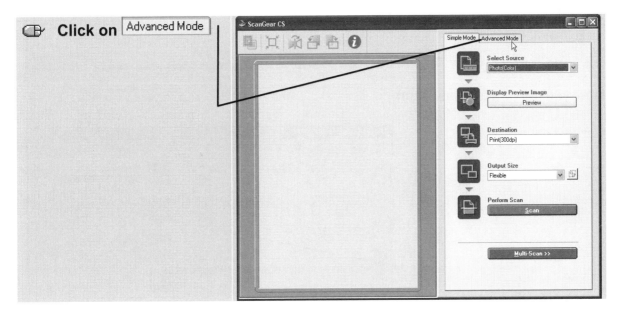

On the *Advanced Mode* tab, you can adjust not only the resolution, but also the brightness and contrast. Go ahead and choose the 300 DPI setting.

☞ **Check that**
Output Resolution : **is at** 300

You don't need to change any other settings.

☞ **Click on** Simple Mode

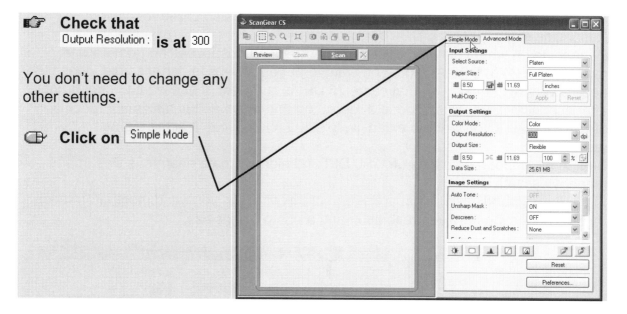

Now you can make a test scan.

☞ **Click on**
Preview

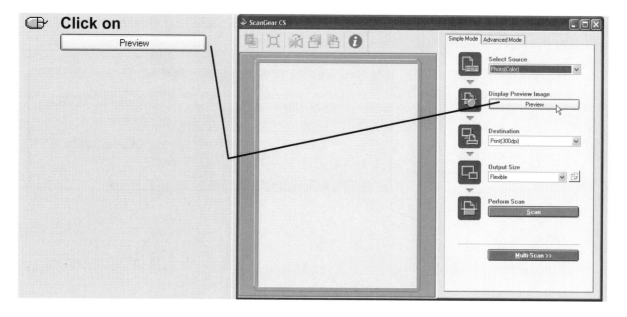

You see the scan preview appear. This scanning program has automatically selected just the photo, leaving out the white around it:

💡 **Tip**

Adjusting the Scan Preview

You can still adjust the size of the surface that will be scanned. This might be necessary if the scan program has captured too large an area, or if you only want to scan a small part of the photo. Using the square corner handles in the corners of the scan preview, you can adjust the area to be scanned.

- **Place the mouse pointer on a corner handle**

- **Drag the corner handle until you reach the desired size**

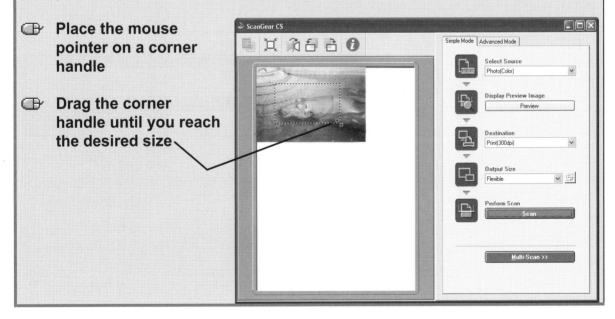

Now you can start the real scan.

Click on

| Scan |

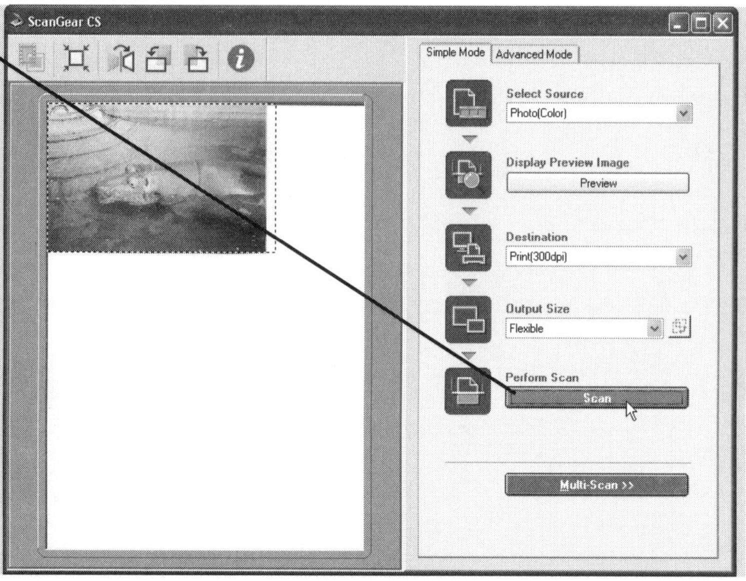

You see the progress of the scan:

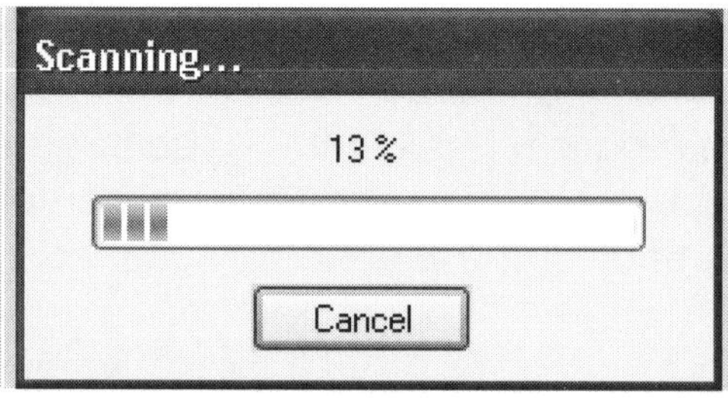

The scan automatically appears in *PhotoStudio*:

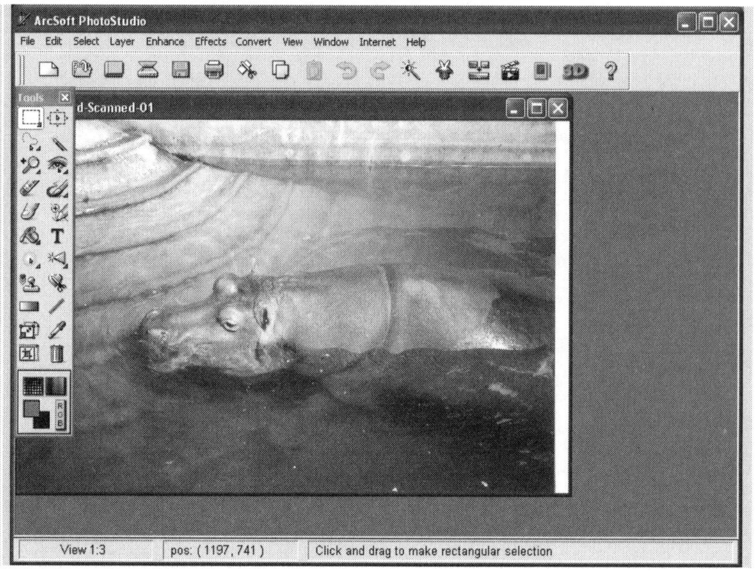

The scanning program for some scanners automatically closes. If yours doesn't, then:

Close your scanning program's window *ll*23

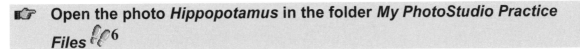

⇒ **Please note:**

If you've scanned one of your own photos, it will of course be different from the example photo. You can keep working with your own photo in the next section, or you can close your photo and continue working with one of this book's practice photos. If you don't have a scanner and have just read through this section, you can work through the following section now using the practice photo *Hippopotamus.*

Editing a Scanned Photo

A scanned photo usually needs a little editing, such as rotating, straightening, shrinking, or cropping. You've already been introduced to these techniques in *PhotoStudio.*

☞ **Open the photo *Hippopotamus* in the folder *My PhotoStudio Practice Files*** $\ell\ell^6$

☞ **Maximize the window containing the photo** $\ell\ell^4$

You see the scanned photo of a hippopotamus:

The scanning process left behind a white border on the right side of this photo:

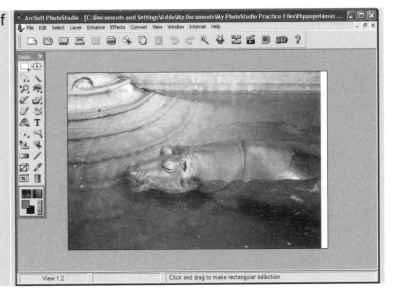

You can get rid of this white border by cropping the photo.

☞ **Select the *Rectangle Select* tool** ✐15

☞ **Hide the *Options Palette*** ✐1

🖰 **Drag the selection boundary from the top left to the bottom right to enclose the photo**

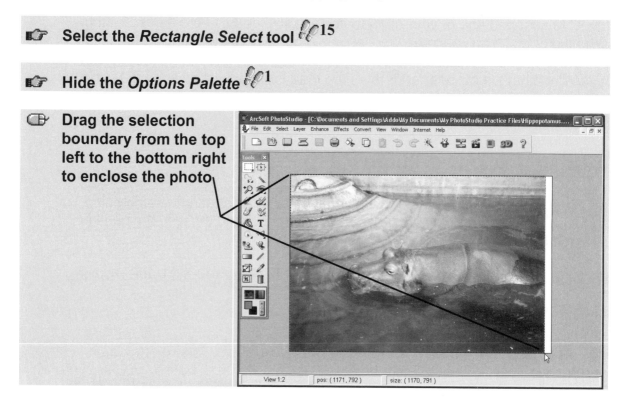

Now you can crop this selection.

🖰 **Click on** ⬚

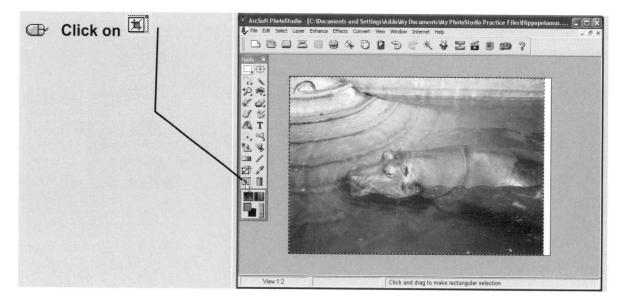

The scanned photo of the hippo looks good now:

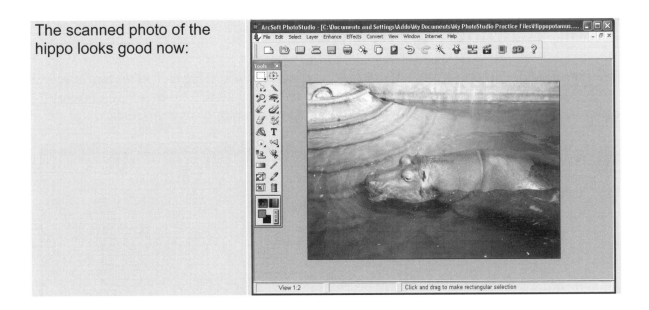

File Types

You've already encountered two file types in *PhotoStudio*. The *PhotoStudio* proprietary file type, the PSF file, is mostly useful when you want to save a photo with several layers. Then you can edit these layers again later. You've also encountered JPEG files. The practice photos on the CD-ROM are all JPEGs, except for the photo of the hippo. That photo is a BMP file.

BMP is the standard file type for images in *Windows*, called a *bitmap*. You can recognize a bitmap by the *.bmp* extension. Essentially, BMP files are of a high quality and contain many colors, but BMP isn't a very efficient file type in terms of storage. That's why two other file types are often used, particularly on the Internet. These two types are much better in terms of file size than a BMP file. The first file type is GIF; the second is JPEG.

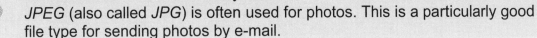

GIF is often used for drawings on the Internet. The little animated drawings you sometimes see are also usually GIFs.

JPEG (also called *JPG*) is often used for photos. This is a particularly good file type for sending photos by e-mail.

Saving as a Different File Type

In *PhotoStudio*, you can save a file of one type as a different type. You've already done this once with PSF files; you saved them as JPEG files. You can also convert a bulky BMP file to a JPEG file. Here's how you save the hippo as a JPEG file:

Click on File

Click on Save As...

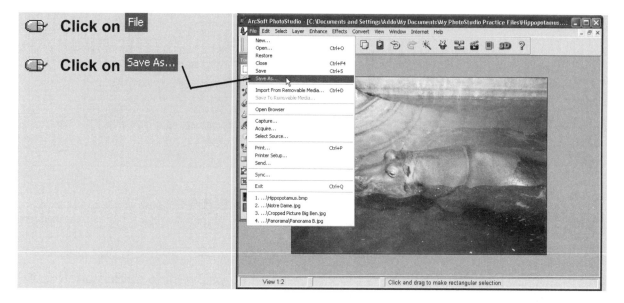

In the *Save As* window, select JPEG.

Click beside Save as type: on ⌄

Click on Jpeg File (*.JPG)

You can now specify in the *Save As* window the quality setting with which you want to save the photo as a JPEG. The default setting for the quality is 90%. The 10% loss in quality makes the JPEG file somewhat smaller. Of course, you can also choose to save the photo at 100%, without any loss of quality.

☞ **Drag the slider** ▦ **for** Quality: **to the right until 100**

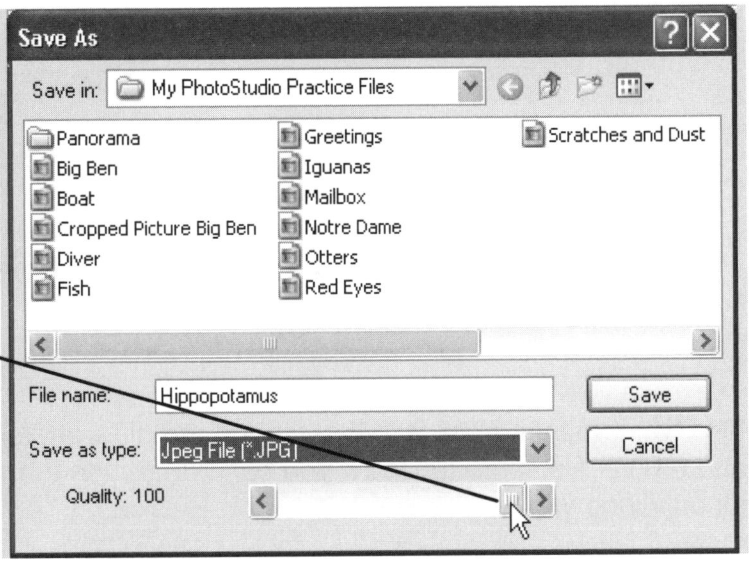

Now you can save the photo.

☞ **Click on** [Save]

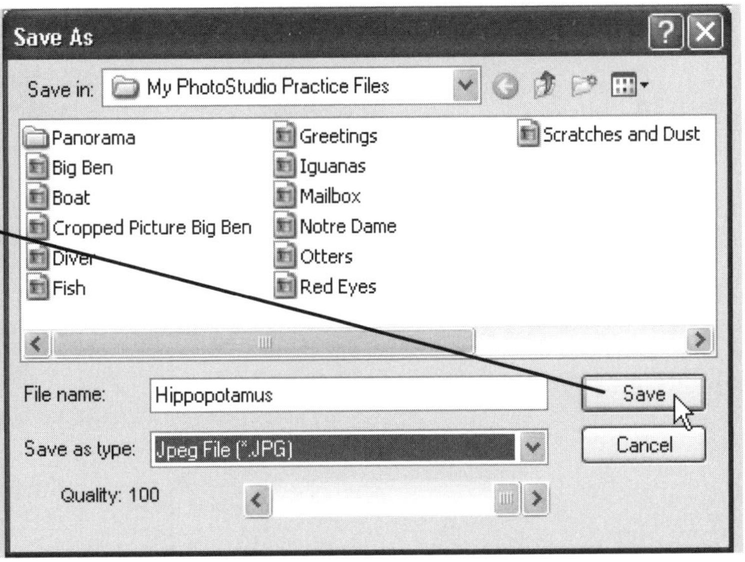

☞ **Close the photo** ℓℓ²¹

☞ **Open the *Browser*** ℓℓ³

Now you have two versions of the hippo photo in the *My PhotoStudio Practice Files* folder: *Hippopotamus.bmp* and *Hippopotamus.jpg*:

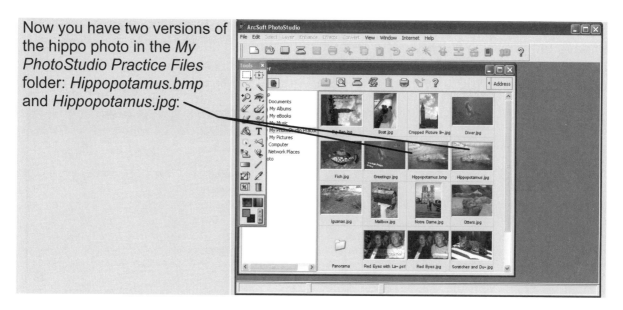

You can use these two files to examine the difference in size between a JPEG file and a BMP file. Unfortunately, you can't do that in the *Browser*. You can see it in the *Open* window, however.

Click on `File`

Click on `Open...`

⎙ Tip

Opening a File
Up until now, you've always used the *Browser* to open photos. Of course, you could just as well have used the *Open* window. On the *Quick Access Bar*, you'll find a

button you can use to open a file directly: 📂

You see the names of the various photo files. You're going to display them in a different way:

👆 **Click on** 🔽

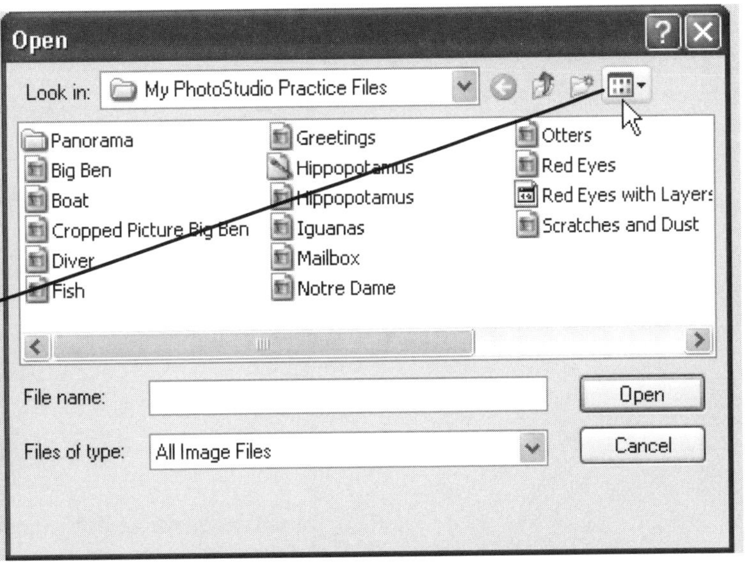

👆 **Click on** Details

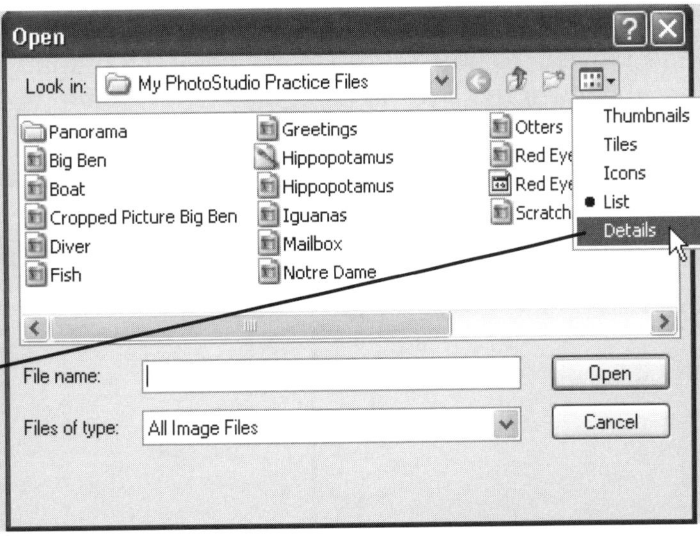

Now you see the size in KB (kilobytes) beside each photo:

👆 **Drag the slider** down to the photos of the hippo

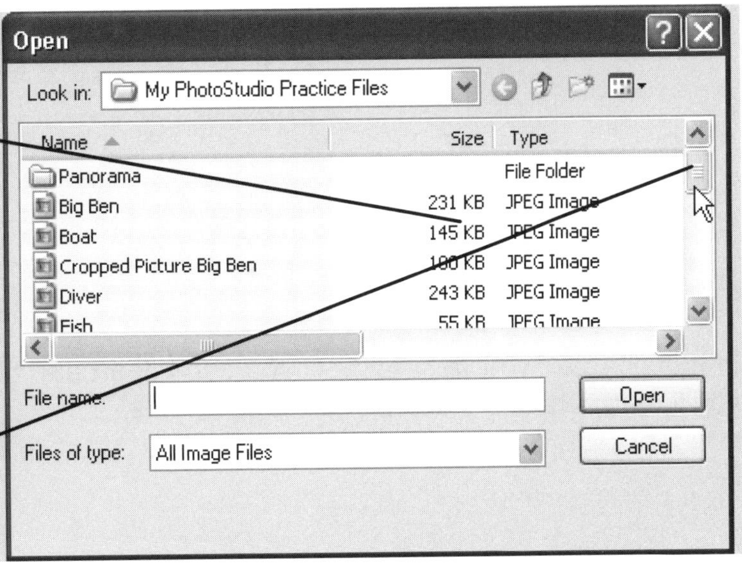

The photo
Hippopotamus.bmp is 2,781
KB:

The photo *Hippopotamus.jpg*
is only 589 KB:

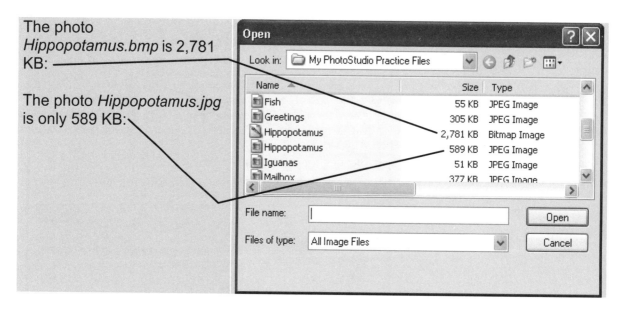

By changing the file type, you've reduced the file size from 2,781 KB (approximately 2.7 megabytes) to 589 KB (approximately 0.5 megabytes). If you had saved the photo at a lower quality, the JPEG file would have been even smaller.

You can close this window now.

☞ **Click on** [Cancel]

☞ **Close the *Browser*** ✐²³

In this chapter, you've seen how you can import and edit photos. In the next chapter, you'll learn about printing and sharing photos.

Background Information

Importing Photos from a Memory Card

Most digital cameras store photos in an internal memory or on a memory card. You can import photos from a memory card in the following way:

Take the memory card out of the camera:

Put the card in a card reader that's connected to your computer via the USB port:

Of course, you can also transfer your photos to the computer over a USB cable. To do this, stick the narrow plug into your camera and the wide plug into your computer's USB port.
The memory card stays in the camera while the photos are transferred to the computer over the cable.

The large and small USB plugs

The USB ports

For this method, it's important that the drivers for the digital camera have been properly installed.
In this chapter, you've learned that whenever *PhotoStudio* recognizes the attached camera or memory card, the photos can be read directly into the program.

Scan Resolution

A photo's resolution is expressed in DPI. That means *dots per inch*. You select the resolution at which you're going to scan depending on the intended use for the photo you're scanning. For example:

75 DPI	Your computer screen, the Internet
200-300 DPI	Color print from an inkjet printer
720 DPI	High-resolution inkjet printer
600-1200 DPI	Laser printer
2400 DPI	Professional printing

Suppose you select color photo quality, for example 300 DPI.
The dimensions of a standard print photo are 4 inches high and 6 inches wide.
That translates to 4 x 300 = 1200 scanned pixels high and
6 x 300 = 1800 pixels wide.
In total, that's 1200 x 1800 = 2,160,000 pixels.

In practice, these measurements won't match exactly.

Resolution and Print Size

The more pixels a photo contains, the larger you can print it at a high quality (300 DPI).
In the table below, you can see the connection between the resolution and the maximum print size.

Resolution	Pixels	Print Size
VGA (Webcam)	640 x 480	For the monitor only
1 megapixel	1280 x 960	3.5" x 5"
2 megapixels	1600 x 1200	4" x 6"
3 megapixels	2048 x 1536	5" x 7"
4 megapixels	2272 x 1704	8" x 10"
5 megapixels	2560 x 1930	11" x 14"

From the table, you can see that a photo should contain at least 2 megapixels for a standard 4" x 6" print.

Scanning Slides and Negatives

In the background information for Chapter 4, you read that there are different types of scanners, including a type that can also scan slides and negatives. You can adjust the software settings for this type of scanner based on the type of medium you're going to scan, for example "negative film" or "positive film." The software automatically converts these files into regular photo files which you can edit and print.

The Video Camera

You can also take photos with a video camera and then import them into your computer. To do so, you need video-editing software and a special interface card in your computer. Many video cameras are connected to the computer via a *firewire* or *i-link* connection. Using this kind of connection, you can quickly import and edit videos, then return them to the videotape.

Digital video cameras often have a built-in feature for taking photos and storing them on the videotape or on a memory card similar to the one for a digital photo camera. There are also digital video cameras that can record onto a DVD.

A digital video camera's memory card is read the same way as a memory card of a digital photo camera. Many cameras have a USB port for this. The quality of photos taken with a digital video camera is lower than that of photos taken with a digital photo camera. This is because video cameras use a different kind of lens and a different kind of chip.

Webcams

The Internet has made *webcams* very popular.

These mini-cameras have a permanent location near the computer and send a regular stream of moving video images or still shots over a cable to your computer. If you use a program such as *MSN Messenger*, you can simultaneously send messages and images *online* to your conversational partner. The resolution of these images is, however, very low, and can't be compared with that of a videocamera.

Tips

Tip

Importing a Photo with the File / Open Command (in Windows XP)
When your camera or memory card reader is connected to the USB port of a computer running *Windows XP*, you have a second option for importing photos into *PhotoStudio*. Instead of using the *File / Acquire* method described in this chapter, you can do the following:

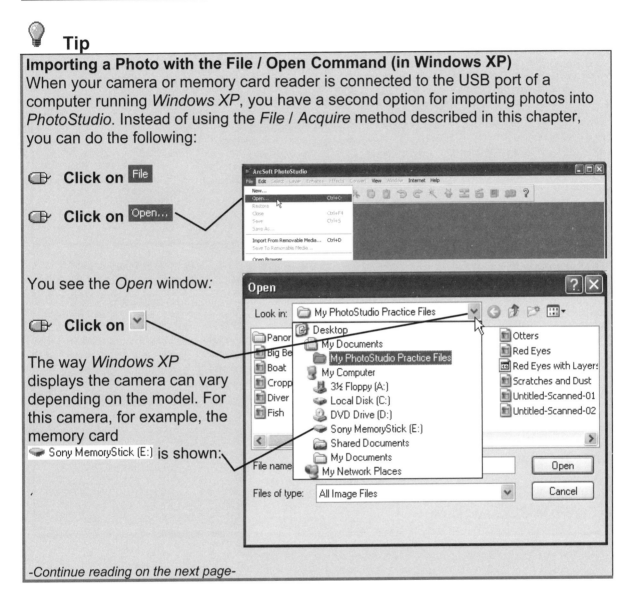

- 👆 **Click on** File

- 👆 **Click on** Open...

You see the *Open* window:

- 👆 **Click on** ⌄

The way *Windows XP* displays the camera can vary depending on the model. For this camera, for example, the memory card
💾 Sony MemoryStick (E:) is shown:

-Continue reading on the next page-

For other types of cameras, the camera itself **hp photosmart 735** is shown:

- ☞ **Click on your camera or memory card**

Open	? ✕
Look in: 📁 My PhotoStudio Practice Files ▾ ◯ 🔾 📂 ▥▾	

Desktop
  📁 My Documents
    📁 My PhotoStudio Practice Files
  💻 My Computer
    💾 3½ Floppy (A:)
    💿 Local Disk (C:)
    💿 DVD Drive (D:)
    📷 hp photosmart 735
  📁 Shared Documents
  📁 My Documents
  💻 My Network Places
  📁 Share-to-Web Upload Folder

Panor   Otters
Big Be   Red Eyes
Boat   Red Eyes with Layers
Crop   Scratches and Dust
Diver   Untitled-Scanned-01
Fish   Untitled-Scanned-02

File name   Open
Files of type: All Image Files   ▾   Cancel

Now you see the contents of the camera or memory card:

A memory card can be organized into folders, but need not be. The photos themselves are usually numbered consecutively:

- ☞ **Click on a photo**
- ☞ **Click on** [Open]

Now the photo will be opened in the *PhotoStudio* window.

Open	? ✕
Look in: 📷 hp photosmart 735 ▾ ◯ 🔾 📂 ▥▾	

HPIM0061 HPIM0084 HPIM0090 HPIM0098 HPIM0104
HPIM0063 HPIM0085 HPIM0091 HPIM0099 HPIM0105
HPIM0064 HPIM0086 HPIM0092 HPIM0100 HPIM0106
HPIM0065 HPIM0087 HPIM0093 HPIM0101 HPIM0107
HPIM0082 HPIM0088 HPIM0094 HPIM0102 HPIM0108
HPIM0083 HPIM0089 HPIM0097 HPIM0103 HPIM0109

File name: 0000\Root\HPIM0064   Open
Files of type: All Image Files   ▾   Cancel

💡 Tip

Opening a Photo from a CD-ROM

If you have photos stored on a CD-ROM, you can open them in *PhotoStudio* as follows:

☞ **Place the CD-ROM in the CD-ROM drive**

👆 **Click on** File

👆 **Click on** Open...

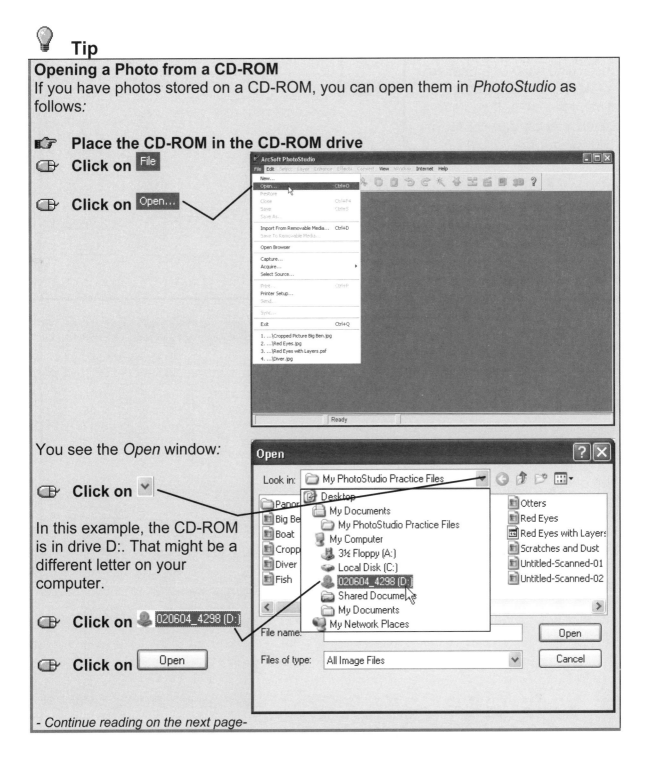

You see the *Open* window:

👆 **Click on** ⌄

In this example, the CD-ROM is in drive D:. That might be a different letter on your computer.

👆 **Click on** 📷 020604_4298 (D:)

👆 **Click on** Open

- Continue reading on the next page-

Now you see the contents of the CD-ROM. Sometimes the photo files have been saved in folders, but that isn't always the case. If you see a folder, you can open it as follows:

👉 **Click on** 📁PICTURES

👉 **Click on** [Open]

Sometimes you'll see more folders, which you can open in the same way.

Eventually you see the photo files stored on the CD-ROM. Now you can select a photo:

👉 **Click on a photo**

👉 **Click on** [Open]

The photo will now be opened in the *PhotoStudio* window.

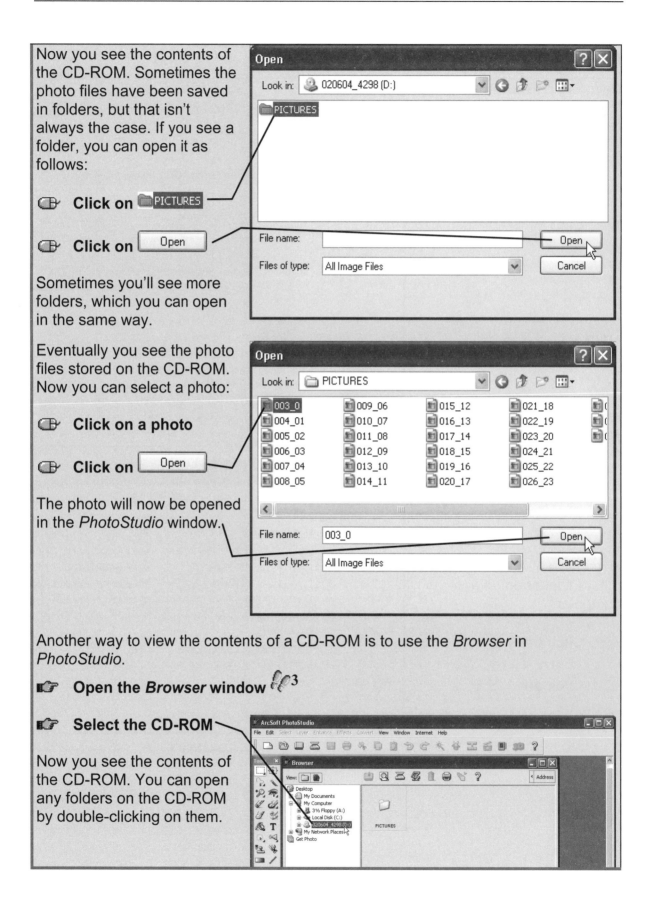

Another way to view the contents of a CD-ROM is to use the *Browser* in *PhotoStudio*.

☞ **Open the *Browser* window** 🦶³

☞ **Select the CD-ROM**

Now you see the contents of the CD-ROM. You can open any folders on the CD-ROM by double-clicking on them.

💡 Tip

Copying Directly from the Camera to the Hard Disk (Windows XP)
In *Windows XP*, you can also save photos directly from your camera to your hard disk. If your camera and *PhotoStudio* aren't working together well, you can copy your photos to your computer this way instead. After transferring them to the hard disk, you can start *PhotoStudio* and open the photos in the program.
The way *Windows XP* displays your camera depends on its make and model. *Windows XP* immediately recognizes some cameras. You can directly access such a camera in the *My Computer* window. You can see that in this example:

☞ **Open the *My Computer* window**

You see your camera under the heading `Scanners and Cameras`. It will probably be a different camera than the one in this example.

👆 **Double-click on**

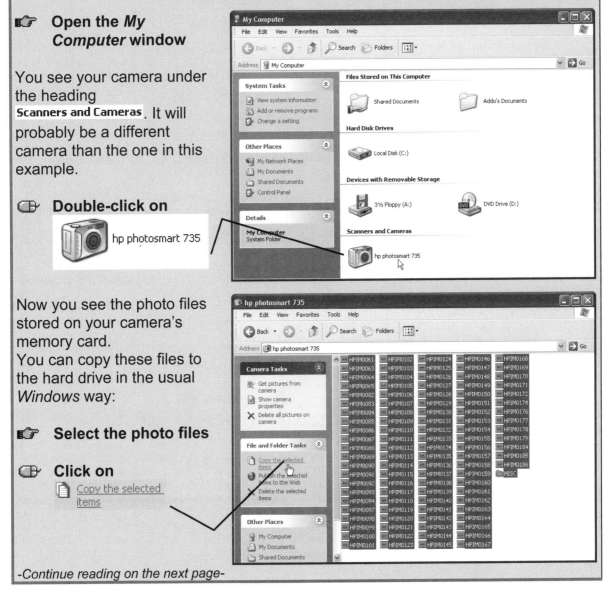

Now you see the photo files stored on your camera's memory card.
You can copy these files to the hard drive in the usual *Windows* way:

☞ **Select the photo files**

👆 **Click on**
📄 Copy the selected items

-*Continue reading on the next page-*

In the *Copy Items* window, you can specify where you want to copy the files. In this example, the folder 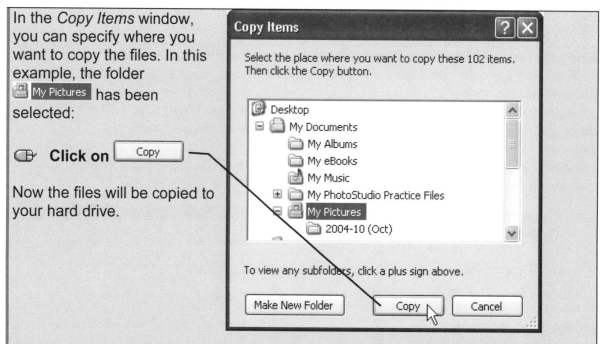 My Pictures has been selected:

☞ **Click on** [Copy]

Now the files will be copied to your hard drive.

Windows XP displays other types of cameras as *Removable Disk* or *Removable Storage.* You can see that in this example:

☞ **Open the *My Computer* window**

This camera is displayed as a device with removable storage. *Windows XP* is actually recognizing the camera's memory stick here:

☞ **Double-click on**
 Sony MemoryStick (E:)

After that, you'll see the same windows as in the above example. You can take the same steps to copy the photos to your hard disk.

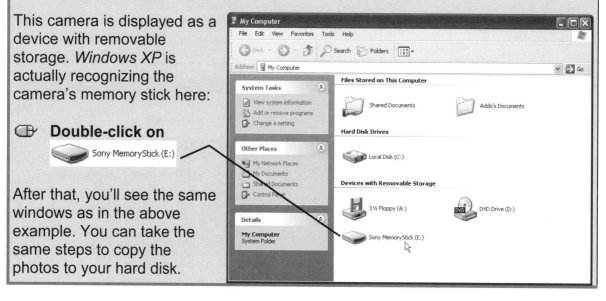

Tip

Your Camera and Windows 98
On computers running *Windows 98*, you always have to install the software that came with your digital photo camera. *Windows 98* doesn't recognize your camera as a removable disk or camera the way *Windows XP* usually does.
If *PhotoStudio* doesn't recognize your camera, you can always use your camera's software to transfer the files to your computer.
Then you can start *PhotoStudio* and open the files on the hard drive in the program.

Tip

Traveling with Your Memory Card
You've seen that the contents of a memory card can easily be copied to a computer's hard disk. Bear in mind that you probably won't have this option when you're traveling. You might want to consider an extra memory card, because you usually end up taking more photos than you thought you would beforehand.

Tip

Adjusting the Photo Quality on the Camera
Many digital cameras can take photos at different resolutions. A high resolution gives the highest-quality photos. The disadvantage is that your memory card can fill up quickly. Consider beforehand what you're going to use the photos for, and choose a fitting resolution. If you only want to display your photos on the screen or send them to friends by e-mail, for example, a lower resolution will suffice. You always need a high resolution for photos you want to enlarge and print. Consult your camera's manual for how to adjust the resolution.

Tip

Climate, Condensation, and Your Camera
When traveling to a warm vacation spot, bear in mind that you'll need to keep your extra memory cards cool.
If you enter an air-conditioned room from the heat, condensation can form on the camera. You can dry the outside of the camera with a paper towel. You should always dry the lens and the viewfinder with a lens cloth, because the wood fibers in paper can scratch them.
When you go skiing, make sure your digital camera doesn't get too cold. This can cause the batteries to discharge. So keep it in an inner pocket and take reserve batteries with you.

💡 **Tip**

Plug-ins on the ArcSoft Website

Patches with which you can expand and update your version of *PhotoStudio* are published regularly. These small additions to the program can be downloaded free of charge from the *ArcSoft* website. You can do that as follows:

☞ **Start** *Internet Explorer*

👆 **Click beside** : Address :

⌨ **Type on one line:**
`www.arcsoft.com/en/`
`products/photostudio`

👆 **Click on** → Go

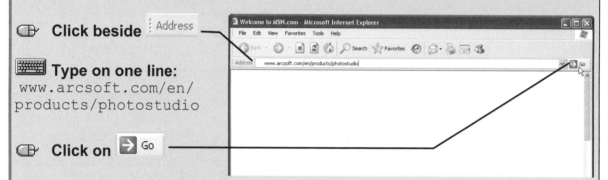

The website for the program *PhotoStudio* will now open. You'll see the available patches on this page.

👆 **Click on** → Patches

Websites are constantly changing, so the page you see might look different than pictured here.

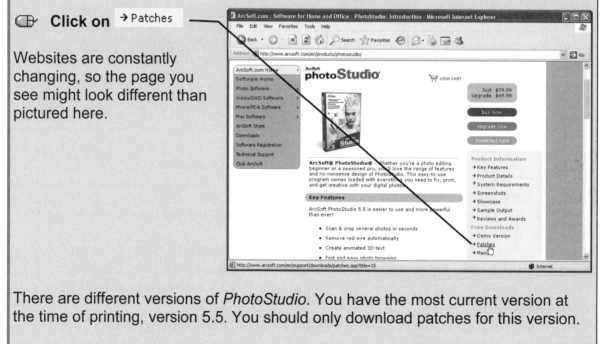

There are different versions of *PhotoStudio*. You have the most current version at the time of printing, version 5.5. You should only download patches for this version.

-Continue reading on the next page-

In this example, you see that there's an update available for *PhotoStudio 5.5*.

☞ **Click on**

PhotoStudio 5.5 Update

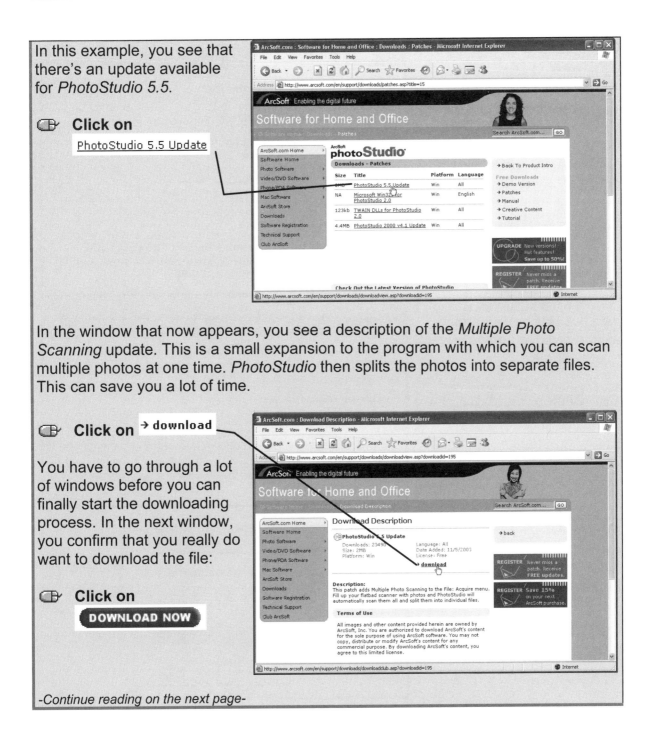

In the window that now appears, you see a description of the *Multiple Photo Scanning* update. This is a small expansion to the program with which you can scan multiple photos at one time. *PhotoStudio* then splits the photos into separate files. This can save you a lot of time.

☞ **Click on** → download

You have to go through a lot of windows before you can finally start the downloading process. In the next window, you confirm that you really do want to download the file:

☞ **Click on**

DOWNLOAD NOW

-Continue reading on the next page-

Go ahead and open the file right away:

⌨ **Click on** ⎘ Run ⎗

In the window that now appears, you can follow the progress of the download.

You see one more warning asking if you're sure you want to open the file:

⌨ **Click on** ⎘ Run ⎗

Installation begins and you can specify the language for the installation. Select English:

⌨ **Click on** ⎘ OK ⎗

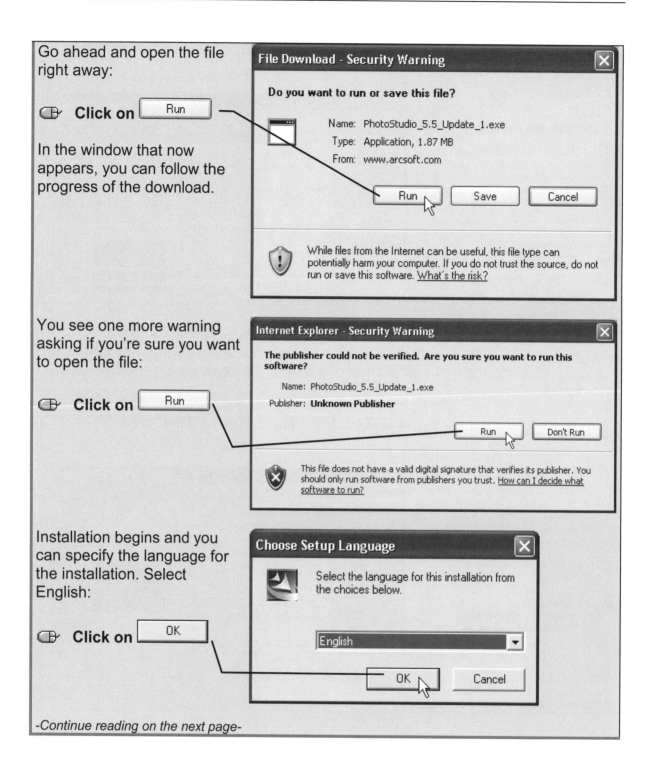

File Download - Security Warning

Do you want to run or save this file?

Name: PhotoStudio_5.5_Update_1.exe
Type: Application, 1.87 MB
From: www.arcsoft.com

[Run] [Save] [Cancel]

While files from the Internet can be useful, this file type can potentially harm your computer. If you do not trust the source, do not run or save this software. What's the risk?

Internet Explorer - Security Warning

The publisher could not be verified. Are you sure you want to run this software?

Name: PhotoStudio_5.5_Update_1.exe
Publisher: **Unknown Publisher**

[Run] [Don't Run]

This file does not have a valid digital signature that verifies its publisher. You should only run software from publishers you trust. How can I decide what software to run?

Choose Setup Language

Select the language for this installation from the choices below.

English ▼

[OK] [Cancel]

-Continue reading on the next page-

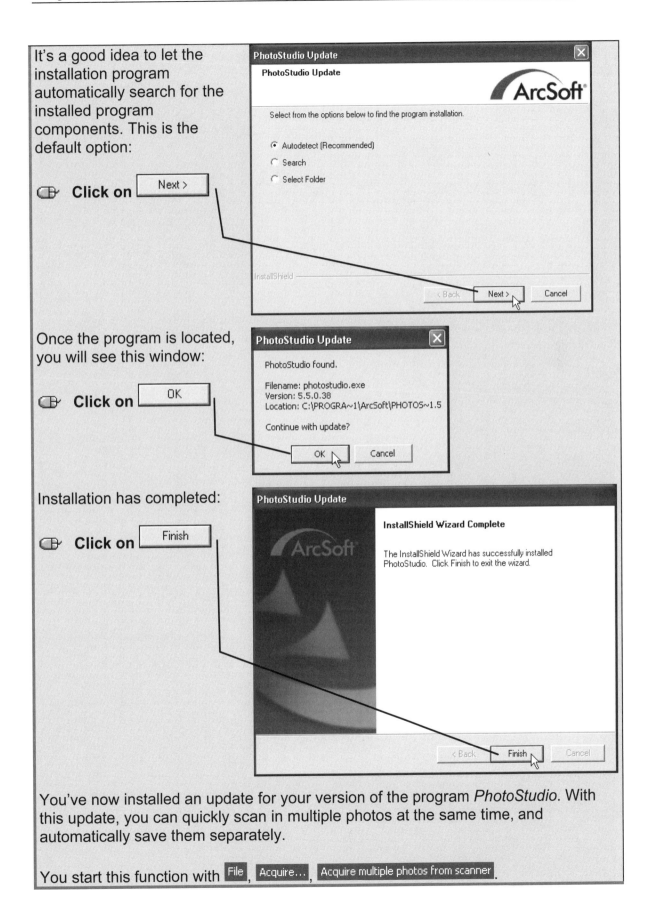

It's a good idea to let the installation program automatically search for the installed program components. This is the default option:

Click on Next >

Once the program is located, you will see this window:

Click on OK

Installation has completed:

Click on Finish

You've now installed an update for your version of the program *PhotoStudio*. With this update, you can quickly scan in multiple photos at the same time, and automatically save them separately.

You start this function with File , Acquire... , Acquire multiple photos from scanner .

9. Printing and Sharing Photos

Frequently you'll want to make nice prints of your digital photos. With today's printers, you can approach the quality of a photo printed in the conventional way. There are a few details involved, however. Not only are there all kinds of photo paper, but you can also adjust the printer settings in various ways.

In *PhotoStudio*, you can easily alter the size of your printed photo. You can also print out a contact sheet, with miniature versions of the photos. This is useful if you archive your photos on CD-ROMs.

In addition to printing, there's another way to share your photos with others: you can send a photo as an e-mail attachment.

In short, there are plenty of options for sharing photos with others in this program. In this chapter, you'll find all the information you need to get good results.

In this chapter, you'll learn how to:

- view and adjust the page settings
- adjust the printer settings
- print a single photo
- print a contact sheet
- send a photo by e-mail

Viewing the Page Settings

After you have imported and edited a photo on your computer you are ready to do more with it. Share the photo with others right on your computer screen, send it in an e-mail or print it out.

For best results when printing your photo, you can adjust the way the photo appears on the printed page. Do this as follows:

☞ **Open the photo *Diver* in the folder *My PhotoStudio Practice Files*** 🖐6

☞ **Maximize the window containing the photo** 🖐4

You see the photo of a diver again:

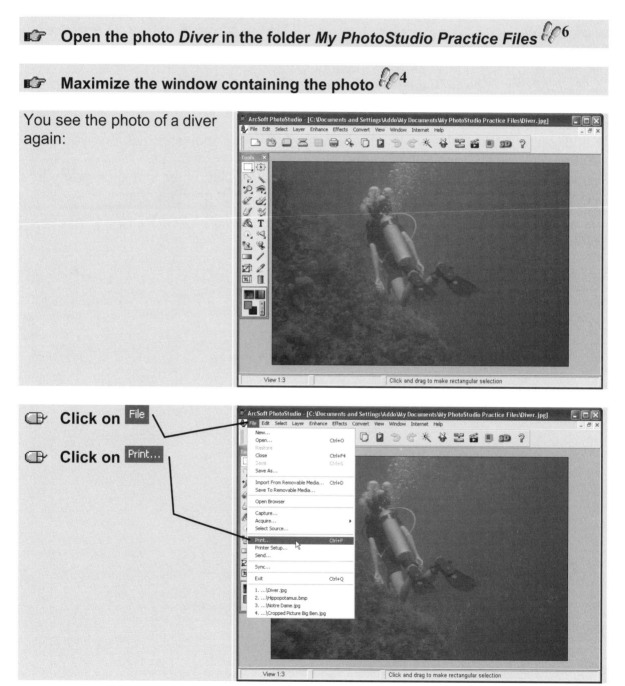

👆 **Click on** `File`

👆 **Click on** `Print...`

In the *Print* window, you can adjust various print settings:

On the preview page you see how the photo will be printed on the paper using the current settings:

Width: 8.2 Inch
Height: 5.4 Inch is the current print size:

Output: 251 dpi is the resolution at which the photo will be sent to the printer:

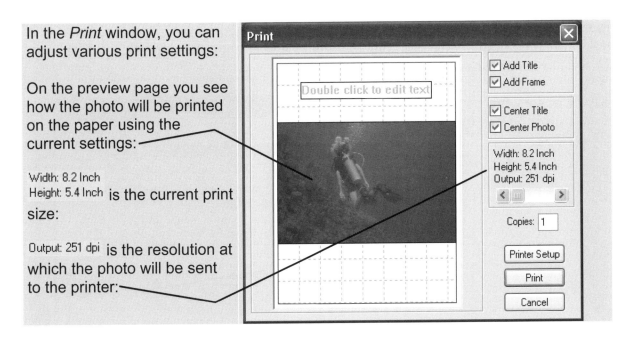

Please note:

The measurements on your screen may differ from the measurements in the example. They depend upon the printer you're using.

Adjusting the Printer Settings

The photo of the diver is in the middle of the page, with a white border above and below. It'll look better if you turn the page 90 degrees.

Click on Printer Setup

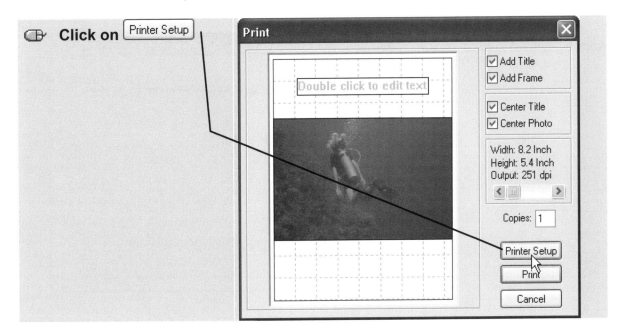

In the *Print Setup* window, you see the name of your own printer. That may be a different name than in this example. Go ahead and change the page orientation from *Portrait* to *Landscape* in this window.

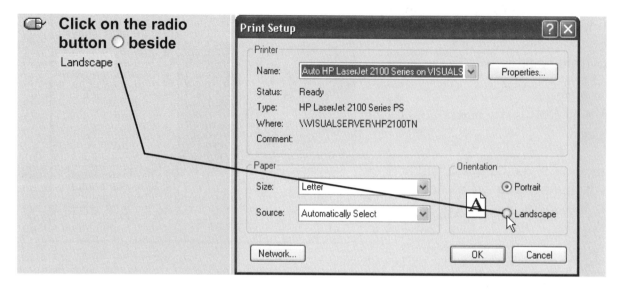

The photo will now be printed lengthwise on the paper. This makes much better use of the paper. You don't have to put the paper lengthwise into the printer to print this way. The printer will take care of printing the photo lengthwise.

Printer Properties

For best results, it's important that you understand the features of (color) printers. You can view these features this way:

Please note:

The next printer window will differ from manufacturer to manufacturer, and even from model to model. It might therefore look different on your screen. The settings options differ from printer to printer, too. The most important features, however, are the same for every printer program.

In any case, you can adjust the following settings in most color printer programs:

- the print quality
- the kind of paper you're using

Printers have different *print qualities*: from simple color drawings to exceptionally high photo quality prints. The difference is in the number of color dots that are printed. It makes sense that a large number of very fine points of many different colors will be printed for a high quality color photo. For a simple color drawing, that isn't necessary. The print quality also depends greatly on the *paper* you use. For a crude color drawing, regular inkjet paper is sufficient. If you use this paper for a photo, however, too much ink will be sprayed onto the paper and it will smudge. The colors will run into one another as a result. That's why there's high-quality paper for printing photos.

You can adjust both settings (print quality and type of paper) in a window like this on every inkjet printer:

For example, you can choose the type of paper here:

Auto HP 2500C Series PS3 on VISUALSERVER Document Prop...

Layout | Paper/Quality

Tray Selection

Paper Source: | Automatically Select

Click on ⌄

Media: | Plain Paper

You can choose from these types of paper, for example:

Plain Paper
HP Rapid-Dry Transparency
HP Transparency
HP Premium Inkjet Paper
HP Premium Inkjet Heavyweight Paper
HP Premium Photo Paper
HP Iron-on T-shirt Transfers

Click on
HP Premium Photo Paper

The list of paper types differs from printer manufacturer to printer manufacturer.

Advanced...

OK | Cancel

☞ **Examine your own printer's options**

💡 **Tip**

Choose a print quality and paper type that go together. For a nice photo, that means you'll choose a high print quality and special photo paper. For a test print, choose a low quality and regular printer paper.

💡 **Tip**

Printing in Black and White
You can also make a nice black-and-white print from a color photo with your printer. You don't have to convert the photo to black and white first.

If you want to print a photo in black and white, select the Black & White option:

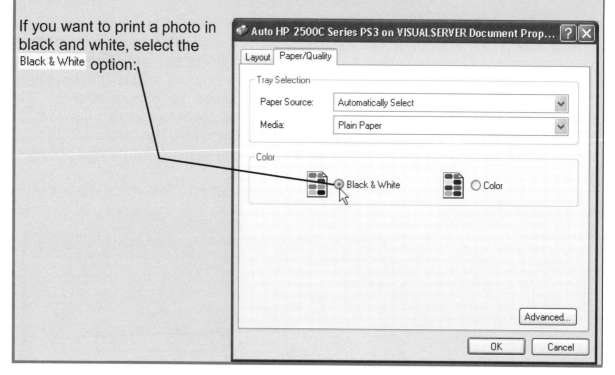

You don't need to change any settings right now.

☞ **Close the *Properties* window** 𝓁𝓁²³

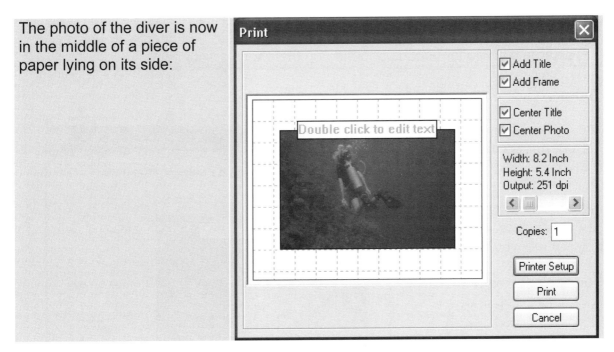

Adjusting the Page Setup

Now that you've altered the paper orientation, this will be indicated in the *Print* window.

The photo of the diver is now in the middle of a piece of paper lying on its side:

In *PhotoStudio*, you can quickly change the size of the photo you're going to print.

You do that as follows:

☞ **Drag the slider ▥ to the left**

You see the size of the photo change right away in the preview window:

As a result of enlarging the photo, the resolution has dropped to Output: 192 dpi .

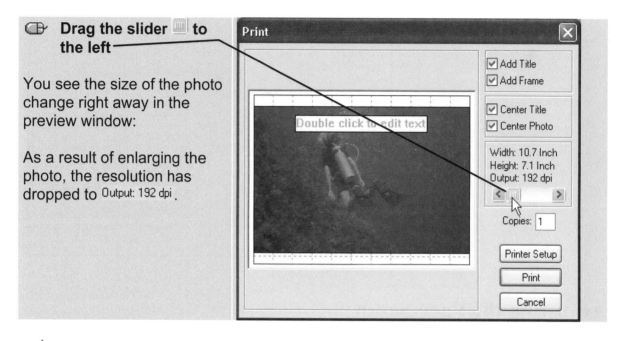

⇨ **Please note:**

Keep in mind that you can't print a small photo too large. The larger you print a photo, the lower the *dots per inch* (DPI) will be. This results in a lesser print quality. As the DPI drops under 200, the photo becomes grainier. The degree to which you can enlarge a photo for printing depends on the photo's resolution.

You won't add a title to the photo this time.

☞ **Click on the check box ☑ beside** Add Title

In the field beside Copies:, you can specify how many copies of the photo you want to print:

You can print the photo using the [Print] button:

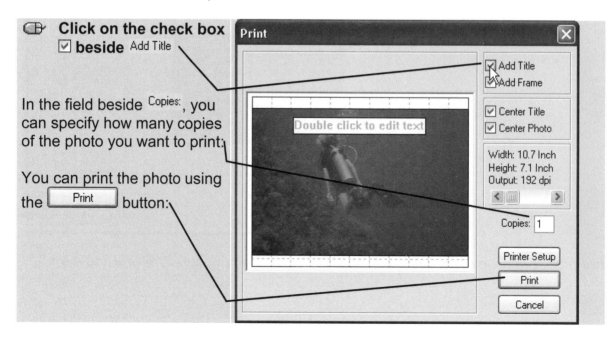

You don't have to print this photo.

☞ **Close the** *Print* **window** 𝓁𝓁23

☞ **Close the photo** 𝓁𝓁21

Printing a Contact Sheet

A useful feature of *PhotoStudio* is the ability to print a *contact sheet*. On a contact sheet, miniature versions (called *thumbnails*) of a group of photos are printed. You can use a contact sheet to catalog your photos, for example. You can print out a contact sheet using the *Browser*.

☞ **Open the** *Browser* 𝓁𝓁3

☞ **Hide the** *Tools Palette* 𝓁𝓁12

You see the contents of the *My PhotoStudio Practice Files* folder:

👆 **Click on** 🖨

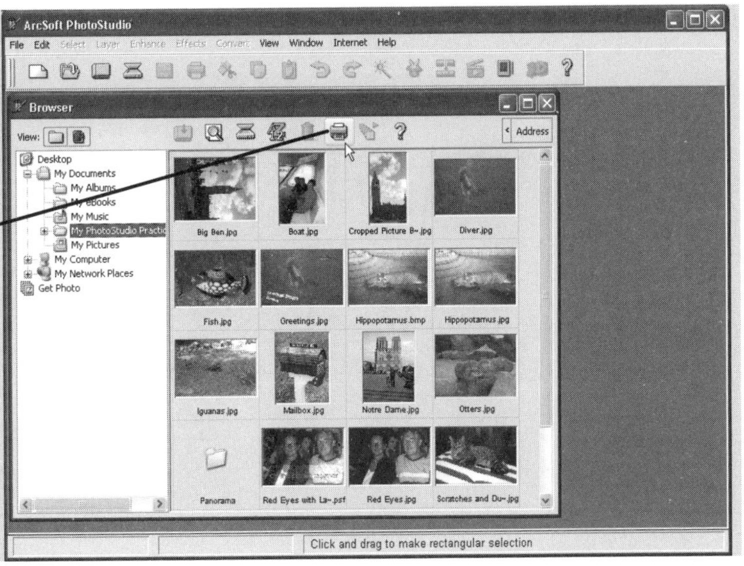

In the *Print Thumbnails* window, you see the settings for printing the contact sheet.

The option ⦿ Print All Thumbnails has been selected because you haven't selected any photos in the *Browser*.

The thumbnail size is set to a default width of 2 inches per thumbnail. You can, of course, change this:

The file name will be printed beneath each thumbnail:

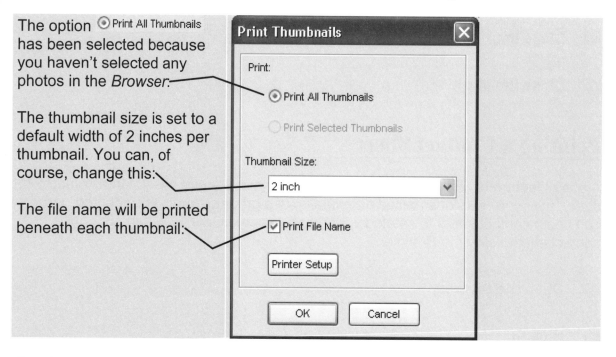

Go ahead and choose a smaller thumbnail.

☞ **Click on** ⌄

☞ **Click on** 1 1/2 inch

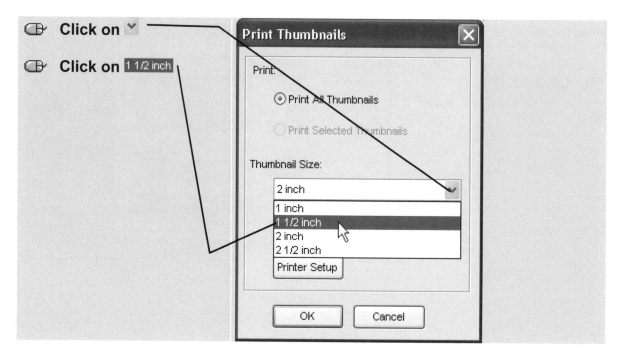

Now you can print the thumbnails.

⬅️ **Click on** ⌷ OK ⌷

Print Thumbnails

Print:

◉ Print All Thumbnails

◯ Print Selected Thumbnails

Thumbnail Size:

| 1 1/2 inch | ▾ |

☑ Print File Name

Printer Setup

OK   Cancel

PhotoStudio informs you that one or more of the file types is not supported. That's true: *PhotoStudio* can only recognize individual photo files right now, and can't do anything with the folder *Panorama*.

⬅️ **Click on** ⌷ OK ⌷

PhotoStudio

One or more files are invalid or unsupported.

OK

The contact sheet containing the thumbnails will now be printed. Because you changed the paper orientation from portrait to landscape earlier, the contact sheet will also be printed lengthwise on the paper.

If you have large numbers of digital photos, it's definitely a good idea to record them on contact sheets. That way you can find a photo you're looking for more easily.

👉 **Close the *Browser*** ✍23

Sending a Photo by E-mail

PhotoStudio has a special command for sending a photo by e-mail.

☞ **Open the photo *Red Eyes* in the folder *My PhotoStudio Practice Files*** *ℓℓ*6

☞ **Maximize the window containing the photo** *ℓℓ*4

🖱 **Click on** File

🖱 **Click on** Send...

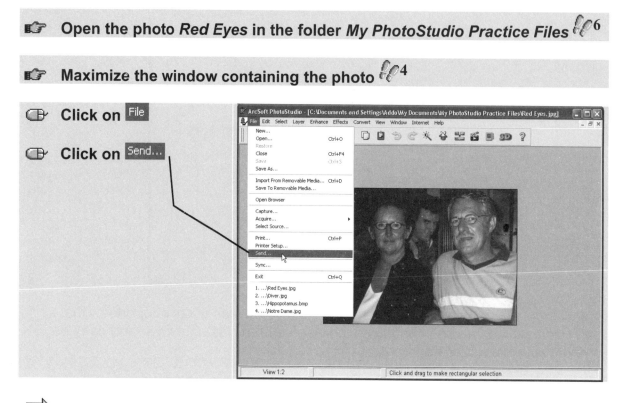

⇨ **Please note:**

This function works with your existing Internet service subscription and e-mail program. If you haven't already set up an e-mail account, the program will ask you to enter this information.

In some cases, the following window will appear when you use the *Send* option for the first time.

You can use your *Microsoft Outlook* settings:

🖱 **Click on** OK

The photo has been added as an attachment to a *New Message*:

Now you can choose a recipient, type a message, and then send the e-mail.

☞ **Close the message and <u>don't</u> save the changes** 📖⁹

☞ **Close the photo** 📖²¹

☞ **Close *PhotoStudio*** 📖¹⁰

💡 **Tip**

Automatic Conversion to JPEG
If a file you want to attach to an e-mail is not a (small) JPEG file, it can take a lot of time to send the e-mail. From now on, you don't have to worry about that any more. *PhotoStudio* will automatically covert a BMP or PSF file to JPEG, thereby reducing the file size.

In this example, the file *Red Eyes with Layers.psf* is being sent. This file is a little more than 535 KB.

PhotoStudio automatically creates the smaller attachment *Red Eyes with Layers_tmp.jpg* from it:

In this chapter you've seen how you can print and send your photos. You now have enough experience to experiment with your photos on your own.

Exercises

The following exercises will help you master what you've just learned. Have you forgotten how to perform a particular action? Use the number beside the footsteps to look it up in the appendix *How Do I Do That Again?*

Exercise: Printing

In this exercise, you'll practice readying a photo for printing.

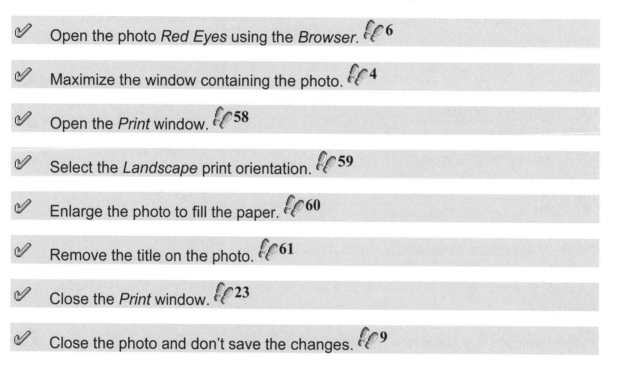

☑ Open the photo *Red Eyes* using the *Browser.* ℓℓ6

☑ Maximize the window containing the photo. ℓℓ4

☑ Open the *Print* window. ℓℓ58

☑ Select the *Landscape* print orientation. ℓℓ59

☑ Enlarge the photo to fill the paper. ℓℓ60

☑ Remove the title on the photo. ℓℓ61

☑ Close the *Print* window. ℓℓ23

☑ Close the photo and don't save the changes. ℓℓ9

Exercise: Printing a Contact Sheet

In this exercise, you'll practice printing a contact sheet.

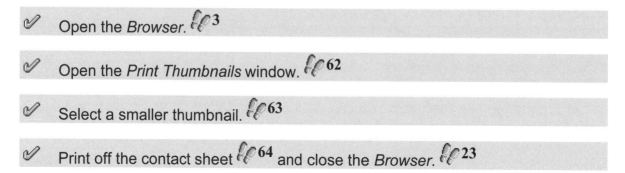

☑ Open the *Browser.* ℓℓ3

☑ Open the *Print Thumbnails* window. ℓℓ62

☑ Select a smaller thumbnail. ℓℓ63

☑ Print off the contact sheet ℓℓ64 and close the *Browser.* ℓℓ23

Background Information

How Does an Inkjet Printer Work?

An inkjet printer is sometimes called a bubble-jet printer. It has a head that moves back and forth horizontally over the paper. The print develops line by line. In each passage, the head sprays tiny drops of ink onto the paper. The amount of ink sprayed each time equals one one-millionth of a water droplet!

Because the ink is sprayed, there's no direct contact between the head and the paper. That's also why an inkjet works fairly noiselessly. All modern inkjet printers are color printers. You can choose to print only in black and white if you wish.

Inkjet printers usually use ink cartridges containing different colors (for example cyan, magenta, yellow, and black) which can be mixed to produce all other colors.

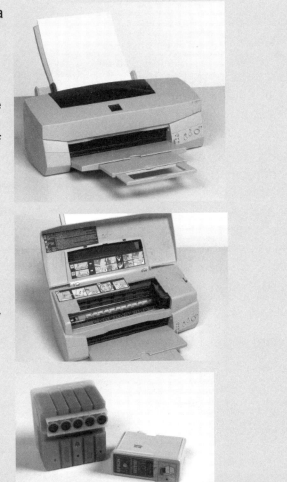

The print consists of countless tiny droplets of ink. The smaller these droplets are, the higher the resolution and the sharper the print. This is expressed in droplets (dots) per inch. Sharpness values include 300, 600, and even 1200 DPI. Because the spraying mechanism is often built into the ink cartridge, an empty ink cartridge almost always means replacing the sprayer too. This partially explains why ink cartridges are so expensive. One advantage is that an inkjet printer needs practically no maintenance.

How Does a Laser Printer Work?

A laser printer greatly resembles a photocopier. The manner in which the print is produced is nearly identical. In an inkjet printer, the print is created line by line. A laser printer is a "page printer," printing the entire page at once.

A laser printer

The technology behind the laser printer is fairly complicated. A laser printer works with toner, a black powder. A laser beam electrically charges parts of a cylinder (the drum).

The printer opened

This charge then attracts the fine toner powder. When the paper is pressed against the drum, the toner transfers from the drum to the paper and is then melted onto the paper at a high temperature.

The toner cartridge

Just as with the inkjet printer, print sharpness is measured in *dots per inch* (DPI), and values here also range from 300 to 1200 DPI and higher.

Laser printers operate quietly and the print quality is the best that can be found. It comes very close to the quality of professional printing.

There are also *color laser printers*, but they're very expensive. This kind of printer is usually used in professional settings.

Fixative

There's a lot of discussion about the perishability of photos printed with inkjet printers. The ink quality is constantly improving, and the "shelf life" of prints is also getting longer and longer. Prints made with the first generation of inkjet printers were very perishable. Even a few months' exposure to sunlight caused bleaching. If you want to be on the safe side, however, you can always spray your prints with fixative.

Photos on CD

These days, you can also have your photos put onto a CD-ROM when you develop 35mm or APS film.

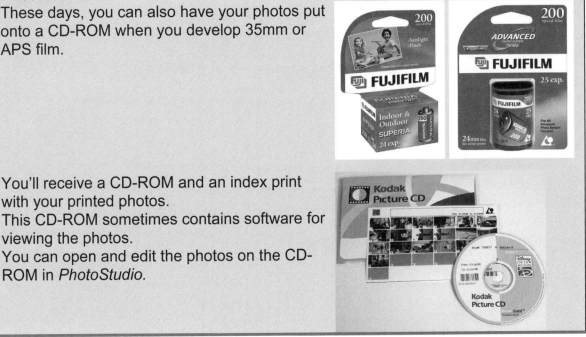

You'll receive a CD-ROM and an index print with your printed photos.
This CD-ROM sometimes contains software for viewing the photos.
You can open and edit the photos on the CD-ROM in *PhotoStudio.*

Inkjet Paper

For daily use, such as printing letters, you can use the regular paper for sale in 500-sheet packs in every office supply store. There is a difference between paper for laser printers and copiers and paper for inkjet printers. The latter is often a little more expensive, but it's also less coarse, so that the ink runs less. That gives you a better result than you'd get using regular copier paper. Photos, however, require a different kind of printing paper.

You can buy special photo paper for printing photos. This photo paper is extra white and has a very fine structure. It's sometimes called *Brilliant White Paper*.

The most expensive kind of paper is *Glossy Paper*, named for its shiny surface. Using this kind of paper will make your print look like a conventional photo.

This paper is sometimes called *High Resolution* or *720 DPI Paper*.

Photo paper is also sold in the familiar 4" x 6" photo size. A package usually contains 20 to 25 sheets.

You can also buy it on perforated standard letter size sheets, each of which can hold two 4" x 6" prints.

Photo paper is sold by printer manufacturers, paper manufacturers, and store chains. You certainly aren't limited to using only paper of the same brandname as your printer. In some cases, however, the paper has been optimized for certain types of printers. This primarily concerns the print resolution and the quantity of ink that's used. But a different brand of paper can give very good results too.

T-shirt Transfer Paper

You can also print your photos onto special paper that lets you iron the image onto fabric, for example a T-shirt. This paper is called *Iron-on Transfer Paper*. It has a special layer that transfers the ink onto the fabric when heated by an iron. The photo should be printed in mirror image on the paper, so that it's in the proper orientation after being ironed onto the fabric. If the photo isn't printed in mirror image, it will be ironed onto the fabric in mirror image instead.

Transfer Paper is sold in packs of just a few sheets. Each sheet is standard paper size. There's still quite a bit of work to be done after you've printed onto the sheet. First, you have to cut out the figure or photo. Then it's placed face down on the fabric and heated with the iron. The paper is usually accompanied by a folder containing specific instructions.

Maintaining Inkjet Cartridges

Cartridges dry out. That's why they're packed in airtight foil. An expiration date is also printed on the packaging.

When you take a cartridge out of the printer, to exchange it for a photo cartridge, for example, be sure to place it in the extra cartridge holder. This keeps it from drying out.

If a cartridge has dried out, try to clean it with a cotton swab dipped in alcohol or benzine. If you're printer isn't working properly, you can let it run through its cleaning procedure. Every inkjet printer has this type of process for removing air bubbles and dirt.

Tips

 Tip

ArcSoft PhotoBase and PhotoPrinter
With *PhotoStudio*, you have an excellent photo-editing package at your disposal. *ArcSoft* has a special program for managing and presenting your photo collections: *PhotoBase*. Using *PhotoBase*, you can organize your photos into albums. This helps you keep track of your photos. You can also create slide shows to play on your computer.

In the *PhotoStudio Browser*, you'll see a special button ▦ you can use to display the albums you've created in *PhotoBase*: That gives you quick access to your albums.

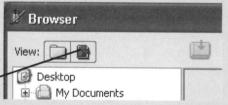

Are you looking for more printing features than *PhotoStudio* offers? Then you can use a special photo-printing program such as *ArcSoft PhotoPrinter*. With this program, you can create all kinds of prints from your photos. How about printing a single photo multiple times on one page, possibly in different sizes? Or printing different photos on one page, so you can use your photo paper optimally? With the help of the built-in print templates, you can print your photos in any size you wish.

Tip

Photo Sizes and Image Sizes
Conventional photos have an aspect ratio of 2:3 or 3:2.
The following are some standard photo sizes:

4" x 6"
5" x 7"
8" x 10"

Digital cameras, however, often have a different aspect ratio, such as 4:3.
The following are some standard digital photo sizes:

640 x 480
1024 x 768
1152 x 864
1280 x 960
1600 x 1200
2048 x 1536

This means not every digital photo can be printed on conventionally sized photo paper. In certain situations part of the photo will be omitted, or conversely, the photo may acquire a white border. Some photo labs offer separate printing sizes for digital photos. In that case, the entire photo will be printed.

💡 Tip

The Right Printer Driver Is Indispensable

Every piece of hardware has its own *driver(s)*, including the photo camera, the scanner, and the printer. Without the driver, the device simply won't work. When you install a new piece of hardware, *Windows* searches for the associated driver. *Windows* itself has a large collection of drivers. Most of them are stored on the *Windows* CD-ROM. Usually, however, the hardware comes with a CD-ROM or floppy disk containing the appropriate drivers. You can find out which driver you need, and how to install it, in your printer's manual. Incidentally, driver problems often cause a device to malfunction. In that case, it sometimes helps to install a new version of the driver. These days you can often download the new version from the Internet.

You're going to visit the website of your printer's manufacturer. The web address is usually listed in the manual.

Once you get there, search the page for "Download drivers" (or similar wording):

Eventually, you'll get to a screen where you can type in your printer model in order to download the proper driver:

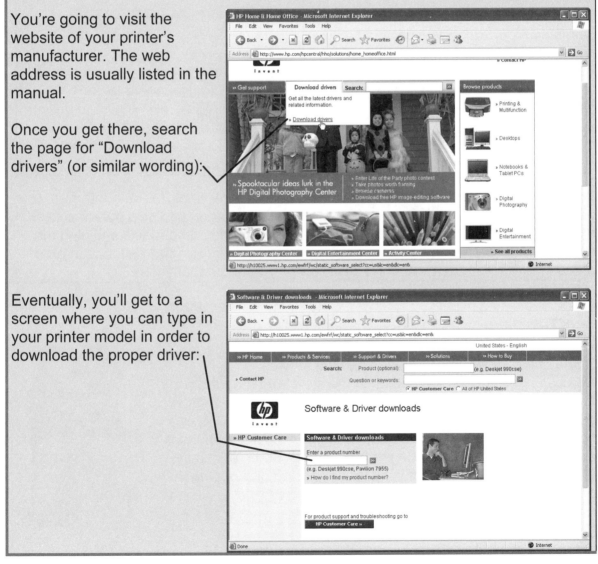

💡 Tip

The Online Photo Lab

If you have Internet access, then you have a good alternative to printing your photos: the online photo lab.

This service has a number of advantages. Printing your own photos is fairly expensive due to the high cost of photo paper and ink cartridges. An online printing service is therefore relatively cheap, especially if you want to print a series of standard-sized photos. Moreover, your photos will be professionally printed on high-quality photo paper, which also increases their "shelf life."

Several retailers such as *Wal-Mart* and *K-Mart* currently offer an online printing service.
You can send your photos to the company's website. A few days later, you can pick up the printed photos in the store. The printing service's website lists the required pixel dimensions for printing a photo at a certain size.

Some online photo services will also let you publish your photos on the Internet. You get your own web page, where your photos are stored. You can give others access to your images this way: you send your family and friends an e-mail containing the hyperlink to your photo web page. One handy feature is that your visitors can order prints themselves. Then you don't have to worry about that anymore.

💡 Tip

In-store Printing Service

Some photo shops offer a kind of printing service.
You can bring your digital photos to the store and read them into a computer there. Depending on the particular printing service, your photos can be stored on a memory card, a CD-ROM, or a floppy disk. Using the store's computer, you select the photos and sizes you want, then give the print command. Some printing services even offer a few options for enhancing or cropping the photo before you print it.

💡 **Tip**

Paper Sizes from Small to Large

In the *Print Setup* window, you can choose among a wide variety of paper sizes.

For standard sheets of paper, you can choose among the sizes *Letter*, *Legal*, *Executive*, and the European standard letter size, *A4*. Every type of paper has its own width and length. These sizes are about the largest a household printer can handle. If you want to print out a larger size, such as *A3* (twice the size of A4), you'll need a special A3 printer.

You can print out smaller sizes, however, and there's plenty of choice there, too, from *A5* (half the size of A4) to envelopes and business cards.

Paper

Size: Legal

8.5x13
Source: A4
A5
B5
B5 (JIS)
Network... Double Postcard (JIS)
Envelope #10
Envelope B5
Envelope C5
Envelope DL
Envelope Monarch
Executive
Legal
Letter
Postcard (JIS)
PostScript Custom Page Size

For good print results, it's important that the print settings in *PhotoStudio* agree with the paper that's actually in the printer.

💡 **Tip**

Colors on the Screen and on Your Print

A photo that looks fantastic on the screen might disappoint you when you see the printed results. Along the input-edit-print path, the colors can begin to deviate from their original values. The monitor should be properly adjusted for contrast, brightness, and color. You can change these settings using the buttons on the monitor. If you work using too high a brightness, which often occurs on a regular computer screen, you'll lose a lot of image information. The same thing occurs if the contrast is too high. And of course you understand how important the RGB colors (Red, Green, and Blue) on your monitor are. If these are "off," the colors on the printed paper will look quite different from those on the screen.

You can also adjust the color settings on some inkjet printers.

The proper color reproduction even depends on the type of paper you choose. If you don't use the right paper, the individual colors can run into each other. The best thing is to experiment a little, so you can tailor the colors on the screen and in the printer to one another.

Appendices

Appendix A.
How Do I Do That Again?

In this book, many tasks and exercises are followed by footsteps: 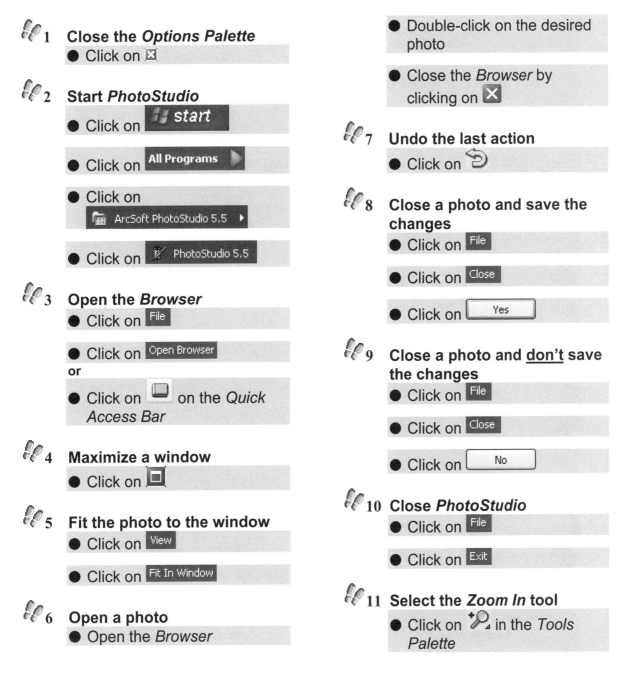 x
You can use the number beside the footsteps to look up how to do these things in this appendix.

1 Close the *Options Palette*
● Click on ☒

2 Start *PhotoStudio*
● Click on **start**
● Click on **All Programs** ▶
● Click on 🔳 ArcSoft PhotoStudio 5.5 ▶
● Click on 📷 PhotoStudio 5.5

3 Open the *Browser*
● Click on File
● Click on Open Browser
or
● Click on 🔲 on the *Quick Access Bar*

4 Maximize a window
● Click on 🔲

5 Fit the photo to the window
● Click on View
● Click on Fit In Window

6 Open a photo
● Open the *Browser*

● Double-click on the desired photo
● Close the *Browser* by clicking on ☒

7 Undo the last action
● Click on ↺

8 Close a photo and save the changes
● Click on File
● Click on Close
● Click on Yes

9 Close a photo and <u>don't</u> save the changes
● Click on File
● Click on Close
● Click on No

10 Close *PhotoStudio*
● Click on File
● Click on Exit

11 Select the *Zoom In* tool
● Click on ⚲ in the *Tools Palette*

12 **Hide the *Tools Palette***
- Click on ⊠

13 **Display the *Options Palette***
- Click on View
- Click on Show Options Palette

14 **Display the *Tools Palette***
- Click on View
- Click on Show Tools Palette

15 **Select the *Rectangle Select* tool**
- Click on ⬚

16 **Select the *Move* tool**
- Click on ⊹

17 **Remove the selection boundary**
- Click on Select
- Click on None

18 **Select the *Magic Wand* tool**
- Click on ✎

19 **Merge the different layers in the photo**
- Click on Layer
- Click on Merge All

20 **Save a file with a new name**
- Click on File
- Click on Save As...
- Select the desired location beside Save in:

- Type a name beside File name:
- Adjust the Quality: setting if desired
- Click on [Save]

21 **Close a photo**
- Click on × (maximized window) or on ⊠ (small window)

22 **Close the *Layers Palette***
- Click on ⊠

23 **Close the *Browser I* window**
- Click on ⊠

24 **Save a file with the current name**
- Click on File
- Click on Save As...
- Select the desired location beside Save in:
- Adjust the Quality: setting if desired
- Click on [Save]

25 **Close all photos**
- Click in each photo on × (maximized window) or on ⊠ (small window)

26 **Create a new folder**
- Click on the folder 📇 My Pictures
- Right-click on 📇 My Pictures
- Click on New

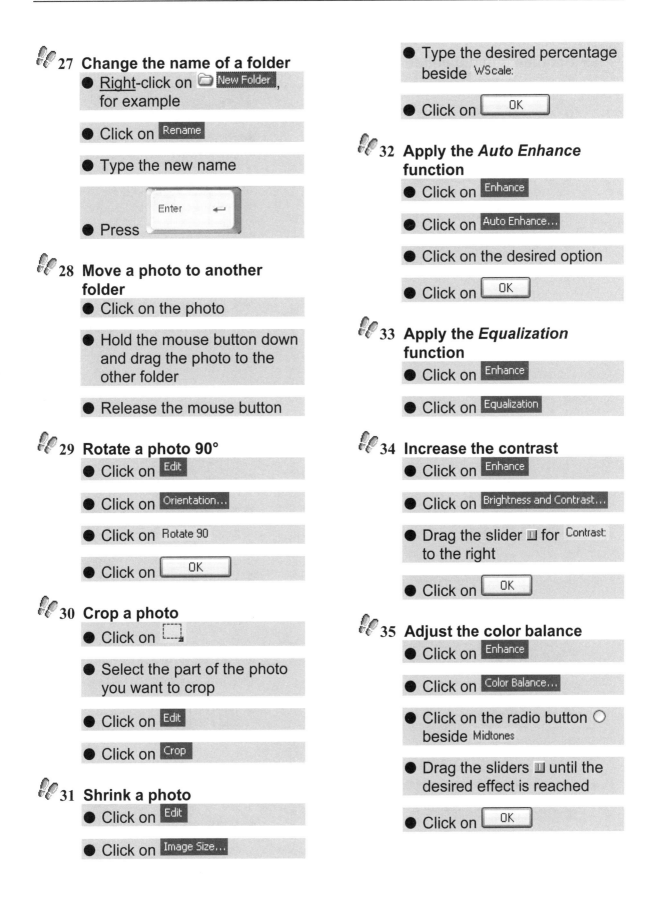

27 Change the name of a folder
- <u>Right</u>-click on 📁 New Folder, for example
- Click on Rename
- Type the new name
- Press [Enter ←]

28 Move a photo to another folder
- Click on the photo
- Hold the mouse button down and drag the photo to the other folder
- Release the mouse button

29 Rotate a photo 90°
- Click on Edit
- Click on Orientation...
- Click on Rotate 90
- Click on [OK]

30 Crop a photo
- Click on ⬚
- Select the part of the photo you want to crop
- Click on Edit
- Click on Crop

31 Shrink a photo
- Click on Edit
- Click on Image Size...

- Type the desired percentage beside WScale:
- Click on [OK]

32 Apply the *Auto Enhance* function
- Click on Enhance
- Click on Auto Enhance...
- Click on the desired option
- Click on [OK]

33 Apply the *Equalization* function
- Click on Enhance
- Click on Equalization

34 Increase the contrast
- Click on Enhance
- Click on Brightness and Contrast...
- Drag the slider ⬚ for Contrast: to the right
- Click on [OK]

35 Adjust the color balance
- Click on Enhance
- Click on Color Balance...
- Click on the radio button ○ beside Midtones
- Drag the sliders ⬚ until the desired effect is reached
- Click on [OK]

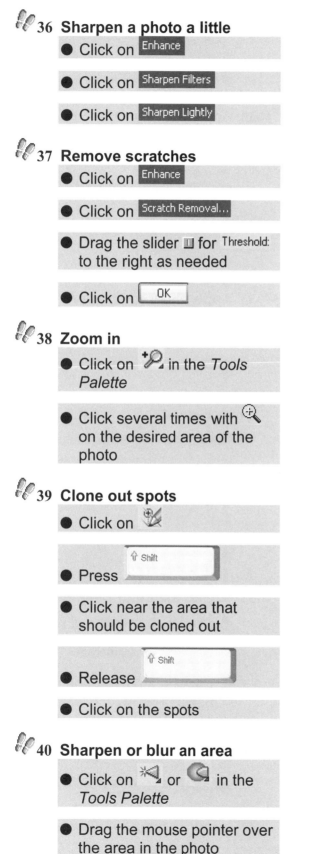

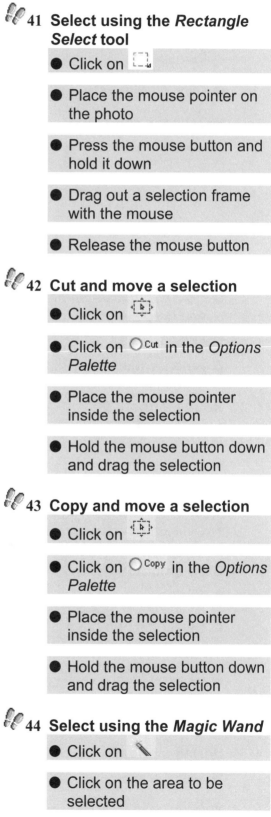

36 Sharpen a photo a little
- Click on `Enhance`
- Click on `Sharpen Filters`
- Click on `Sharpen Lightly`

37 Remove scratches
- Click on `Enhance`
- Click on `Scratch Removal...`
- Drag the slider ▯ for `Threshold:` to the right as needed
- Click on `OK`

38 Zoom in
- Click on ⌖ in the *Tools Palette*
- Click several times with ⌕ on the desired area of the photo

39 Clone out spots
- Click on ✎
- Press `⇧ Shift`
- Click near the area that should be cloned out
- Release `⇧ Shift`
- Click on the spots

40 Sharpen or blur an area
- Click on ◁ or ◔ in the *Tools Palette*
- Drag the mouse pointer over the area in the photo

41 Select using the *Rectangle Select* tool
- Click on ⬚
- Place the mouse pointer on the photo
- Press the mouse button and hold it down
- Drag out a selection frame with the mouse
- Release the mouse button

42 Cut and move a selection
- Click on ✛
- Click on ○ Cut in the *Options Palette*
- Place the mouse pointer inside the selection
- Hold the mouse button down and drag the selection

43 Copy and move a selection
- Click on ✛
- Click on ○ Copy in the *Options Palette*
- Place the mouse pointer inside the selection
- Hold the mouse button down and drag the selection

44 Select using the *Magic Wand*
- Click on ✎
- Click on the area to be selected

45 Extend a selection
- Press ⇧ Shift
- Click on the photo until all desired areas are selected
- Release ⇧ Shift

46 Select the entire photo
- Click on Select
- Click on All

47 Copy a photo and paste it as a new layer
- Click on Edit
- Click on Copy
- Click on Edit
- Click on Paste

48 Crop part of a layer using the *Shape* tool
- Click on the layer you want to crop
- Click on ✎
- Click on the desired shape
- Select the area you want to crop

49 Apply the *Charcoal* effect
- Click on Effects
- Click on Fine Art
- Click on Charcoal...

50 Add a text layer
- Click on T
- Click in the white box on the *Options Palette*
- Type the desired text

51 Move text
- Click on ⊕
- Place the mouse pointer on the text
- Drag the text to the desired location

52 Merge layers
- Click on Layer
- Click on Merge All

53 Apply the *Moonlight* effect
- Click on Effects
- Click on Lighting
- Click on Moonlight

54 Using the *Transform* function
- Click on ▣
- Click on ˅ in the *Options Palette*
- Click on Skew, for example
- Place the mouse pointer on a corner handle
- Hold the mouse button down and drag the corner handle

55 Apply the *Twist* effect
- Click on `Effects`
- Click on `Distort`
- Click on `Twist...`
- Click on `OK`

56 Apply the *Old Photo* effect
- Click on `Effects`
- Click on `Old Photo...`
- Click on `OK`

57 Add a frame
- Click on `Effects`
- Click on `Framing`
- Click on `Clear Frame...`, for example
- Click on `OK`

58 Open the *Print* window
- Click on `File`
- Click on `Print...`

59 Select the *Landscape* print orientation
In the *Print* window:
- Click on `Printer Setup`
- Click on the radio button ○ beside Landscape
- Click on `OK`

60 Adjust the print size
In the *Print* window:
- Drag the slider ▥ until the desired effect is reached

61 Remove the title on the print
In the *Print* window:
- Remove the check mark beside Add Title

62 Open the *Print Thumbnails* window
In the *Browser*:
- Click on 🖶

63 Select smaller thumbnails
In the *Print Thumbnails* window:
- Click on ⌄ beside
  Thumbnail Size:
- Click on a smaller size

64 Print a contact sheet
In the *Print Thumbnails* window:
- Click on `OK`

Appendix B. Index

Appendix C. Color Supplement

Plate 1
The original photo:

Plate 2
After applying the *Auto Enhance* function:

Plate 3
After applying the *Equalization* function:

Plate 4
The original photo:

Plate 5
After applying the *Equalization* function:

Plate 6
After adjusting the brightness:

Plate 7
After a second brightness adjustment:

Plate 8
After adjusting the contrast:

Plate 9
The original photo:

Plate 10
The color wheel:

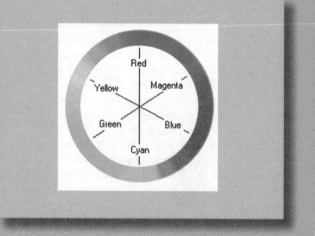

Plate 11
After adjusting the color balance:

Plate 12
After adjusting the brightness and contrast:

Plate 13
The original photo:

Plate 14
After sharpening:

Plate 15
The original photo:

Plate 16
After smoothing:

Plate 17
The previously edited photo:

Plate 18
After fixing one red eye:

Plate 19
After fixing both eyes:

Plate 20
After fixing both eyes:

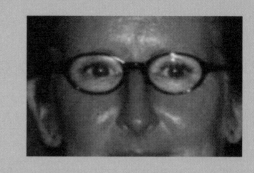

Plate 21
After fixing all four red eyes:

Plate 22
After applying the *Lighten* tool:

Plate 23
The final result:

Plate 24
After cloning out the damaged spots:

Plate 25
After sharpening the letters:

Plate 26
After blurring the letters:

Plate 27
The original photo with dust and scratches:

Plate 28
After removing the small spots:

Plate 29
After removing the large scratch:

Plate 30
The copied fish:

Digital Photo Editing
for SENIORS

Plate 31
After applying a soft edge:

Plate 32
After adding shadow:

Plate 33
After replacing the original sky color:

Plate 34
After applying the *Charcoal* effect to Layer-0:

Plate 35
After lightening the layer:

Plate 36
The translucent fish: